It was not lon… n to the
House of Cor… of the
women was al… y voted
the wrong wa… ove all,
they were accu… e failed
women.

Drawing on in… Labour
women MPs, … d being
MPs, and expl… ir con-
stituencies, in … nsights
into theories of … elation-
ship between … tion is
complicated, t… omen's
differences mu… ht not
always be possi… even if
they want to.

Including secti… vomen
MPs act as ro… uld be
present in polit… men's
substantive rep… eading
for all those inte… olitical
behaviour and r…

Sarah Childs i…

NEW LABOUR'S WOMEN MPs:
Women Representing Women

Sarah Childs
University of Bristol

LONDON AND NEW YORK

First published 2004 by Routledge, an imprint of Taylor & Francis
11 New Fetter Lane, London EC4P 4EE

Simultaneously published in the USA and Canada
by Routledge
29 West 35th Street, New York, NY 10001

Routledge is an imprint of the Taylor & Francis Group

Typeset in Ehrhardt 11 on 13 pt by Cambridge Photosetting Services
Printed in Great Britain by MPG Books Ltd, Bodmin, Cornwall

British Library Cataloguing in Publication Data
A catalogue record for this book is available from the British Library

Library of Congress Cataloguing in Publication Data

Childs, Sarah, 1969–
New Labour's women MPs: women representing women/Sarah Childs.
p. cm.
Includes bibliographical references and index.
ISBN 0-7146-5661-5 (cloth) – ISBN 0-7146-8566-6 (pbk)
1. Women in politics–Great Britain. 2. Women legislators–Great Britain–Interviews. 3. Labour Party (Great Britain) 4. Women–Great Britain–Social conditions. 5. Representative government and representation–Great Britain. 6. Great Britain–Politics

HQ1391.G7C48 2003
320′.082′0941–dc22 2003062074

ISBN 0-7146-5661-5 (Hb)
ISSN 0-7146-8566-6 (Pb)

Contents

Foreword

When I was first elected as MP for Peckham 20 years ago, I joined a House of Commons which was 97 per cent men.

When I look at the new Labour women MPs – still outnumbered four to one by their male colleagues – I am in no doubt how important are the changes that they have made to our party, to our parliament and to our country. Of course we have yet to achieve all we want to – and many battles lie ahead, but the women MPs have transformed the face of parliament and with it the agenda of politics and government.

At the time of writing this introduction we are just introducing into parliament our Domestic Violence Bill. I am in no doubt that it is the backing of the Labour women MPs which enabled the ideas of the bill to be turned into legislation. I remember only too well the response of the House to Jo Richardson's campaigns on domestic violence in the late 1970s and early 1980s. If you mentioned domestic violence once it could be ignored – mention it twice and you were regarded as obsessed. That has changed, and now domestic violence has found its rightful place on the law and order agenda.

In the early 1980s when I spoke in the House of Commons calling for more nurseries and after-school clubs, I was jeered – by my own side as well as by the Tories. The overwhelmingly male parliament just could not see the point of even discussing it. Now, we have a National Childcare Strategy to spread nurseries and a new Children's Minister to spearhead it. That would have been unthinkable in a House of Commons with only 3 per cent women. The presence of the Labour women has changed the definition of what is political – what is appropriate for parliamentary business. Having more women in the House of Commons also makes it much easier for the women to go about their business, and to succeed in the difficult struggle of balancing home and work.

When I was in the House of Commons in the early 1980s with three young children, there was no one to share ideas about how to succeed in being a good MP and a good mother. When I was in a standing committee considering a Bill, the Chair congratulated one MP whose wife had had a baby that morning. I wondered why he was at the committee rather than being at home. Now it is not unusual to see young women MPs pregnant or to welcome back those who've had a baby – usually well-timed to coincide with the Summer Recess. And men MPs take some time off for paternity leave – as well as doing their work in a parliament which has introduced a new right to paternity leave for all men at work.

Since I entered the House of Commons the proceedings have become televised. We want women as well as men to see that they are represented. Why should any woman watching an all-male parliament think that it has anything to do with her? Now the grey suits that used to dominate the Commons are interspersed with women. The Conservatives – still with hardly any women MPs – are embarrassed about their overwhelmingly male face being caught on camera, so they cluster their few women around the male shadow minister who is speaking.

When I was first elected I was warned not to speak about women's concerns in case I might get 'pigeon-holed'. But if there are so few women, those who are there have to speak up for women's concerns – who else will? We are still in a minority. So I still feel that it is our responsibility as women in the House to raise issues about women outside the House. Of course we have made mistakes. We are still in the minority so our mistakes are more visible. A mistake by a man passes, usually, without comment. A woman's mistake will be in the next day's papers. Some of the men in the Commons are excellent and some just do a good job. Being an 'ordinary' woman MP will not be possible until we have equal numbers.

Women MPs have changed the face, and the priorities, of government as well as parliament. I remember when John Major announced the names of his first cabinet. Not one woman. What did that say about the Conservative party? That there were no women in the Conservative party? That there were, but they had nothing to say? We denounced the all-male cabinet. There never has been an all-male cabinet since and nor will there be – of any party.

It was downright embarrassing for Labour – supposedly the party of equality – to have so few women MPs. And we couldn't get women to vote for us. We believed women in parliament was right in principle but we hoped too that it would enable women voters to take a fresh look at the Labour party they had turned their back on. We tried everything to get women into the seats that Labour hoped to win. We tried giving women extra training, we tried rule changes which required a woman on every selection shortlist. We tried persuading local parties, but as each new seat came up for selection the women only ever seemed to come second. So we took the drastic step of excluding men altogether from the selections in half of the constituencies which we expected to win. This was such a controversial measure – reverse discrimination – that the women selected under these rules had to work doubly hard to prove themselves as candidates. And when they were elected in 1997 – below the surface of the welcome for the new women was the suggestion that they were second rate. So they had to prove themselves all over again. Now, no one can remember which women were selected from all-women shortlists and which came through selections which included men.

All the facts and figures are well set out in Sarah Child's book; our setbacks as well as our successes. But I am in no doubt; parliament would have not a shred of credibility without the women MPs. A parliament of men – such as we had 20 years ago – would be unfair and unrepresentative. We are a country of women as well as men, and our parliament must be a parliament of women as well as men.

The Rt Hon Harriet Harman QC, MP

Preface

One of the most striking features of the 1997 British general election was the arrival in the House of Commons of a record number of women MPs. Numbering 120, of whom 101 were Labour, women were finally present in Parliament in sufficient numbers for them to make a difference.

Feminist conceptions of representation argue for women's political presence in a number of different ways – in terms of justice, for symbolic reasons, on the basis that women politicians have a different style of politics, and because women representatives are more likely to act for women than men.

Taking Labour's new women MPs as a case study and drawing on in-depth interviews with more than half of them, this book subjects these claims to empirical analysis. Without the participation of these 34 MPs this book simply could not have been written. I thank them for giving up their precious time to talk to me, particularly those who agreed to participate in both 1997 and 2000. Their openness when discussing these ideas and their friendliness also made the project an enjoyable one and stands in contrast to the (often critical) media depiction of them. I hope they find the book both interesting and fair.

This book is the culmination of research that began nearly ten years ago. My interest in the relationship between gender and politics was formed while I studied politics and then women's studies at the Universities of Sussex and York. Kingston University provided me with the opportunity to undertake post-graduate study and particular thanks must go to my PhD supervisor, Ian Gordon. Joni Lovenduski and Vicky Randall's supportive comments when I first presented my research proved a critical moment – they know how much I appreciated their support at that time and since. My book has also benefited enormously from the comments of participants at various conferences where I have presented papers – especially the PSA Women and Politics annual conference, which provides a stimulating, demanding, but none the less safe, space in which to discuss ideas.

The following read and offered comments on drafts of the book or helped with the research, and I am grateful to them for their input: Joe

Bailey, Peter Beck, Janice Childs, Philip Cowley (who also co-wrote Chapter 8), Heather Deegan, Adam Fagin, Justin Fisher, Ian Gordon, Mike Hawkins, Fraser King, Joni Lovenduski, Dan Lyndon, Fiona MacKay, Philip Norton, Vicky Randall, Meg Russell, Judith Squires, Wendy Stokes, Terry Sullivan and Mark Wickham-Jones. I'd also like to thank Ben Kisby, who compiled the index.

An earlier version of Chapter 8 appeared as 'Too Spineless to Rebel? New Labour's Women MPs', *British Journal of Political Science*, Vol. 33, No. 3, pp. 345–65 (2003), copyright Cambridge University Press.

An earlier version of Chapter 10 appeared as 'A Feminised Style of Politics? Women MPs in the House of Commons', *British Journal of Politics and International Relations*, Vol. 6, No. 1 (2004), Copyright Blackwell Publishing.

I am also grateful to my family and friends, whose support I depend on – be it in the form of reading my work or just accompanying me in retail therapy. Although I have benefited from the insight and advice of many others over the years I acknowledge that I am responsible for what follows.

In memory of Marion Avril Childs (1942–1979)

1

Introduction

The Labour Party's landslide at the 1997 general election saw 120 women Members of Parliament elected to the House of Commons, doubling the number of women MPs overnight. Women now constituted 18 per cent of all MPs. This was unprecedented: for most of the twentieth century women MPs had accounted for less than 5 per cent, and less than 10 per cent even at the previous general election in 1992. So 1997 was the 'year of the woman MP'. Yet it was, in truth, the 'year of the Labour woman MP'. For 101 of the 120 women MPs in the 1997 Parliament were Labour, only 13 were Conservative, three were Liberal Democrat and two were Scottish Nationalists.[1]

The election of Labour's 101 women MPs was met with a great media fanfare. Pictures of the women MPs were widely printed in the British press in the days after the election. And then there was *that* picture: Blair surrounded by 'his' women MPs. Here was proof that something enormous had changed in British politics. It was no longer about 'men in grey suits'. Women had arrived, and it looked as though they wanted to do business.

Indeed, there was a clear expectation that they would do business. Headlines, from newspapers across the political spectrum, promised a feminization of Parliament:

> 'Women storm the most exclusive club in town'
> 'Women start to beat back pinstripe hordes'
> 'Sweeping change for male bastion'
> 'Winning women to overturn male culture of the commons'
> 'Sisterhood signals end to macho politics'[2]

Yet it was not only the press who claimed that the presence of these women MPs would make a difference. Feminists expected them to bring with them a 'new agenda'.[3] They would break 'the rules of the gentleman's club'.[4] There was talk of the 'difference those extra women will make',[5] and, to paraphrase the Spice Girls, of 'what we [women] really, really want'.[6]

The new Labour women MPs were also happy to talk about the effect their presence would have: 'All the intake of '97 believes there will be changes both physical and cultural ... more opportunities to raise issues which matter to women.'[7] Jacqui Smith, soon to be elected MP for Redditch, declared that women MPs would 'bring a perspective that is not always considered in political discussion'.[8] Natasha Walter, writing in the *Observer*, interviewed five of the youngest new Labour women MPs – Lorna Fitzsimmons, Yvette Cooper, Ruth Kelly, Claire Ward and Oona King – and concluded that 'they take it for granted that they will speak out on what are generally seen as women's issues'.[9] She quoted Oona King directly: 'For a long time I thought I could dodge women's issues but you do have that responsibility to all women in Britain, because they are still under-represented in Parliament.'

Such sentiments were not restricted to the newly elected Labour women MPs. Record numbers of women were appointed to Blair's Cabinet and government and the post of Women's Minister was established. Harriet Harman (then Secretary of State for Health and Women's Minister) argued that for the first time 'women's issues have been put at the heart of government'. Individual women MPs – Angela Eagle, Glenda Jackson, Helen Liddell, Estelle Morris, Mo Mowlam and Clare Short – were identified in the media as re-elected women MPs who would be 'working for women'.[10] Moreover, experienced women politicians from both the Liberal Democrat and the Conservative Parties agreed. Baroness Williams and Edwina Currie MP agreed that the presence of so many more women MPs would transform the political agenda; moving issues such as childcare, domestic violence and healthcare up the government's agenda.[11]

However, the backlash against the women MPs, and especially the new ones, was not long in coming. Less than two weeks after the election, the *Times* columnist Jane Shilling decried the fashion sense of the Labour women MPs: 'Cherie, your country needs you, who will save Labour's idealistic, visionary and utterly dowdy Class of '97 from years of brightly coloured polyester?' Next to a photograph of three French women ministers 'all comfortable in their skins', individual Labour women MPs were taken to task for what they had worn for the infamous photograph:

> Margaret Beckett in shrieking geranium pink; Ann Taylor in blinding lobelia blue; Linda Perham in cruel French marigold orange and Patricia Hewitt in a jacket covered in writhing herbiage of a kind usually heralded by a sign reading 'Britain in Bloom, runner up, 1997'.[12]

Nor was it only their 'fashion sense' that was criticized. Their very presence in Parliament was questioned. In the Chamber the women were subjected to sexual harassment: comments were made about women MPs' 'legs and breasts' and when women spoke in debates it was reported that Conservative MPs 'put their hands out in front of them as if they are weighing melons'.[13]

Furthermore, critics of all-women shortlists (AWS) – the method by which some of the new Labour women MPs had been elected in 1997 – resurfaced. But this time the criticism of this method of selection was linked to wider criticisms of the new Labour women MPs' behaviour in Parliament. Ann Widdecombe, a leading Conservative MP, stated:

> Serious politicians arrive in the House already battled-hardened ... Blair's Babes have arrived with starry eyes and a pager, shielded by positive discrimination from any real competition. They nod in unison behind the front bench ... some of the dear little souls have even whinged that Madam Speaker is too hard on them and indeed has caused more than one to burst into tears. Can anyone imagine Bessie Braddock, Barbara Castle or Margaret Thatcher dissolving at a ticking off from the speaker?[14]

The impression created was clear: the new Labour women MPs were simply not up to the job. The implication was, as Betty Boothroyd (Speaker of the House) put it, if you can't stand the heat you should get out of the kitchen,[15] to which one new Labour woman MP replied, 'New Labour: New Kitchen'.

The House of Commons was especially uncomfortable for the new Labour women MPs in December 1997. Pledged as it was to the Conservative government's spending commitments for the first two years of the 1997 Parliament, the government introduced, as part of the Social Security Bill, a reduction in lone parent benefit. Forty-seven Labour MPs voted against the reduction. But only one of these, Ann Cryer, was a newly elected Labour woman MP. This was *the* moment when the new Labour women MPs were considered to have failed women. Women's faith in them appeared to have been misplaced. The honeymoon was well and truly over.

Henceforth the behaviour of all of the new Labour MPs was under constant scrutiny and a litany of derogatory terms was used to describe them, the *Daily Mail*'s term, 'Blair's Babes', being the most (in)famous.[16] 'Part of a deliberate strategy' by its editor to set the new Labour women up to fail – to 'see if Labour could deliver' – 'Blair's Babes' stuck.[17] It continued to be used regularly throughout, and beyond, the 1997 Parliament. But other terms were no less harsh and many were distinctly misogynistic: Milbankettes,[18] Barbie dolls,[19] bleeper fodder and empty vessels.[20]

And these labels were not just the product or parlance of the media. Their parliamentary colleagues – male and female – also played their part.[21] One MP, Brian Sedgemore, repeated *Times* columnist Matthew Parris's depiction of the new Labour women MPs as Blair's 'Stepford Wives'.[22] Sedgemore stated that the new Labour women MPs had had a 'chip inserted into their brain to keep them on-message' – an analogy Ann Widdecombe considered an insult to the Stepford Wives rather than to the women MPs. Another male Labour MP called the new women MPs an 'uncritical mass', and Austin Mitchell MP referred to them as a 'monstrous mini-regiment of women'.[23] Some re-elected Labour women MPs were also less than sisterly. One found them 'very depressing', another considered them 'clones' while a third wondered why they had even bothered to come into Parliament.[24]

Individual new women MPs singled out by the media were vilified. Following an appearance on BBC2's *Newsnight*, where she stated that Peter Mandelson's greatest achievement was ensuring that the Labour Party spoke with one voice, Helen Brinton[25] (MP for Peterborough) was described as an 'alien life form designed in the Millbank lab by Baron Mandy von Mandelson to stay on message for 1,000 years without new batteries'.[26] Henceforth she was depicted as the 'Android MP for Peterborough'.[27]

Early in the Parliament Caroline Flint (MP for Don Valley) was identified in an article in the *Guardian* as a 'Blairite' who 'might well have been among those' whom Sedgemore had in mind when he railed against the so-called 'Stepford Wives'. Although the article was more balanced – it mentioned Flint having established the Commons childcare group – it was accompanied with the unflattering headline, 'Super-loyalist leaves old guard fuming'.[28] Furthermore, Simon Hoggart, parliamentary sketch writer for the *Guardian*, seemed to have it in for Flint. He awarded her the title of the 'greasiest Labour MP of all' and devoted considerable column inches to her apparent failure, in November 2000, to ask a question at Prime Minister's Questions.[29] Hoggart's sketch was pointed: 'Even in the new Labour Party Ms Flint is regarded as something of a hard-line toady, an aardvark-tongued bootlicker, a member of an active service unit in the greasers' provisional wing.'[30] But according to Flint her 'failure' to ask a question at PMQs was accounted for by the simple fact that it had already been asked by a colleague. Indeed, she was not on the Order Paper (a list of MPs who will be called to ask a question). Neither was she still standing (and therefore seeking the opportunity to ask a supplementary question), so the Speaker should technically not have called her. Nevertheless, the *Telegraph* suggested a less honourable interpretation, namely, that 'another female Blair loyalist had got her grovel in before Miss Flint could grovel in her own right'.[31]

Yet if the women MPs' loyalty to Blair in general was questioned, it was their behaviour in respect of women's concerns and especially their failure to vote against the cut in lone parent benefit that garnered the most opprobrium.[32] More than a year after the cut it was still being cited as the reason the new women MPs had earned 'the reputation of betraying women who needed them'.[33] Baroness Williams's critique went to the heart of the matter: 'How ironic that, less than eight months after the election [of 120 women MPs], the day for alleluias, MPs have cut lone parents' benefit, when poverty in Britain has the face of a woman and the face of a child. Those women MPs have to ask themselves what they are there for.'[34] 'Blair's Babes', it seemed, were 'a big disappointment':[35] they had 'turned out to be all but invisible', had 'beat a retreat' and 'failed women in politics'.[36]

If the new Labour women MPs were 'useless' at acting on the concerns of women outside the House, they appeared busy mobilizing around their own 'problems' in Westminster. The press repeatedly reported how they 'whinged' about the hours of the House, the 'laddish' behaviour in the Chamber, the inadequacy of the childcare provisions and the fact that the Speaker would not allow them to breastfeed their newborn babies.[37]

Even feminists, who had previously been optimistic about the presence of 101 women, became critical. Natasha Walter admitted in 1998:

> I was startled by my optimistic response to the sight of 100 [*sic*] female Labour MPs in Parliament. I was sympathetic when I heard them talk about what they intended to do for the women of Britain. They too seemed full of optimism ... But in December [1997] these new women MPs showed that they couldn't deliver. Ignoring the needs of the women who had put them in power, they failed against that pointless and callous decision to remove premiums from lone-parent benefits. For a while, any idealism that had attached to those women looked ridiculous.[38]

Germaine Greer – doyenne of 1970s feminism – was even less sympathetic: 'Blair Babes? They're just his backing singers.'[39]

Was the faith in Labour's women MPs misplaced? Why had women expected these MPs to make a difference? And what kind of difference was being expected from the women?

The expectation that the presence of 120 women MPs would make a difference has intuitive appeal. It also reflects the fact that in the past, women MPs appeared to have made a difference. In the (auto)biographies of women MPs and in early studies of women in Westminster a tradition of women MPs raising women's concerns both individually and collectively is apparent. Nancy Astor, in 1919 the first woman MP to take her seat in the House of Commons, stated that, although she would represent all her constituents, she saw herself as having a special responsibility towards women and children.[40] In her maiden speech she declared: 'I am simply trying to speak for hundreds of women and children throughout the country who cannot speak for themselves.'[41]

Women MPs in the pre-war period similarly showed a concern with women's concerns. Women MPs supported Margaret Blondfield's private member's bill in 1928 to provide shoes to children in deprived areas.[42] Moreover, in the period 1939–45 it is claimed that women MPs came closest to working as a 'women's party' when they demanded that women be given a greater role in the war effort.[43]

Later research also indicated that women MPs, although few in number, had made a difference. Elizabeth Vallance's interviews with most of the women MPs in the 1974 Parliament led her to conclude that many of the women, but especially the Labour women MPs, felt a 'sense of unity' with women. She noted that there was 'almost' a tradition of women MPs attending the maiden speeches of other women MPs – a tradition that even Lady Thatcher is said to have followed.[44] More importantly, Vallance found that the women MPs were 'almost' united behind the Equal Pay Act, and other equality legislation in the 1970s, although it was the threat to the 1967 abortion law that saw the Labour women MPs fully mobilized.[45]

Melville Currell's study in the 1970s, *Political Woman*, which also drew on interviews with women MPs, found once again that women MPs appeared to make a difference.[46] A third of her (admittedly unrepresentative) sample thought that women MPs brought 'distinctive qualities', 'experiences', 'interests' and a 'peculiarly feminine contribution' to politics.[47]

More recently, Joni Lovenduski and Pippa Norris's studies of the 1987 and 1992 British Candidate Surveys (BCS) and the 1997 British Representation Survey (BRS) have provided greater evidence that the sex of our representatives matters. Examining the question of women's liberal and/or feminist attitudes and priorities, the 1987 analysis concluded that there was 'tentative support for the view that in Britain women representatives may prove substantially different to their male colleagues' because women were more liberal within each of the political parties.[48] The 1992 BCS reinforced these findings. The sex of the representative was also positively associated with a concern with social policy and the prioritization of constituency work.[49] The 1997 BRS, again, suggested that 'women politicians are more likely to take a pro-woman line than men'.[50]

Experience from abroad also supports the claim that the presence of women makes a difference. In the United States there has been extensive analysis of how women representatives vote in legislatures (roll call analysis), much of which suggests that women do 'make a difference', particularly on women's concerns.[51] Other research has established *inter alia* that women are more likely to express 'some sort of commitment to representing women and/or women's concerns' and that women representatives understand their ability to represent women as derived from their shared gender.[52]

Contrary to the overwhelmingly critical representations of the new Labour women MPs in the media, historical precedent, recent attitudinal data and comparative research appear to suggest that the presence of the unprecedented number of women MPs in the 1997 Parliament had made a difference.

Alongside, and often elided with, the claim that women MPs will make a difference is the assertion that women would, in some way, be better 'represented' by women representatives. But what is being claimed when it is stated that the enhanced, albeit still unequal, presence of women MPs in Westminster means that women in the UK are better 'represented'?

The concept of representation has a long history and there is no agreement about what the concept refers to. Different dimensions of representation include formal representation, where the representative is given authority to represent others; symbolic representation, where the representative symbolizes those they represent; descriptive representation, where political fora reflect the social characteristics of the represented; and acting for representation, where the representatives act in the interests of the represented.[53]

The contested nature of the concept of representation raises the question of what women's political representation means. Should it be taken to refer to the simple fact that there are more women MPs in the House of Commons? Or does it mean that these women MPs symbolically represent women? And what does that mean anyway? Alternatively, does representation mean that the women MPs will somehow 'act for' women? But how do women representatives 'know' what women 'really, really, want'? Can they know what women who are different from them – in terms of class and ethnicity at the very least – want? Finally, how does one contend with the acknowledgement that women MPs have been elected as representatives of particular political parties for individual constituencies?

In recent years, feminists have expended considerable energy in reconsidering the concept of representation, and, in particular, the question of why women's presence in politics might matter.[54] Four arguments are usually given. Briefly, the justice argument claims that women's absence from elected political fora is evidence of a *prima facie* case of injustice that should be redressed. This argument does not rely upon the representatives having any differential impact upon politics; it matters simply that women are present. The second argument is that the presence of women in our political fora is important for symbolic reasons. An overwhelmingly male political body 'looks wrong' and 'suggests' that women are not capable of being representatives. In addition, women's presence enhances, and their absence diminishes, the legitimacy of the political institution. Again, this argument does not require that the newly present women representatives make a difference in any substantive sense (although they may be said to have some effect as 'role models'). The third argument is that women will bring a different, more consensual, style to politics. Finally, and most contested, is the argument that women representatives are more likely than male representatives to act for women. It is this latter argument – the claim that women's descriptive and substantive representation are related – that engages many feminists and underpins the presumption that the presence of 120 women MPs (and Labour's 101 women MPs) means that women will be better represented.

The conceptual framework that is usually employed to hypothesize the relationship between women's political presence and their effect is known as 'critical mass'. This suggests that once women reach 'critical mass' 'political behaviour, institutions, and public policy' will be feminized.[55] Rosabeth Moss Kanter's classic typology outlines four different kinds of group: the *uniform* group has 'only one significant social group and its culture dominates the organizations'; in the *skewed* group, the minority constitutes a maximum of 15 per cent and is 'controlled by the dominant group and its culture' while the minority are 'tokens'; in the *tilted* group, where the minority is between 15 and 40 per cent, 'the minority is becoming strong enough to begin to influence the culture of the group'; in the *balanced* group with ratios of 60:40 down to 50:50 the culture and interaction reflect the balanced nature of the group.[56]

After the 1997 general election women MPs constituted 18 per cent of all MPs and Labour's 101 women MPs constituted 24 per cent of the Parliamentary Labour Party (PLP). In both cases they constitute a 'tilted group' and therefore would be considered capable of effecting change.[57] Arguably, those who claim that a significant presence of women is important for substantive change could be confident that the 1997 Parliament would see such changes.

As the women MPs took their seats in the House it had looked as though there were plenty of them, but over time some commentators began to question whether they did, in fact, constitute a critical mass. Rather than simply blaming the women MPs for their apparent failure to act for women, they looked to the government, the House of Commons itself and the wider political environment for explanations for their behaviour. Anna Coote (academic, journalist and activist) concluded that 'feminism just doesn't fit into Blair's vision';[58] Cristina Odone (*Observer* columnist) recognized that New Labour had failed women, in society *and* as members of Parliament;[59] while Jeanette Winterson (author of the novel *Oranges are Not the Only Fruit*) agreed that the problem lay, at least in part, with the government when she asked: 'why are women sidelined to the constituencies while men take the big platforms?'[60] Even Germaine Greer acknowledged that if the new women MPs had let women down, they themselves were 'seriously let down' by the government.[61] Yet Natasha Walter, in her article, 'If faith falters be charitable and hope', retained her belief that the women MPs would make a difference: 'If anything is really going to change for women in Britain, it's just too early to give up on them.'[62]

The need for an empirical study that explores the relationship between women's political presence and the representation of women (in all its dimensions) is self-evident. Politicians, the media, women's groups, feminist theorists, and women in general want to know what difference, if any, the women MPs have made since their election: are women better represented as a consequence of the election of the 120 women MPs (or 101 Labour women MPs) in 1997? In what ways have these women representatives represented women – numerically, symbolically, substantively? And did they act in a feminized way?

This book constitutes one answer to these questions. Analysing how the women MPs conceive of and practise representation through talking to them provides fresh insights (situated knowledge) into the theoretical literature on women's political representation.[63] It should also make us more confident about the claim that the presence of greater numbers of women representatives is important and enable us to theorize more assuredly the relationship between women's descriptive and substantive representation.

This book is based on data drawn from in-depth interviews with Labour women MPs first elected to the House of Commons in 1997. They were undertaken at two different points in the 1997 Parliament. The first round of interviews in 1997 involved 34 of the 65 newly elected Labour women MPs. A second round of interviews was undertaken in the summer of 2000. Of the original 34 interviewees 23 agreed to participate again. The research strategy and methods are outlined in Appendix 1.

THE STRUCTURE OF THE BOOK

The next chapter examines traditional and feminist conceptions of representation. A brief homage to Hanna Pitkin's seminal *The Concept of Representation* (1967) is undertaken as this is part of a well-established formula for books on representation but, more importantly, because it serves as the context within which contemporary feminist conceptions have developed.[64] The chapter focuses on the work of Anne Phillips, whose *The Politics of Presence* outlines a case for women's political presence that, *inter alia*, makes the claim that women's descriptive and substantive representation are linked.[65]

Although women's political representation does not simply refer to the numbers of women in a given political institution, this remains one important dimension of the concept and is the subject of Chapter 3. given that the 1997 general election saw the doubling of the numbers of women MPs, a re-examination of women's numerical representation in the House of Commons is timely. That the women MPs were overwhelmingly Labour makes this even more imperative: the Labour Party's policy of all-women shortlists (AWS) appears to be a key factor in explaining their success in returning increased numbers of women in the 1997 general election, relative to both previous Parliaments and the other main political parties.

The new Labour women MPs' thoughts on women's numerical representation in general, their own experiences of legislative recruitment in 1997 and the implementation and, where appropriate, their experiences of AWS are discussed.[66] They also reflect on these concerns in respect of the 2001 general election.

Whether women's presence in politics matters symbolically is addressed in Chapter 4, which explores whether the new Labour women MPs considered that their presence legitimized Parliament and whether they felt it 'says something' about women's place in society. The women MPs' thoughts regarding the role model effect of women MPs is also extensively discussed, in particular, whether they consider that they act as role models and whether their presence means that greater numbers of women will seek to be selected as parliamentary candidates in subsequent elections.

The women MPs' discussion of symbolic representation often slipped into discussions of descriptive representation – the argument that political institutions should broadly reflect the make-up of society. The latter part of the chapter therefore considers whether, and for what reasons, the new Labour women MPs considered that women's descriptive representation matters. Did they, for example, agree that there is a link between a representative's identity and attitudes?

Chapter 5 is about women's substantive representation: establishing whether women representatives seek to act for women can be determined by asking them what or whom they represent and whether they consider that they have a responsibility to act for women. The claim that women representatives act for women also needs to contend with the acknowledgement of women's differences. In this chapter, the bases upon which the women MPs claim they are able to act for women who are different from them were sought, as was whether they considered that men could substantively represent women.

This chapter also explores the attitudes of the new Labour women MPs towards feminism. Establishing the extent to which they are 'attitudinally feminist' enables us to envisage how they might act for women; in other words, it tells us the likely direction of their effect. The question of how party differences determine this is also explored: do all women MPs seek to act for women, and in the same way?

The next four chapters (Chapters 6–9) shift the focus towards the ways in which women MPs consider that women representatives substantively represent women in their constituencies, in Parliament and in government. Unpacking the representative roles of British MPs enables a more sophisticated analysis of whether women representatives seek and are able to 'act for' women. It may be the case that the different sites of representation influence the substantive representation of women.

Chapter 6 opens with a discussion of the new Labour women MPs' perceptions of whether their presence determines the extent and nature of the links between themselves and their women constituents. With many more women constituents represented by women MPs it is important to establish whether claims that women representatives act for women hold in the constituency. Whether this is the same for women constituents who are different from their representatives is also explored. The second round of interviews in 2000 enabled the new Labour women MPs to reflect on their experiences of constituency representation since their election.

There are two chapters that consider the substantive representation of women in Parliament. Chapter 7 explores whether the new Labour women MPs sought to and were able to feminize the parliamentary agenda. By drawing on two data sets it is possible to examine the extent to which the women MPs considered that they had acted for women during the 1997 Parliament. Did they consider that they had voiced women's concerns? Had they been able to effect change?

Chapter 8, co-authored with Philip Cowley, looks at the claim that the new Labour women MPs differed from their male colleagues in terms of their voting behaviour in the House of Commons. Was it true that the new Labour women MPs were more loyal to Blair than were other members of the Parliamentary Labour Party, as their critics (in both the media and in the House) claimed? And if so, how can this be explained? How did the women MPs explain their behaviour?

The new Labour women MPs' thoughts on the Women's Minister are explored in Chapter 9. The Women's Minister constitutes an independent and alternative means by which women's substantive representation can occur.[67] Did the women MPs support the post in principle and the women who have inhabited the post in practice? Did they consider that the Women's Minister is, as one of them suggested, a 'bird on the shoulder of government', acting for women? And how did they evaluate the work of the Women's Ministers between 1997 and 2000?

Chapter 10 explores whether the new Labour women MPs considered that they practise politics differently from their male colleagues – one of the arguments presented to support women's political presence. More importantly, it explores whether the women MPs were able, if they so wanted, to act in a feminized way in Parliament. It also considers whether party identity affects the extent to which women MPs 'act like' women.

Establishing whether women MPs consider that they practise a different style of politics from their male colleagues also helps answer the question of whether the increased presence of women makes a difference: if women MPs consider that their preferred style of politics is less well regarded and effective than the dominant masculinized style, they may be 'forced' to act like men in order to act for women.[68]

The conclusion (Chapter 11) draws together the findings of the research. By exploring the new Labour women MPs' conceptions of representation and by considering their experiences of representation, a more nuanced understanding of women's political representation is advanced. In particular, a more complicated theory of the relationship between women's descriptive and substantive representation is developed.

The Epilogue outlines the Sex Discrimination (Election Candidates) Act. This Act, passed in 2002, has transformed the legal context within which women will be recruited to Westminster in the future – it permits political parties to introduce positive discrimination – and constitutes one example of women MPs acting for women in the 1997 Parliament.

NOTES

1. The other woman MP was the Speaker Betty Boothroyd. On election, the Speaker resigns from his or her political party (House of Commons [2002], *The Speaker, Factsheet M2* [London]). See Table 3.1.
2. *Independent* 13 April 1997; *Financial Times* 3 May 1997; *Telegraph* 2 May 1997; *Guardian* 3 May 1997; *Observer* 4 May 1997.
3. *Guardian* 22 July 1996.
4. *Independent* 17 April 1997.
5. *Guardian* 6 January 1997.
6. *Guardian* 5 May 1997.
7. *Independent* 3 May 1997.
8. *Independent* 13 April 1997.
9. *Observer* 8 June 1997.
10. *Guardian* 5 June 1997.
11. *Independent* 17 April 1997.

12. *Times* 14 May 1997. The women MPs' clothing was commented on regularly thereafter: see, for example, 'Dressing down for Blair babes' (*Daily Mail* 28 December 2001); 'Can the babes wear it anymore?' (*Sunday Times* 30 December 2001).
13. *Mirror* 8 October 1997; *Times* 10 December 1997.
14. *Sunday Times* 4 October 1998. A similar comment is made by Richard Ingrams in the *Observer* (26 January 2003). When discussing Conservative Party efforts to select more women he states: 'Behind all the talk about fairness and having sympathetic candidates, lies, I suspect, another less worthy thought on the part of our political leaders, namely that women MPs are likely to be more docile, more easily led than their male counterparts. Such has certainly proved the case with the huge increase of women MPs on the Labour benches … from Mr Blair's point of view they have been a great success – doing what they are told, not asking awkward questions and trooping obediently into the lobby when required.'
15. *Sunday Mirror* 25 October 1998.
16. A group of young MPs, including Oswald Mosley, elected in 1918, had been nicknamed 'The Babes' (J. Dalley [1999], *Diana Mosley: A Life* [London: Faber and Faber], p. 95).
17. *Guardian* 24 May 2001.
18. *Guardian* 3 August 2000.
19. *Telegraph* 8 April 2001.
20. *Guardian* 29 September 2000.
21. Ibid.
22. Mathew Parris wrote, in an article entitled 'A fragrant army incapable of stepping out of line', 'There is something Orwellian about new Labour women MPs … unsmilingly synchronized, so nervelessly correct, so relentlessly unoriginal, as to be sinister … these are Tony Blair's Stepford Wives' (*The Times* 14 November 1997). See also the *Mirror* 7 February 1998.
23. *Independent* 18 January 1998. John Knox's 1558 pamphlet, 'The First Blast of the Trumpet against the Monstrous Regiment [that is, rule] of Women' was written against the rule of Queen Mary Stuart in Scotland (D. Starkey [2001], *Elizabeth* [London: Vintage], p. 113).
24. P. Cowley and S. Childs (2002), 'An Uncritical Critical Mass', in P. Cowley, *Revolts and Rebellions* (London: Politicos), p. 127.
25. Following her marriage in 2001 Helen Brinton is known as Helen Clark.
26. *Guardian* 14 May 1997; *Telegraph* 21 May 2001.
27. See, for example, Matthew Norman in the *Guardian* May, June and July 1997 and May and June 2001.
28. *Guardian* 4 May 1998.
29. *Guardian* 22 December 2000; 15 March 2001.
30. *Guardian* 16 November 2000.
31. *Telegraph* 16 November 2000; 17 November 2000.
32. The term 'women's concerns' is employed here in preference to the more disputed term 'women's issues'. Women's concerns point 'to issues that bear on women, without in any way presupposing what position any given group of women would take on them' (C. Cockburn [1996] 'Strategies for Gender Democracy', *European Journal of Women's Studies*, 3, 7: 14–15).
33. *Guardian* 29 April 1999.
34. *Guardian* 15 December 1997.
35. *Guardian* 5 January 1998.
36. *Mail on Sunday* 21 January 2001; *Telegraph* 14 February 1998; *Telegraph* 22 July 2000.
37. *Telegraph* 7 April 2001. See also *Telegraph* 22 July 2000; 8 October 2000; *Guardian* 5 January 1998; 3 August 2000.
38. 'If faith falters, be charitable and hope', *Observer* 4 January 1998.
39. *Mail on Sunday* 21 January 2001.
40. P. Brookes (1967), *Women at Westminster* (London: Peter Davies), p. 17.
41. Ibid., p. 23.
42. Ibid., p. 64.
43. Ibid., pp. 135 and 150.
44. E. Vallance (1979), *Women in the House* (London: The Athlone Press), pp. 74–5.
45. Ibid., pp. 39 and 75.
46. M. Currell (1974), *Political Woman* (London: Croom Helm).
47. Ibid., pp. 87–8.

48. P. Norris and J. Lovenduski (1989), 'Women Candidates for Parliament', *British Journal of Political Science*, 19, 1: 114.
49. P. Norris and J. Lovenduski (1995), *Political Recruitment* (Cambridge: Cambridge University Press), pp. 213–24.
50. J. Lovenduski (1997) 'Gender Politics', *Parliamentary Affairs*, 50, 4: 719. For a discussion of the 2001 BRS, see J. Lovenduski and P. Norris, 'Westminster Women: the Politics of Presence', *Political Studies*, 51: 84–102.
51. The terms of the US debate are summarized in S. Caroll (1994), *Women as Candidates in American Politics* (Bloomington and Indianapolis, IN: Indiana University Press); R. Darcy, S. Welch and J. Clark (1994), *Women, Elections and Representation* (Lincoln, NB: University of Nebraska Press). See also B. Reingold (2000), *Representing Women* (Chapel Hill, NC and London: University of North Carolina Press).
52. B. Reingold (1992), 'Concepts of Representation among Female and Male State Legislators', *Legislative Studies Quarterly*, 17: 531. See also K. Tamerius (1995), 'Sex, Gender and Leadership in the Representation of Women', in G. Duerst-Lahti and R. Mae Kelly (eds), *Gender, Power, Leadership and Governance* (Ann Arbor, MI: University of Michigan Press), p. 96.
53. H. F. Pitkin (1967), *The Concept of Representation* (Berkeley, CA: University of California Press); A. Birch (1993), *The Concepts and Theories of Modern Democracy* (London: Routledge); N. Rao (1998), 'Representation in Local Politics', *Political Studies*, 46, 1: 19–35.
54. A. Phillips (1995), *The Politics of Presence* (Oxford: Oxford University Press); J. Mansbridge (1999), 'Should Blacks Represent Blacks and Women Represent Women?', *The Journal of Politics*, 61, 3: 628–57.
55. D. T. Studlar and I. McAllister (2002), 'Does a Critical Mass Exist?', *European Journal of Political Research*, 41, 2: 234.
56. D. Dahlerup (1988), 'From a Small to a Large Minority', *Scandinavian Political Studies*, 11, 4: 280; J. Lovenduski (2001), 'Women and Politics', in P. Norris (ed.), *Britain Votes 2001* (Oxford: Oxford University Press).
57. P. Norris (1996), 'Women Politicians', in J. Lovenduski and P. Norris (eds), *Women in Politics* (Oxford: Oxford University Press), p. 94.
58. *Guardian* 11 May 1999.
59. *Observer* 27 May 2001, emphasis added.
60. *Guardian* 29 May 2001; J. Winterson (1991), *Oranges are Not the Only Fruit* (London: Vintage).
61. *Mail on Sunday* 21 January 2001.
62. *Observer* 4 January 1998.
63. F. Mackay (2001), *Love and Politics* (London: Continuum), pp. 3, 6; J. Squires (1999), *Gender in Political Theory* (Cambridge: Polity Press), p. 227.
64. D. Judge (1999), *Representation* (London: Routledge), p. 1.
65. Phillips, *A Politics of Presence.*
66. Norris and Lovenduski, *Political Recruitment.*
67. J. Squires and M. Wickham-Jones (2002), 'Mainstreaming in Westminster and Whitehall', *Parliamentary Affairs*, 55, 1: 59; C. Short (1996), 'Women in the Labour Party', in J. Lovenduski and P. Norris (eds), *Women in Politics* (Oxford: Oxford University Press), pp. 24–5.
68. K. Ross (2002), 'Women's Place in "Male" Space', *Parliamentary Affairs*, 55, 1: 195.

2

Women's Political Representation

Traditionally the sex of our representatives was not deemed to matter. In her seminal work on representation Hanna F. Pitkin declared that the concept of representation did not mean descriptive representation: it meant 'acting for'.[1] As long as the representative acted for the represented – 'the represented must be somehow logically prior; the representative must be responsive to him rather than the other way around'[2] – it did not seem to matter who the representative was.[3]

Moreover, Pitkin was forthright in her criticism of descriptive representation: it was, in her opinion, wrongly premised upon an assumed link between the representative's characteristics and their actions.[4] Any resemblance between the representative and the represented is misleading.[5] The descriptive representative cannot 'act for' the represented because the representative '"stands for" them by virtue of a correspondence or connection between them, a resemblance or reflection'.[6] Neither can the represented hold representatives to account under descriptive representation: 'a man can only be held to account for what he has done' and 'not for what he is'.[7]

Many feminists, however, disagree with traditional conceptions of descriptive representation. The idea that representation has occurred when a representative acts in the interests of the represented has served 'to justify' the dominance of 'white males'.[8] And on closer inspection, descriptive representation turns out to have had its historical supporters all along; even Pitkin acknowledged that there was some kind of expectation of a relationship between who and what was represented.[9] Indeed, descriptive representation played a part in the extension of the franchise to previously excluded categories of people (which raises the question of why it was thought necessary to extend the franchise to the working classes and women if rich white men were representing them).[10]

Yet, claims that women *should* be present in our political fora do not, in themselves, explain *why* women should be present. The normative case for women's political presence is variously made, in terms of justice, symbolic representation, substantive representation, and on the basis that women politicians have a different style of politics.[11] But it is the claim that there is a relationship between women's descriptive and substantive representation that is the most considered and contested. This argument, that there is a relationship between women's descriptive and substantive representation, is appealing. To suggest that there is no link between women's gender identity and behaviour is counter-intuitive to most women.[12] Similarly, Anne Phillips's presumption that women representatives are more likely than male representatives to act for women seems reasonable.[13]

Ironically, feminist demands for women's descriptive representation (for whichever reason) have occurred at the same time that some feminists have begun to question the theoretical coherency of the category 'woman'.[14] Differences between women, said to have been played down by second-wave feminist ideas of 'sisterhood', are now widely acknowledged. Women are never simply women: 'real' women's identities are multiple, differentiated in terms of class, ethnicity and sexuality (at the very least). In this context it seems naïve to be demanding women's political presence. Do not demands for women's descriptive representation reify sex differences and, once again, incorrectly assume 'direct and uncomplicated links between sex and gender'?[15]

Advocates of women's descriptive representation must, therefore, contend with the theoretical problems thrown up by contemporary feminist understandings of sex and gender,[16] namely, whether it is possible to talk about representing women while avoiding the charge of essentialism.[17] Jane Mansbridge's refinement of the concept of representation suggests, at least at the level of theory, that this can be achieved: descriptive representation should be considered as denoting 'shared experiences' and 'not only visible characteristics'.[18]

Empirical study of women representatives acting in particular political fora should reveal what differences, if any, follow from the presence of women representatives: what the relationship is between women's descriptive, symbolic and substantive representation and women's style of politics; whether an appreciation of women's differences disrupts or prevents the representation of women (in all its dimensions) in practice; and whether the difference women representatives make is, as critical mass theory suggests, simply a result of the effect of the increased numbers of women present (that is, the result of sex) or whether other determinants are at play.[19]

ANNE PHILLIPS: THE POLITICS OF PRESENCE[20]

The politics of presence is the demand for the equal representation of groups. Unlike the politics of ideas, it rejects a 'detached understanding of political ideas' in which no link is acknowledged between one's ideas and one's material existence.[21] Rather, it reflects the fact that difference is, in contemporary times, increasingly framed not around different ideas, but around different identities.

The politics of presence is grounded in existing structures of exclusion.[22] Women's, minority ethnic groups' and other disadvantaged groups' presence cannot be deduced from the democratic principles of popular control or political equality because representative democracy has challenged a direct association between being a representative and being represented and because the concept of political equality is too 'slippery'.[23]

The demand for presence can be regarded as being both at odds with, and an extension of, liberal democracy.[24] It is at odds with liberal democracy when it seeks the guarantee of political office for certain groups of people – this goes against the 'classically liberal principle that requires all citizens to have the same civil and political rights'.[25] At the same time, the politics of presence is 'merely an extension of this basic idea', namely that no one should be 'excluded by virtue of gender, ethnicity or language' and that therefore 'certain guarantees have to be set in place'.[26]

The normative case for a politics of presence is argued, first, in terms of symbolic representation; second, it is premised upon the need to tackle exclusions that derive from party representation; third, it is claimed that disadvantaged groups need more aggressive advocates; and finally, presence is said to be needed to ensure a transformation of the political agenda.[27]

The case for women's political presence is made on four more specific bases:[28] first, principles of justice between the sexes; second, the role model effect; third, the realist argument that women's interests are discounted in the absence of women's political presence;[29] and finally, women's different relationship to politics, in which women will introduce a different set of values and concerns.[30]

It is increasingly accepted that for justice reasons our political fora should be descriptively representative in terms of sex. Women's absence raises the question of discrimination against women and is regarded as evidence of a *prima facie* case of injustice that should be redressed.[31]

Although this interpretation is reliant upon acceptance of the feminist insight that the current sexual division of labour between women and men is 'inequitable', 'unnatural' and 'unjust', it is largely uncontested.[32] Nevertheless, criticisms regarding the method to achieve women's numerical representation remain (as Chapter 3 and the Epilogue discuss).[33]

It is also increasingly accepted that the absence of women undermines the legitimacy of our political institutions.[34] An overwhelmingly male House of Commons simply 'looks wrong' and 'suggests' that women are not capable of being MPs, a contention that is untenable, if not risible, in the twenty-first century. Thus women need to be physically present to symbolize that they are as capable as those (that is, men) who are already present.[35]

These arguments clearly contest traditional analysis of symbolic representation. *Contra* Pitkin, who held that symbols are often arbitrary, symbols frequently have a clear relationship with their referents. As Duerst-Lahti and Verstegen note, the US flag has the same number of stars as the number of states: they contend that it could not have any other number of stars, nor change its colour, and retain its symbolic representativeness.[36] In the same way, the symbolic representation of women requires the presence of women representatives; those who have different bodies cannot symbolically represent women.[37] Furthermore, the claim that women *are* represented when they believe *that they are* irrespective of the sex of the representative is unconvincing.[38]

Although symbolic arguments do not require that the newly present women representatives make a difference, in any substantive sense, women's symbolic representation nevertheless offers the possibility of a substantive as well as symbolic effect.[39] As Sapiro states: 'Women and men continue to think of politics as a male domain because the empirical truth at this moment is that politics *is* a male domain.'[40] Women's presence might change this. Women representatives might act as role models and women can gain political experience by working for women representatives. In these ways women's numerical representation might be greatly enhanced.[41]

The need to tackle the exclusions that derive from party representation is the second argument for the politics of presence. Party representation has eclipsed traditional concerns regarding how much autonomy representatives should have.[42] Yet party representation becomes problematic when a representative is forced by party discipline and/or an electoral mandate to vote with their party and against the apparent interests of the constituency and their own beliefs.[43] Moreover, if party representation is predominant, as it is in the UK, then the sex of the representative seems irrelevant once again.

However, even in the British political system MPs act on areas and issues that are not explicitly discussed in the electoral campaign and/or manifesto.[44] Therefore, even if party representation usually dominates, the sex of the representative may still matter. MPs have more than one representative role. As constituency representatives, they are able to represent the interests of their constituents and in the constituency the influence of party identity is said to be less important.[45] Furthermore, when an MP shares the opinions and interests of a particular group these interests are even more likely to be represented.[46] Consequently, having women representatives may not only make a difference, but may be particularly important in the constituency.

The third argument in support of the politics of presence is the disadvantaged groups' need for more assertive advocacy. This is not to say that no one ever acts on behalf of others, but, as Phillips argues, 'there is something distinctly odd about a democracy that accepts a responsibility for redressing disadvantage, but never sees the disadvantaged as the appropriate people to carry this through'.[47] Moreover, she makes it clear that 'when policies are worked out *for* rather than *with* a politically excluded constituency, they are unlikely to engage with all relevant concerns'.[48]

The argument that the presence of the previously excluded will transform the political agenda focuses upon the realm of preferences not yet formulated, articulated or legitimated on the political agenda and therefore unable to be part of the packages of political ideas.[49] In this context, presence really matters:

> Since all options are *not* already in play, we need to ensure a more even handed balance of society's groups in the arenas of political discussion. The social construction of political preferences means that some possibilities will have been opened up and other ones closed down, and relying only on what is registered through the vote (through the initial choice of representatives) will then reinforce what is already dominant.[50]

The argument that women should be present in politics because they will bring a different style to politics is usually based on one of two arguments, which, despite their different starting points, agree that women in politics will seek to be consensual rather than confrontational.[51] The first relies upon traditional notions of women's sex, while the second makes reference to the way in which women in the Women's Liberation Movement rejected notions of individual leadership and emphasized deliberation and collective decision-making.[52]

However, whether women should seek to base their claims for political presence on women's 'superior' mode of political engagement is questionable, as it risks reproducing essentialist notions of sex and gender.[53] It may also be risky because when the feminized style is no longer in demand, demand for greater numbers of women politicians might similarly be reduced.

Notwithstanding these various arguments for women's political presence, many feminists consider that women should be present in politics because of a perceived relationship between women's descriptive and substantive representation. Indeed, it might be the case that this is a necessary argument to make in order to secure women's greater numerical representation, through mobilizing women to participate and engendering women's (s)election.[54] Yet this claim is the most contested argument, for it contends (at least in a strong interpretation) that women representatives will act for women. But is it plausible to move from arguing that the sex of the representative does not matter to claiming that the sex of the representative is *all* that matters? Phillips is concerned that a strong argument that women representatives will act for women is dependent upon essentialism:[55]

> I could argue some fundamental unity between women, some essential set of experiences and interests that can be represented by any interchangeable combination of women. But if I prefer to keep off this terrain, in what sense are women represented by women?[56]

Although at the intuitive level it is 'hard to fault' the contention that women have particular needs, interests and concerns that derive from women's different experiences, that these concerns will be inadequately addressed in political fora dominated by men and that the case is further strengthened with an appreciation of women's interests as 'varied, unstable, perhaps still in the process of formation', these points do not negate essentialist concerns.[57] Phillips is also concerned about accountability.[58] When the House of Commons is descriptively representative in terms of sex, there can be no complaints if the women MPs do not act for women because 'the only possible criteria [*sic*] of sex representativeness' – that half the representatives should be women – has been met.[59]

Acknowledging these concerns leads Phillips to conclude that there is no 'empirical or theoretical plausibility' to the notion that women share experiences or that women's shared experiences translate into shared beliefs or goals.[60] Neither is it likely that women will organize themselves into a group with group opinions and goals that can be represented.[61]

Yet if Phillips turns away from a strong sense of women's politics of presence, she looks towards gender parity. Achieved by sex quotas, gender parity identifies additional barriers and obstacles to women's political participation, including those associated with and/or located in the private sphere, and supports the introduction of mechanisms that some liberals might consider to constitute affirmative, and therefore illiberal, action.[62]

Gender parity operates in a framework of probabilities rather than certainties – it is 'a shot in the dark' – although it does claim that women representatives, while shooting in the dark, are still more likely than men 'to hit the target'.[63] Gender parity therefore remains underpinned by a relationship between women's descriptive and substantive representation. There is still a guarantee, albeit unguaranteed, that women representatives will 'act for' women. That women representatives are more likely to act for women because of their 'general (and inevitably more tenuous) perception' of women's gender-differentiated experiences seems, to Phillips, a fair presumption.[64]

THE COMPLICATED RELATIONSHIP BETWEEN SEX, GENDER AND THE SUBSTANTIVE REPRESENTATION OF WOMEN

More questions must, however, be asked about the relationship between women's descriptive and substantive representation. The danger remains of simply, but nevertheless mistakenly, reducing a representative's likelihood to act for women to their sex and/or gender.[65] As Phillips admits: 'to treat class and gender composition as just a proxy for opinion and ideas' 'begs some important questions'.[66] And while it is 'methodological individualism run wild to think that Margaret Thatcher as Prime Minister is better for women than some man who wants more nurseries or a higher minimum wage', her point is clear.[67]

Jane Mansbridge's work is useful here. Like Phillips, Mansbridge argues that the case for women's political presence should be based not on a simple or essentialist interpretation of descriptive representation, but on the basis of women's former exclusion from politics.[68] If women can demonstrate that they are under-represented, if they consider themselves capable of representing themselves, and if there is evidence that dominant groups have 'intentionally made it difficult or illegal' for women 'to represent themselves', then the case can be made for their presence – what she terms 'affirmative selective representation'.[69] Mansbridge emphasizes the contingent nature of this argument; it is not a case for permanent quotas.[70]

The reasons why Mansbridge favours descriptive representation are, again, similar to those of Phillips: 'disadvantaged groups gain from descriptive representation' in contexts of group mistrust, uncrystallised interests, historical political subordination and low *de facto* legitimacy'.[71] She too emphasizes substantive effects of women's political presence. Women representatives will improve deliberation between the represented and their representative (vertical deliberation) and among representatives (horizontal deliberation).[72]

Furthermore, Mansbridge makes the case for women's full rather than token presence. This is necessary because token presence cannot guarantee the voicing of 'minority perspectives'; because there needs to be sufficient numbers of representatives present in all the different fora where representation occurs; and, because 'deliberation is often synergistic', more representatives 'usually produce more and sometimes better information and insight'.[73] Importantly, the case is also made on the basis that it ensures that the diversity of women's perspectives is included.[74]

Notwithstanding her commitment to the presence of different women in politics, Manbridge's argument, like Phillips's, holds that there is a relationship between women's descriptive and substantive representation. Yet the continuing difficulty in conceiving of the substantive representation of women once we take the acknowledgement of women's differences seriously must be addressed.[75] If women are a heterogeneous and not a homogeneous group, who experience the world in different ways, mediated, at the minimum, by class and ethnic identities, the basis upon which women can substantively represent other women is rendered problematic.[76] Securing women's descriptive representation begins to look as though it cannot ensure the substantive representation of women because women are not a homogeneous group with a singular interest to be represented. Indeed, as Voet argues, if sex descriptiveness does not make reference to other differences between women, then the ensuing 'rough approximation' means that the representation of women is merely symbolic and inadequate.[77]

To be sure, feminist theories have sought to refine conceptions of women's difference and asserted that women's 'social group membership is very real in practical terms to all of us'.[78] Young, for example, defines difference as 'less like the icing bordering the layers of cake, however, and more like a marble cake, in which the flavours remain recognisably different, but thoroughly insinuated in one another',[79] while Phillips argues that it is establishing that women have different interests from men rather than establishing that all women share the same interests that is important.[80]

Again, Mansbridge's analysis is helpful. Mindful of essentialist criticism, she maintains that women representatives can act for other women notwithstanding the differences between them.[81] Women representatives need not have personally shared the same experiences before they can act for other women because their wider shared experience gives them 'communicative and informational advantages':

> Representatives and voters who share some version of a set of common experiences and the outward signs of having lived through those experiences can often read one another's signals relatively easily and engage in relatively accurate forms of shorthand communication. Representatives and voters who share membership in a subordinate group can also forge bonds of trust based specifically on the shared experience of subordination.[82]

Accordingly, descriptive representation should be considered as denoting 'shared experiences' and 'not only visible characteristics'.[83] This claim – that women's descriptive representation does not require a sameness between women representatives and the women who are being represented – combined with her assertion that women representatives can be held to account through the competitive nature of the existing electoral system, constitutes a strong and helpful counter-challenge to critics of descriptive representation.[84] Indeed, if Mansbridge is correct – and only empirical study will demonstrate this – then the class and ethnic identity of the women representatives present in our political fora is less problematic, at least in terms of conceptualizing women's substantive representation.

APPLYING IDEAS

If the assumption of many feminist theorists is that there is a relationship between women's descriptive and symbolic and substantive representation, the relationship is, for the most part, acknowledged as a 'probabilistic rather than deterministic' one:[85] Phillips's guarantee *is* unguaranteed.[86] What remain under-theorized are the determinants of women representatives 'acting for' women.[87]

As was made clear in the Introduction, the concept of critical mass is the dominant framework that purports to explain the relationship between women's political presence and their effect.[88] Unfortunately, there is little agreement as to the precise figure that constitutes critical mass.[89] Consequently, it is not at all clear whether there were sufficient Labour women MPs, either newly elected or re-elected, in the 1997 Parliament to effect change. Moreover, because critical mass simply counts the numbers of biological females and males present in a particular political institution it tells us nothing about the women representatives' attitudes and (likely) behaviour. Neither does it tell us anything about the environment in which they act. Critical mass arguably hides more than it reveals.

Not all women accept gendered analysis; neither are all women representatives feminists (and feminism has multiple interpretations anyway).[90] It is important, therefore, not to elide the substantive representation of women by women representatives with the feminist substantive representation of women by feminist women representatives; women's bodies must not be confused with feminist minds. A more complex understanding of gender identity – one that does not posit a feminist/non-feminist dichotomy – is necessary. We need to be able to conceptualize women representatives who 'act for women' but whose gendered analysis is in conflict with what is considered to be 'in the interests of women'[91] and women representatives who reject the link between the substantive representation of women by women (those who deny that their gender determines their actions in any way).[92] This is not to say that the actions of women representatives cannot be evaluated in terms of feminist analysis.[93] But if the aim is to theorize the relationship between women's descriptive and substantive representation, then we need to include within in our conceptual frameworks non-feminist women representatives.

Critical mass also fails to tell us to which political parties the women representatives belong. Yet in the UK women MPs are first and foremost party members. They are selected and elected in the same way as their male colleagues, as party representatives of a geographical and not a sex-based constituency.[94] It is therefore important to explore whether, and in what ways, the party identity of women representatives qualifies the claim that women representatives represent women (in all its dimensions),[95] although this should not be taken to imply that women representatives' views on women's concerns are simply reducible to their parties' views. Intuitively, it makes sense to argue that had the 101 Labour women MPs returned in the 1997 general election been Conservative women MPs then any claims about what difference they would make would have been qualitatively different. Thus, rather than downplaying party identity or regarding it as confusing the issue, it is necessary to centre women representatives' party identity (at least in systems where party identity is dominant) and consider how this complicates the relationship between women's descriptive, symbolic and substantive representation.

Critical mass also fails to give sufficient acknowledgement to the gendered context within which women representatives operate,[96] and yet whether women representatives who want to make a difference are able to effect change may well depend upon the political environment they inhabit.[97] Where women and men representatives face the 'same institutional norms and expectations and share the same status', it is likely that they will 'exhibit similar representational priorities'.[98] Where political institutions are characterized by masculinist norms, and when inter-party conflict is heightened, the ability of women representatives to act for women may be reduced.[99] For example, women representatives may 'downplay' their perspectives to gain the 'acceptance of their colleagues who control access to rewards'.[100] Thus situating women representatives within their particular political institutions and acknowledging the larger political environment can only improve our theorizing.[101]

Accordingly, exploring whether women representatives do politics differently is not only interesting in itself, but central to a more comprehensive consideration of the relationship between women's presence and their effect. It is important to establish whether women MPs can act differently and effect change in environments characterized by established and gendered norms of behaviour or whether they are forced to adopt the masculinized modes of political behaviour. This question is particularly significant because it is said that women are 'turned off' by the 'willy-jousting' that characterizes the House of Commons.[102] Consequently, if women representatives adopt this style of politics it may prevent a relationship developing between themselves and women.

It may also reduce the numbers of women seeking selection and/or those selected as candidates.

Rather than relying upon a simple claim that women representatives act for women, I contend, then, that the nature of the relationship between women's descriptive and substantive representation should be more easily determinable with the adoption of a conceptual framework in which the relationship between women's descriptive and substantive representation is understood as reflecting women representatives' gender and party identities and one that acknowledges that women representatives act in particular gendered environments. This approach recognizes that the substantive representation of women will vary according to the different sites of representation and over time.[103]

Examining in practice how the new Labour women MPs' gender and party identities determine their attitudes and behaviours and exploring whether they consider the House of Commons a conducive environment should enable us to theorize with greater confidence the relationship between women's enhanced political presence in the 1997 Parliament and whether the women MPs could make a difference – in terms of women's numerical, symbolic and, most importantly of all, substantive representation.

Questions of women's differences can also be more fully explored at the practical rather than theoretical level. If Mansbridge's claim that women representatives need not have personally shared the same particular experiences because of women's wider shared experiences and their more diffuse consciousness of 'being a woman' in a gendered society is correct – and this book offers the new Labour women MPs' insights on this – then this should enable us to refine our understanding of women's multiple identities and explore how feminist theory might conceive of the substantive representation of women even when it takes the acknowledgement of women's differences seriously.

NOTES

1. H. F. Pitkin (1967), *The Concept of Representation* (Berkeley, CA: University of California Press), Chapters 6 and 7. Neither did it mean formalistic representation (when an individual has the authority to act for others bestowed upon them or when an individual is held to account and has to answer to another for what they do) nor symbolic representation (ibid., Chapters 2, 3 and 5).
2. Ibid., p. 140.
3. Ibid., p. 163.
4. Ibid., p. 89.

5. Ibid., pp. 66–72.
6. Ibid., pp. 61, 226.
7. Ibid., p. 90; I. Mclean (1991), 'Forms of Representation and Systems of Voting', in D. Held (ed.), *Political Theory Today* (Cambridge: Polity Press), p. 175; N. Rao (1998), 'Representation in Local Politics', *Political Studies* 46, 1: 25.
8. G. Duerst-Lahti and D. Verstegen (1995), 'Making Something of Absence', in G. Duerst-Lahti and R. Mae Kelly (eds), *Gender, Power, Leadership and Governance* (Ann Arbor, MI: University of Michigan Press), p. 218; C. S. King (1995), 'Sex-role Identity and Decision-styles: How Gender Helps Explain the Paucity of Women at the Top', in G. Duerst-Lahti and R. M. Kelly (eds), *Gender, Power, Leadership and Governance* (Ann Arbor, MI: University of Michigan Press), p. 67.
9. Pitkin, *The Concept of Representation*, p. 63; D. Judge (1999), *Representation* (London: Routledge), p. 22.
10. Pitkin, *The Concept of Representation*, pp. 62–3; A. H. Birch (1993), *The Concepts and Theories of Modern Democracy* (London: Routledge), p. 72; Judge, *Representation*, pp. 22–33.
11. A. Phillips (1995), *The Politics of Presence* (Oxford: Oxford University Press).
12. J. Vickers (1997), 'Towards a Feminist Understanding of Representation', in J. Arscott and L. Trimble (eds), *In the Presence of Women* (Toronto: Harcourt Brace), p. 23.
13. Phillips, *The Politics of Presence*, p. 82.
14. M. Sawer (2002), 'The Representation of Women in Australia', *Parliamentary Affairs* 55, 1: 5.
15. B. Reingold (2000), *Representing Women* (Chapel Hill, NC: University of North Carolina Press), pp. 45, 49; J. Squires (1999), *Gender in Political Theory* (Cambridge: Polity Press), p. 215.
16. Reingold, *Representing Women*, p. 49; Fiona Mackay, private correspondence.
17. F. Mackay (2001), *Love and Politics* (London: Continuum), p. 10. Essentialism refers to any account that 'theorises women as a category with a set of essential attributes' (I. M. Young [1990], *Throwing Like a Girl* [Bloomington and Indianapolis, IN: Indiana University Press], p. 87).
18. J. Mansbridge (1999), 'Should Blacks Represent Blacks and Women Represent Women?', *Journal of Politics*, 6, 3: 629.
19. Reingold, *Representing Women*; D. Dodson (2001), 'The Impact of Women in Congress', paper presented to the Annual Meeting of APSA Women and Politics Special Session, San Francisco; G. Duerst-Lahti (2001), 'Institutions, Ideologies, and the Possibility of Equal Political Participation', paper presented to the Annual Meeting of APSA Women and Politics Special Session, San Francisco; J. Lovenduski (1990), 'Feminism and West European Politics', in D. W. Urwin and W. E. Paterson (eds), *Politics and West Europe Today* (London: Longman).
20. This chapter draws extensively on Phillips, *The Politics of Presence*.
21. Phillips, *The Politics of Presence*, pp. 1–2.
22. Ibid., p. 25.
23. Ibid., pp. 28–34.
24. Ibid., p. 121.
25. Ibid.
26. Ibid., p. 121.
27. Ibid., pp. 39–44.
28. Ibid., pp. 62–3.
29. The concept of interest is a contested concept with a long and distinguished history of feminist engagement (V. Sapiro [1998], 'When are Interests Interesting', in A. Phillips [ed.], *Feminism and Politics* [Oxford: Oxford University Press]; I. Diamond and N. Hartsock [1998], 'Beyond Interests in Politics', in A. Phillips [ed.] *Feminism and Politics* [Oxford: Oxford University Press]; A. G. Jonasdottir [1990], 'On the Concept of Interest, Women's Interests, and the Limitations of Interest Theory', in K. B. Jones and A. G. Jonasdottir [eds], *The Political Interests of Gender, Developing Theory and Research with a Feminist Face* [London: Sage], pp. 33–65; C. Cockburn [1996], 'Strategies for Gender Democracy', *European Journal of Women's Studies*, 3, 7).
30. In her later work Phillips reframes the fourth point and makes reference to a revitalization of democracy that bridges the gap between representation and participation – the establishment of additional decision-making bodies, open fora or 'just the extraordinary energy so many women politicians devote to what they see as their responsibilities for representing women' (A. Phillips [1998], 'Democracy and Representation', in A. Phillips [ed.], *Feminism and Politics* [Oxford: Oxford University Press], p. 238; Phillips, *The Politics of Presence*).

31. Phillips, *The Politics of Presence*, p. 65.
32. Ibid., pp. 63–5.
33. Ibid., p. 60; Judge, *Representation*, pp. 44–5; S. Childs (2002), 'Conceptions of Representation and the Passage of the Sex Discrimination (Election Candidates) Bill', *Journal of Legislative Studies* 8, 3.
34. Phillips, *The Politics of Presence*, pp. 40, 65; Mansbridge, 'Should Blacks Represent Blacks?', p. 628; A. High-Pippert and J. Cromer (1998) 'Female Empowerment', *Women and Politics* 19, 4; Reingold, *Representing Women*, pp. 31–2.
35. Birch, *The Concepts and Theories of Modern Democracy*, p. 74; Phillips cited in H. F. Pitkin (ed.) (1969), *Representation* (New York: Atherton Press), p. 135; Phillips, *The Politics of Presence*, pp. 40, 45; Mansbridge, 'Should Blacks Represent Blacks?', p. 636.
36. Duerst-Lahti and Verstegen, 'Making Something of Absence', pp. 216–17.
37. Pitkin, *The Concept of Representation*, p. 97.
38. Ibid., pp. 99–100, 104. It is this aspect – whether or not people support or believe a specific symbol, whether a leader is pleasing or acceptable to the represented – which, pushed to its limits, justifies fascist theories of representation (Pitkin, *The Concept of Representation*, pp. 107–11; Pitkin, *Representation*, p. 13).
39. Phillips, *The Politics of Presence*, pp. 40–1.
40. Sapiro, 'When are Interests Interesting?', p. 183, emphasis in the original; S. J. Carroll (1994), *Women as Candidates in American Politics* (Bloomington and Indianapolis, IN: Indiana University Press).
41. J. Clark (1994), 'Getting There', in M. Githens, P. Norris and J. Lovenduski (eds), *Different Roles, Different Voices* (New York: HarperCollins), p. 100.
42. Pitkin, *The Concept of Representation*, pp. 165–6; A. H. Birch (1971), *Representation* (Basingstoke: Macmillan), pp. 15–16; Rao, 'Representation in Local Politics', pp. 29, 31.
43. R. J. Pennock (1968), 'Political Representation', in J. R. Pennock and J. W. Chapman (eds), *Representation* (New York: Atherton Press), p. 24.
44. Phillips, 'Democracy and Representation', pp. 235–6; Phillips, *The Politics of Presence*, pp. 43, 8; Mansbridge, 'Should Blacks Represent Blacks?', pp. 644–6; D. Beetham (1992), 'The Plant Report and the Theory of Political Representation', *Political Quarterly*, 63, 4; A. Reeve and A. Ware (1992), *Electoral Systems* (London: Routledge); J. Squires (1996), 'Quotas for Women', in J. Lovenduski and P. Norris (eds), *Women in Politics* (Oxford: Oxford University Press).
45. D. D. Searing (1985), 'The Role of the Good Constituency Member and the Practice of Representation in Great Britain', *Journal of Politics*, 47: 348.
46. Beetham, 'The Plant Report and the Theory of Political Representation', p. 462; Reeve and Ware, *Electoral Systems*, p. 82.
47. Phillips, *The Politics of Presence*, pp. 43–4, 66.
48. Ibid., p. 13, emphasis in the original.
49. Ibid., pp. 44, 176.
50. Ibid., p. 45.
51. P. Norris (1996), 'Women Politicians', in J. Lovenduski and P. Norris (eds), *Women in Politics*; Mackay, *Love and Politics*; C. Bochel and J. Briggs (2000), 'Do Women Make a Difference?', *Politics* 20, 2: 63–8; Sawer, 'The Representation of Women in Australia'.
52. A. Phillips (1991), *Engendering Democracy* (Cambridge: Polity Press), Chapter 5.
53. K. Ross (2002), 'Women's Place in "Male" Space', *Parliamentary Affairs*, 55, 1: 189–201.
54. Mackay, *Love and Politics*, p. 3.
55. Phillips, *The Politics of Presence*, p. 23.
56. Ibid., p. 54.
57. Phillips, 'Democracy and Representation', pp. 233–5.
58. Ibid., pp. 234–5.
59. R. Voet (1992), 'Political Representation and Quotas', *Acta Politica*, 27, 4: 393.
60. Phillips, *The Politics of Presence*, pp. 53–5.
61. Ibid., p. 55.
62. Phillips, *Democracy and Difference*, p. 132; Phillips, *Engendering Democracy*, pp. 150–1. See also Chapter 3.
63. Phillips, *The Politics of Presence*, pp. 82–3.
64. Ibid., pp. 56, 158.
65. Judge, *Representation*, p. 22; R. Voet (1994), 'Women as Citizens', *Australian Feminist Studies*, 19: 71.

66. Phillips, *The Politics of Presence*, p. 49.
67. Phillips, *Engendering Democracy*, pp. 69–70; Voet, 'Political Representation and Quotas', p. 391; Squires, 'Quotas for Women'; J. Pilcher (1995), 'The Gender Significance of Women in Power', *European Journal of Women's Studies*, 2, 4: 506; Sapiro, 'When are Interests Interesting', p. 164.
68. Mansbridge, 'Should Blacks Represent Blacks?', p. 638.
69. Ibid., pp. 638–9. Mansbridge draws a distinction between microcosmic representation achieved by lottery and which might throw up 'legislators with less ability, expertise' and 'commitment to the public good' and selective descriptive representatives where representatives 'need not be significantly less skilled' than other representatives (pp. 631–3).
70. Mansbridge, 'Should Blacks Represent Blacks?', pp. 652, 639.
71. Ibid.
72. Ibid., pp. 629, 644.
73. Ibid., p. 636; Cockburn, cited in Mackay, *Love and Politics*, p. 85.
74. Mansbridge, 'Should Blacks Represent Blacks?', p. 636.
75. Phillips, *Engendering Democracy*, p. 155.
76. Clark, 'Getting There', p. 99; Voet, 'Women as Citizens', p. 71.
77. Voet, 'Political Representation and Quotas', p. 392.
78. Cockburn, 'Strategies for Gender Democracy', pp. 15, 21.
79. Young, *Throwing Like a Girl*, p. 88; see also E. Frazer and N. Lacey (1993), *The Politics of Community* (Hemel Hempstead: Harvester Wheatsheaf), p. 197.
80. Phillips, *The Politics of Presence*, pp. 67–9.
81. Mansbridge, 'Should Blacks Represent Blacks?', p. 637.
82. Ibid., p. 641.
83. Ibid., p. 629.
84. Ibid., pp. 635–6, 640. Mackay argues that 'we should not discount ideas of substantive representation because we cannot envisage conditions for perfect accountability' and argues that feminist organizations and 'women in the community' may 'offer one sort of accountability' (Mackay, *Love and Politics*, p. 210).
85. Dodson, 'The Impact of Women in Congress', p. 11.
86. Phillips, *The Politics of Presence*, p. 168.
87. Reingold, *Representing Women*, p. 35.
88. D. T. Studlar and I. McAllister (2002), 'Does a Critical Mass Exist?', *European Journal of Political Research*, 41, 2: 234.
89. Studler and McAllister, 'Does a Critical Mass Exist?'; S. Grey (2002), 'Does Size Matter?', in K. Ross (ed.), *Women, Politics and Change* (Oxford: Oxford University Press); Reingold, *Representing Women*; S. Thomas and C. Wilcox (1998), *Women and Elective Office* (Oxford: Oxford University Press); P. Norris and J. Lovenduski (1995), *Political Recruitment* (Cambridge: Cambridge University Press); J. Lovenduski and P. Norris, 'Westminster Women: the Politics of Presence', *Political Studies*, 51: 84–102.
90. Dodson, 'The Impact of Women in Congress', p. 39.
91. See also ibid., pp. 17–20.
92. Duerst-Lahti, 'Institutions, Ideologies, and the Possibility of Equal Political Participation'; Dodson, 'The Impact of Women in Congress'.
93. Reingold claims (and I agree) that 'a feminist definition of women's issues … delineates not only the primary subject matter … (women) but also the general (feminist) directions for answering the questions and solving the problems' (Reingold, *Representing Women*, pp. 138, 166–7).
94. Squires, 'Quotas for Women'; Mackay, *Love and Politics*, p. 99.
95. Phillips, *The Politics of Presence*; C. Hoskyns and S. Rai (1998), 'Gender, Class and Representation', *European Journal of Women's Studies*, 5, 3–4: 345–65. In the USA the presence of women from centre-right parties has sometimes been used to prove the failure of the link between the descriptive and substantive representation of women (Dodson, 'The Impact of Women in Congress').
96. Duerst-Lahti, 'Institutions, Ideologies, and the Possibility of Equal Political Participation'; Grey, 'Does Size Matter?'; Dodson, 'The Impact of Women in Congress'; Reingold, *Representing Women.*
97. Mackay, *Love and Politics*, p. 98; Dodson, 'The Impact of Women in Congress', p. 38.
98. Reingold, *Representing Women*, p. 116; Mackay discusses this in respect of UK politics (Mackay, *Love and Politics*, p. 98).

99. Dodson, 'The Impact of Women in Congress', pp. 22–3, 7.
100. Ibid., p. 23; Mackay, *Love and Politics*, p. 97.
101. Dodson, 'The Impact of Women in Congress', pp. 14, 20.
102. See, for example, *Observer* 27 May 2001; *Guardian* 23 May 2001; *Guardian* 6 August 2001; *Guardian* 20 June 2001.
103. Dodson, 'The Impact of Women in Congress', pp. 23–5, 28.

Women's Numerical Representation

The 120 women MPs returned to Westminster in 1997 constituted 18.2 per cent of all MPs and doubled the numbers of women overnight (Table 3.1).[1] This increase in itself makes it important to reconsider explanations for women's numerical representation in Parliament. That 101 of the 120 were Labour MPs and that 35 of the 65 Labour women MPs elected for the first time in 1997 were selected from all-women shortlists (AWS) makes this task all the more necessary.[2]

Determinants of women's numerical representation are socio-economic (women's labour force participation and participation in the professions), cultural (egalitarian ideology, religion, attitudes towards the state) and political (electoral systems, party organization, quota laws, policy formation process).[3] Norris and Lovenduski identify four levels of analysis of

TABLE 3.1 WOMEN ELECTED IN BRITISH GENERAL ELECTIONS, 1945–2001

Year	*Con*	*Lab*	*Lib*	*SNP*	*Others*	*Total*	*% MPs*
1945	1	21	1	0	1	23	3.8
1950	6	14	1	0	0	21	3.4
1951	6	11	0	0	0	17	2.7
1955	10	14	0	0	0	24	3.8
1959	12	13	0	0	0	25	4.0
1964	11	18	0	0	0	29	4.6
1966	7	19	0	0	0	26	4.1
1970	15	10	0	0	1	26	4.1
1974 (Feb.)	9	13	0	1	0	23	3.6
1974 (Oct.)	7	18	0	2	0	27	4.3
1979	8	11	0	0	0	19	3.0
1983	13	10	0	0	0	23	3.5
1987	17	21	2	1	0	41	6.3
1992	20	37	2	1	0	60	9.2
1997	13	101	3	2	1 (Speaker)	120	18.2
2001	14	95	5	1	4	118	17.9

Source: Amended from J. Lovenduski and P. Norris (1993), *Gender and Party Politics* (London: Sage).

legislative recruitment – 'the critical step as individuals move from lower levels of politics into parliamentary careers'.[4] First are the systematic factors that set the broad context within any country: the legal,[5] electoral,[6] party systems and the structure of opportunities (the structure of party competition, the strength of parties and the position of the parties across the ideological divide). Second is the context within parties: their organization, rules and ideology.[7] Third are individual factors such as resources, motivations and the attitudes of gatekeepers (party selectorates). Fourth is the outcome of the process for the composition of parliaments.[8]

Looking at the third level, supply-side explanations 'suggest that the outcome of the selection process reflects the supply of applicants wishing to pursue a political career' while demand-side arguments assume 'selectors choose candidates depending on their perceptions of the applicants' abilities, qualifications and experience', although demand, or perceptions of a demand, may also be an important factor in determining who comes forward.[9]

If 'constraints on resources (such as time, money and experience) and motivational factors (such as drive, ambition and interest) determine who aspires to Westminster', it is important to establish whether women have the necessary resources and motivations to seek selection (supply) *and/or* whether women's resources and motivations are regarded as appropriate by the party selectorates (demand).[10] Indeed, it is likely that women, because of the sexual division of labour, will have 'lower resources of time and money, and lower levels of political ambition and confidence'.[11] At the same time, women may also suffer from selectorate discrimination if candidates with resources primarily associated with men and masculinity are sought by the party selectorates.[12]

The contention that women's political recruitment is determined, at least in part, by negative discrimination by party selectorates finds support in early studies.[13] Yet these were later contested.[14] A study in the late 1970s of Labour Party selection conferences in Scotland and Northern England concluded that 'if more women sought nomination they would have a fair chance of selection'.[15] Analysis of the British Election Study (a random sample of nearly 1,900 respondents from Great Britain) found that 'political activists' showed similar levels of support for women MPs as the general population.[16]

However, 'selectorate self-perception of the absence of sexism' (such as revealed in some studies) 'are only reliable if confirmed by prospective women candidates'.[17] And gender-discriminatory questions have been posed to women at selection committees.[18] Prospective women candidates have also suffered from indirect discrimination, where ideas of what constitutes a good MP have counted against women.[19] There has also been a discrepancy between the number of women seeking candidatures and the numbers selected, an indicator of discrimination.[20] Norris and Lovenduski's comprehensive study of women's legislative recruitment for the 1992 general election suggested that *a lack of demand on behalf of the Labour Party selectorates was more significant than supply-side explanations* of women's legislative recruitment, although their analysis of selectorates' attitudes did not provide strong evidence of discrimination against women.[21]

THE LABOUR PARTY'S ADOPTION OF ALL-WOMEN SHORTLISTS

With the adoption of AWS for the 1997 general election the 'rules of the selection game' in the Labour Party had clearly changed.[22] In 1986 the Labour Party's annual conference had accepted the principle and in 1987 the constitutional requirement that at least one woman should be included on the shortlist of any constituency in which a woman was nominated.[23] Composite 54, which accepted quotas in principle, was passed in 1989 and in 1990 Conference committed the Labour Party to the introduction of quotas for candidate selections with a target of securing 50 per cent of women in the Parliamentary Labour Party (PLP) within ten years or three general elections, whichever was the shorter period of time.[24] Following the failure of the policy to be enforced at the 1992 general election the 1993 Conference committed the party to the introduction of quotas to secure its target. There would be AWS in 50 per cent of all the key seats (defined as winnable on a 6 per cent swing) and in 50 per cent of all vacant Labour-held seats.[25] Implementation would occur through regional 'consensus' meetings. This policy was reaffirmed at Conference the following year.[26]

Yet the adoption of AWS by the Labour Party leadership did not reflect a Damascene conversion to the feminization of the PLP. Rather, it reflected 'instrumental rationality' by the party leadership, who became convinced of the electoral rewards of having greater numbers of women MPs.[27] The pro-Conservative gender gap in voting needed to be closed, and here was a policy that might persuade women to vote Labour.[28]

The implementation of AWS was neither simple nor straightforward. The proposal put at the 1993 Conference was itself a compromise: Labour's women's conferences had wanted AWS in all Labour retirement seats.[29] There was also significant intra-party conflict associated with AWS, focused, in particular, upon local constituency autonomy over selection, especially in safe seats.[30] In addition, there was little support for AWS by the party's new leader, Tony Blair (elected after the death of John Smith in 1994).[31] Indeed, Blair announced on 25 July 1995 that 'the process has not been ideal at all' and claimed that this 'is accepted by the most vociferous supporters of the proposal'.[32]

Even though AWS lacked leadership support and, in the eyes of some, legitimacy, the policy was, nevertheless, in place for selection for the 1997 general election: it established that there would be AWS in 50 per cent of all the key and vacant Labour-held seats. But AWS were short-lived (1993–96). Two disgruntled male members of the Labour Party took the party to an Industrial Tribunal, claiming that the policy was illegal under the Sex Discrimination Act (SDA). Although the Labour Party had been advised that candidate selection was covered by Section 29(1) of the SDA (the provision of services 'to the public or a section of the public'), from which political parties were exempt, the Industrial Tribunal in January 1996 (*Jepson and Dyas-Elliot v. The Labour Party*) found them in breach of Section 13 of Part II of the SDA, which prevents sex discrimination by professional bodies in awarding qualifications.[33] The Labour Party accepted the ruling even though it set no precedent. It was claimed that the party did not challenge the ruling because to do so would have threatened the status of the women already selected on AWS, although this justification was privately criticized as both political obscuration and opportunism.[34]

Notwithstanding the premature ending of the policy, AWS was an important feature of the Labour Party's selection practices for the 1997 general election. By making party selectorates select women, any negative discrimination against women that might be in operation in the selection process would be nullified. Also, and perhaps as an indirect result of AWS, more women might regard themselves, and/or be regarded, as having the 'relevant' resources and seek selection. Interpretations of their impact varied. Criddle claimed that the Rubicon had been crossed.[35] He argued that, despite the ruling, AWS continued to have a positive effect on Labour Party selections. Others were more pessimistic. Eagle and Lovenduski considered that there was 'no

TABLE 3.2 LABOUR CANDIDATES BY TYPE OF SEAT AT THE 1997 GENERAL ELECTION

Type of seat	*No. women*	*No. men*	*Total*	*% Women*
Returned Labour incumbents	**36**	199	235	**15.3**
Labour retirements	**11**	21	32	**34.4**
Key seats	**43**	42	85	**50.6**
Unexpected gains	**11**	55	66	**16.7**
Total MPs	**101**	317	418	**24.2**
Unwinnable seats	**57**	166	223	**25.6**
Total candidates	**158**	483	641	**24.6**

Source: M. Eagle and J. Lovenduski (1998), *High Time or High Tide for Labour Women* (London: Fabian Society), p. 8.

evidence to suggest that the culture of the party has changed in favour of selecting women'.[36]

As Table 3.2 shows, it was only in the key seats that the Labour Party managed to ensure that 50 per cent of the selected candidates were women. In the other seats the percentage of women selected was much lower, ranging from 15 to 35 per cent. Even in the 'unexpected gains', those seats that the Labour Party won because of its landslide, only 11 extra women MPs were returned. Overall, Eagle and Lovenduski argue that only when compelled to do so will selectorates select women in sufficient numbers to 'make a difference'.[37]

THE NEW LABOUR WOMEN MPs TALK ABOUT WOMEN'S NUMERICAL REPRESENTATION AND WOMEN'S LEGISLATIVE RECRUITMENT FOR 1997

What of the opinions of the women selected by the Labour Party for the 1997 general election, selected, that is, on or at the time of AWS? What do they have to say about women's numerical representation? What factors did they regard as determining women's legislative recruitment? How did they experience the Labour Party's recruitment for Parliament?

Although what follows is based on the perceptions and experiences of women who succeeded in being both selected and elected by the Labour Party, and notwithstanding Norris and Lovenduski's disclaimer that perceptions by applicants 'are not direct proof' of discrimination, it is important to analyse these women MPs' views, if only because their perceptions may encourage or discourage other women from seeking selection.[38]

Tables 3.3 and 3.4 show that the new Labour women MPs emphasized supply-side explanations to a greater extent than demand-side explanations in accounting for women's numerical representation in politics: women lack the requisite resources. For example, 15 new Labour women MPs acknowledged the difficulty of combining domestic and familial responsibilities with political participation: 'If you've got children you can't do the things you need to do in the party [to] get to the point of standing for Parliament.'

Tables 3.5 and 3.6 present the responses from the MPs concerning the impact of supply-side factors on their own participation in Westminster politics. In contrast to their views about women's political participation

TABLE 3.3 THE NEW LABOUR WOMEN MPs: REASONS FOR WOMEN'S UNDER-PARTICIPATION IN POLITICS*

Reasons	*Number of responses*
Gendered structure of society	18
Gendered socialization	10
Selectorate discrimination	12
Absence of mechanisms	4
Lack of role models	1
Insufficient supply	1
Motivation	1
Lack of exhortation	1

*The women MPs were asked to discuss their understanding of why women are under-represented in numerical terms in the House of Commons. In respect of the category 'gendered structure of society', the numbers are calculated on the basis of the numbers of MPs who cited at least one fetter to women's political participation derived from the gendered structure of society. Arguably, this underplays the significance of these factors. In less abstract terms, responses in this category refer to women's domestic and familial responsibility. Some women MPs provided multiple responses. N = 23.

TABLE 3.4 THE NEW LABOUR WOMEN MPs: SUPPLY- AND DEMAND-SIDE EXPLANATIONS

Explanation	*Number of responses*
Supply	31
Demand	17

Notes: The responses given by the MPs have been recategorized according to Norris and Lovenduski's supply- and demand-side model of political recruitment (P. Norris and J. Lovenduski [1995], *Political Recruitment* [Cambridge: Cambridge University Press, pp. 14–17]).

TABLE 3.5 THE NEW LABOUR WOMEN MPs: OBSTACLES TO THEIR PARTICIPATION IN PARLIAMENT

Obstacles to participation	*Number of responses*
Familial responsibilities	5
Economic	2
Male culture of politics	2
Selectorate discrimination on basis of age	2

Note: The women MPs were asked to talk about their experiences of seeking and being (s)elected. Some women MPs provided multiple responses. N= 8.

TABLE 3.6 THE NEW LABOUR WOMEN MPs: SUPPLY-SIDE RESOURCES THAT ENABLED THEIR PARTICIPATION IN PARLIAMENT

Supply-side resources	*Number of responses*
Lack of familial responsibilities	12
Local constituency	3
Motivation	4

Note: Some women MPs provided multiple responses. N= 15.

in general, when asked to reflect upon their own experiences they provided a rather different analysis: the MPs do not perceive themselves as experiencing supply-side factors as significant fetters to their participation in the House of Commons. Table 3.5 shows how few obstacles this particular group of women perceived themselves to be faced with. Moreover, Table 3.6 demonstrates that the MPs perceived that they benefited from particular resources that enabled them to participate. For example, 12 women stressed that either they did not carry familial responsibilities or that they benefited from a supportive partner who had an equal or primary role regarding familial/domestic responsibilities. The explanation for this difference between the new Labour women's view of women's numerical representation in general and their own participation is that they appear to differentiate themselves from other women in society; they perceive themselves as atypical in terms of the supply-side factors that influence women's participation in politics.[39]

This perception may have important implications for the ways in which the new Labour women MPs represent women. If they regard themselves as different from other women this might interrupt the relationship between numerical and other conceptions of representation. It raises, for example, the question of whether women representatives can act for women who are different from them and whether symbolic representation, especially in terms of the role model effect, depends on women representatives looking like, and having similar experiences to, other women in society.[40]

Table 3.7, which shows the reasons determining the women MPs' selection as parliamentary candidates in 1997, adds some qualifications to our understanding of women's legislative recruitment for the Labour Party at that time and for women's numerical representation in subsequent elections. The MPs' responses suggest that it is not sufficient for women to acquire the necessary resources and/or be exempt from the 'fetters' that inhibit women's political participation. Rather, it highlights the importance of demand: eight of the new women MPs stated that they were exhorted to participate in 1997. Furthermore, seven women MPs (including two women MPs who also cited 'exhortation') identified the Labour Party's implementation of AWS in order to explain their decision to participate in 1997. When demand for women is overt, with the adoption of AWS and/or when local constituency party members invite participation, women are more likely to consider, and be successful in, the recruitment process for parliamentary candidates. These insights demonstrate the interaction of supply- and demand-side explanations of political recruitment and temper the earlier emphasis placed upon supply-side explanations by the women MPs (Tables 3.3–3.6). Two MPs made the link explicit:

> I feel that had the Party not sent out such a strong message that it wanted more women, that it really want[ed] to ... reach out, *I would have felt less encouraged to do it.*
>
> *[I] deliberately went for [an] all-women shortlist*, [I] partly felt that if the party [had] gone out of its way, [and] wanted women candidate[s], identified certain seats, [it] did need a credible array of women putting in for those seats, so [it] seemed quite important [that] quite a lot of women went for all women shortlist. (emphasis added)[41]

Support for AWS was almost universal among the new Labour women MPs, if not surprising given the numbers who were themselves selected on AWS: 31 of the 34 MPs indicated their support for AWS, with six of these calling for a continuation of the policy and/or

TABLE 3.7 THE NEW LABOUR WOMEN MPs: EXPLANATIONS FOR THEIR LEGISLATIVE RECRUITMENT FOR THE 1997 PARLIAMENT

Explanations	*Number of responses*
Exhortation	8
Institutional mechanisms	7
Unplanned opportunity/luck	4

Note: Some women MPs provided multiple responses. N= 13.

alternative mechanisms,[42] none indicating direct disapproval and only one intimating ambivalence.[43]

The MPs considered that the issue of women's (s)election needed to be directly addressed though positive discrimination. They talked about not being 'prepared to wait [for] organic change'; that increased numbers of women (s)elected for Parliament were not 'going to happen naturally'; that a 'sudden impetus' was necessary; that 'we had tried everything else'; 'persuasion does not work'; and that positive discrimination was 'just [a] natural progression'.[44] Others added: 'If the system does not deliver, you have to force the system', that one needs to 'challenge assumptions' and more specifically: 'You just have to [take] drastic action when you have been trying the subtle approach ... [and] it just isn't working.'[45] Two MPs concluded that had the policy not been implemented for the 1997 general election the numbers of women in the House of Commons would have been greatly reduced: 'It did the business'; 'if [we] hadn't done it ... we would only have half the numbers of women'.[46] Another phrased the sentiment more forcefully: 'What other mechanisms? This has delivered, not to the extent I would like to see, but it has delivered.'[47] Interestingly, one MP stated that her support for AWS derived from her own experiences of Labour Party selections over a number of elections.[48]

Two other MPs, in addition to their support for AWS, discussed the more conducive context for women seeking parliamentary candidature in 1997: 'I think I was fortunate, a woman in the party at that particular time when the party was making an effort';[49] 'Aren't I fortunate, being in the right place at [the] right time in [a] constituency [which] preferred local candidates, when articulate middle-class members said "yes, we need more women in Parliament".'[50] This MP continued by stating that 'one member one vote' 'would have reduced, eliminated [the] negative influence of male-dominated trade union branches'.

The MP whose support for AWS was ambivalent stated that she 'always felt perhaps [what] we should have done is [a] 50:50 [sex quota]'.[51] However, she followed this assertion with a recognition of the 'intractable problem' of the 'constituency party [who] just won't have it [women candidates]'. This MP also indicated that AWS had a positive impact on constituency parties more generally:

> [AWS] did serve a purpose ... [they put ideas] into [the] minds [of] constituencies like mine ... so despite the fact they didn't want to have all women shortlists [they] still thought 'maybe it's not so bad', [there was] pressure to say 'well you have got to see some women, give them a chance'.

Two other women qualified their support for AWS. They considered them a 'blunt instrument' and 'fairly crude'.[52] Another MP was against the imposition, but not the voluntary adoption, of AWS because the 'leadership of the party could [have] used imposition in areas [where the] front-runner [is a] male member of the awkward squad and they wanted to make sure he wasn't selected';[53] and one MP was conscious that 'in individual places it meant that men were excluded'.[54]

The new Labour women MPs' support for AWS was also evident when more than one-third of the women discussed women's numerical representation in the Conservative and Liberal Democrat Parties.[55] Their concern about the lower levels of women (s)elected by these parties indicates a general concern for women's numerical representation in Parliament and not just in the PLP.

A group of the new Labour women MPs who were concerned about the low number of women (s)elected for the Liberal Democrats implied that they expected that party to have greater numbers of women MPs.[56] One MP argued that the small numbers of Liberal Democratic women MPs proved that 'warm words don't get you anywhere' and therefore vindicated the Labour Party's adoption of positive discrimination. Another stated: 'I don't particularly have much truck with the Liberals. I don't doubt their sincerity in wanting [to] have [a] good selection of women [but it] didn't happen, [you] have to positively act to ensure that women get in still.'[57] Other responses demonstrated greater sympathy for the Liberal Democrats' inability to secure the (s)election of greater numbers of women.[58] For example, one MP said that she was 'flabbergasted ... because they [the Liberal Democrats] pretended to be open and democratic and it seems to me [that] they can't possibly be'.[59]

Another MP was even more sympathetic: 'I think that the Liberal Democrats are concerned, genuinely concerned about the fact they've got so few women and are quite shocked about the fact they have got so few women.'[60]

When the MPs discussed the Conservative Party many felt that it would be mistaken to think that the Conservatives were concerned about women's numerical representation and women's legislative recruitment. The Conservative Party was portrayed by the new Labour women MPs as a party whose ideology and traditional views on gender are disadvantageous for women's (s)election in general and antithetical towards positive discrimination in particular.[61] However, two MPs presented accounts of discussions they had had with Conservative women MPs that suggest that some Conservative women MPs are conscious of both the lack of women's numerical representation in their parliamentary party and of the need for greater positive action policies, if not positive discrimination:

> One of the Tory women on [the] first day here, when we met, she said she looked across at us and saw all these women, [it] just hit home, it really hit home how out of touch [the] Conservatives [had] been. She actually said, 'What on earth have we been doing for the last four or five years?'[62]

Finally, one MP thought that the electoral costs of having so few women MPs would force the Conservative Party to (s)elect more women in the future. In her opinion they would realize that 'we had better get some [women] because that will show that we are changing and we need to change and we need to be "new" Conservatives'.[63]

In addition to their support for AWS some of the Labour MPs wanted to talk in greater detail about their experiences of, and feelings about, being selected for the Labour Party at the time of the policy. Three women MPs discussed their perception that they were judged as second-class MPs because of the nature of their selection. The first talked about how AWS had been 'like some talisman' around her neck, the second said that she wanted to 'be judged on the basis of my record' and the third said that 'it would have been nicer not to have been' selected on an AWS.[64] However, these women were in the minority. Indeed, five of the new Labour women MPs rejected the assertion that being selected on an AWS undermined their 'right' to be in the Commons. They questioned the meritocratic nature of male selection and argued that the 'quality of the women going for selection' was very high. Another

MP stated: 'I don't think anybody honestly felt in their hearts of hearts that they didn't have the range of choice of quality of candidates to choose from.'[65]

A couple of the MPs who were selected from AWS proffered interesting interpretations regarding the implementation of, and support for, AWS in their constituencies. They perceived that constituency parties at times subverted the policy of AWS. This occurred when constituencies volunteered to adopt AWS knowing that they would select the woman candidate who had previously stood in the constituency at the 1992 general election. Four women who had previously stood as the candidates in the same constituency, which they won in 1997, felt that it was because they had stood before in that constituency that their local party volunteered to be an AWS.[66] Two other MPs, who had not won but had stood for selection in their current constituencies for the 1992 general election, also indicated that their constituencies opted for AWS knowing that they would seek selection in 1997.[67] Crucially, these MPs felt that this 'undermined' the policy:

> I had some actual misgivings about the fact that my constituency decided to become [an] all-women short list because I had no doubt that they did it in quite a few cases because they felt it was a way of easily helping the party to reach the quota because they knew they were going to select a woman anyway and as I got 92 per cent of the vote in the selection process ... my concern was that there was some people in the local party who felt that it let the rest of the party off the hook.[68]

> When the regional meetings with the constituencies about which constituencies [would] like [to] consider AWS ... [the] constituency [was] happy to put itself forward principally because they had virtually made up their mind ... if I was going to stand again they would select me again, so really [they] didn't mind having [an] all-women shortlist.[69]

These MPs' interpretations suggest that rather than the policy of AWS extending opportunities for the selection of women candidates, its implementation in some instances may have actually foreclosed opportunities elsewhere. Women who had previously stood in a particular constituency and who were likely to be selected as the parliamentary candidate again in 1997 in an open selection process did not need their constituencies to volunteer to have AWS. However, because their constituencies opted for an AWS the regional quota of women candidates was met by constituencies that were going to select a woman in any case. This would leave other constituencies to select their candidates through open shortlists, which are less likely to select women.[70] Had these constituencies, therefore, not opted for AWS, other constituencies would have needed and/or been forced to adopt AWS. This would have had the effect of increasing the numbers of women selected in a region.[71] As noted above, four new Labour women MPs perceived that their constituencies had opted for AWS because they had already stood before in that constituency. So, it can be argued that at least four more Labour women MPs would have been (s)elected in 1997. The addition of four more Labour women MPs would have increased the percentage of Labour women MPs to over 25 per cent of the PLP. Moreover, if one generalizes from this analysis to include the new Labour women MPs selected through endorsed AWS but who did not participate in the research (12), the percentage might have been increased further.

Two MPs also felt that their personal candidacies eased the passage of AWS within their constituencies in other ways. In one instance the MP felt that her candidacy solved the conflict within her constituency party over AWS because she was a 'known' and 'acceptable' woman.[72] The MP retells how her candidature came to pass:

> [A male party member said] 'are you saying you would let your name go forward ... if you would, I know a lot of people in [the constituency] who would be very relieved ... [you would] unite the party, you would get behind you people [from] both sides'.

She continued by stating that a couple of weeks later this particular man came back to her, and revealed that he had 'had a quiet word' and that other constituency activists were happy with her possible candidature *even* on an AWS. Here the criterion of acceptability was being 'known' in the constituency and the woman's relationship with a male Labour MP. Together these positive attributes acted to negate her sex – as she put it, 'I was, I suppose, the least offensive' – and hostility towards AWS.

The second MP felt that despite her background in feminist organizations, and her self-identification as a feminist, she was not perceived as a 'loony feminist' and therefore unacceptable because she was known locally – an interpretation that suggests, however, that other women who might be perceived as feminists would be considered unacceptable.[73]

These MPs' comments highlight the women's perceptions of themselves as acceptable to their party selectorates notwithstanding the fact that they were women. Yet, while some women were seen as 'okay' by local selectorates *despite* the fact that they were women, thereby rendering AWS more acceptable within particular constituencies, these examples show something less than wholehearted support for the policy of AWS.

WOMEN'S NUMERICAL REPRESENTATION IN THE 2001 PARLIAMENT

Labour's second landslide at the 2001 general election saw 118 women MPs returned to the House of Commons (17.9 per cent). This was the first time in over twenty years that the numbers of women MPs had decreased, though the decline was often hidden because the percentage in both the 1997 and 2001 Parliaments is rounded to 18 per cent (down and up respectively).[74] The smallness of the decrease in the numbers of women MPs was due to the fact that many of the Labour women MPs first elected in 1997 were selected in Labour's safe or winnable seats as a result of AWS; very few were elected for the seats the Labour Party won unexpectedly (which were won by Labour's 'unlikely lads') and most were therefore safe even from the small swing away from Labour in 2001.

TABLE 3.8 SEX BREAKDOWN OF HOUSE OF COMMONS, 2001

Party	*Women*	*Men*	*Total*	*% Total*
Labour	95	317	412	23
Conservative	14	152	166	8
Liberal Democrat	5	47	52	10
SNP	1	4	5	20
UUP	1	5	6	17
DUP	1	4	5	20
Sinn Fein	1	3	4	25
Other	0	9	9	0
Total	118	541	659	18

Source: Amended from Centre for the Advancement of Women in Politics, Queen's University Belfast (www.qub.ac.uk/cawp).

The decline in the number of women MPs was not, however, unexpected. If Labour's AWS was the key to explaining the doubling of women's numerical representation in the 1997 Parliament, then their absence in 2001 was not likely to augur well.[75] Those who had found Eagle and Lovenduski's analysis convincing back in 1998 were not surprised by the outcome in 2001.[76]

Reflecting the legal situation post-Jepson (which had established candidate selection as subject to UK employment discrimination legislation), concerns about European and human rights legislation and a lack of political will on behalf of party leaders, none of the political parties adopted 'effective positive action measures'.[77] But the signs should have been clear to all the parties that women were not being selected as parliamentary candidates in greater numbers, particularly in safe or winnable seats. Newspaper reports documented the situation regularly.[78] Feminists and women MPs were also vocal in pointing out the situation and had been doing so since just after the 1997 election.[79] In January 2000 Harriet Harman MP (more than a year after she had been sacked as Minister for Women) called explicitly for more women MPs and in July of that year she declared that 'clearly discrimination is going on'.[80]

Nor was there a lack of other evidence about the necessity of positive discrimination for securing women's proportionate legislative presence following the elections to the Scottish Parliament, the Welsh Assembly and the European elections in 1999 (where the percentage of women MEPs increased from 18 to 24 per cent). The relatively high percentage of women elected to these institutions was, however, the result not of the electoral systems used (proportional representation), but was due to the use of positive discrimination. In Scotland and Wales the Labour Party 'twinned' its constituency seats (constituencies were paired on the basis

TABLE 3.9 THE SCOTTISH PARLIAMENT (129 SEATS)

	Labour		*Liberal Democrats*		*Conservative*		*SNP*		*Other*	
	M	**W**	**M**	**W**	**M**	**W**	**M**	**W**	**M**	**W**
Selected	41	32	53	20	60	13	54	19	37	5
Elected	28	28	15	2	15	3	20	15	3	0
% seats	21.7	21.7	11.6	1.6	11.6	2.3	15.5	11.6	2.3	0
% party group	50	50	88.24	11.76	83.33	16.66	57.14	42.86	100	0

Source: B. Gill (n.d.), *Winning Women: Lessons from Scotland and Wales* (London: Fawcett Society), p. 8.

TABLE 3.10 WOMEN MSPs ELECTED THROUGH REGIONS/CONSTITUENCIES

	Labour	*Liberal Democrats*	*Conservative*	*SNP*
Regions	2	2	3	13
Constituency	26	0	0	2

Source: B. Gill (n.d.), *Winning Women: Lessons from Scotland and Wales* (London: Fawcett Society), p. 8.

TABLE 3.11 THE NATIONAL ASSEMBLY FOR WALES (60 SEATS)

	Labour		*Liberal Democrats*		*Conservative*		*Plaid Cymru*		*Other*	
	M	**W**	**M**	**W**	**M**	**W**	**M**	**W**	**M**	**W**
Selected	31	28	67	32	69	29	57	22	106	28
Elected	13	15	3	3	9	0	11	6	0	0
% seats	21.7	25	5	5	15	0	18.3	10	0	0
% party group	46.43	53.57	50	50	100	0	64.70	35.30	0	0

Source: B. Gill (n.d.), *Winning Women: Lessons from Scotland and Wales* (London: Fawcett Society), p. 7.

TABLE 3.12 WOMEN AMS ELECTED THROUGH REGIONS/CONSTITUENCIES

	Labour	*Liberal Democrats*	*Conservative*	*PC*
Regions	0	2	3	4
Constituency	15	1	0	2

Source: B. Gill (n.d.), *Winning Women: Lessons from Scotland and Wales* (London: Fawcett Society), p. 8.

of 'winnability' and geography and a male and female candidate selected for each pair), though not without significant intra-party hostility, particularly in Wales. In the European elections the Liberal Democrats 'zipped' their candidates (men and women were placed alternately on the lists).[81]

The lessons were simple. Where parties introduce positive discrimination measures, that is, where demand is artificially created, women are selected in greater, if not proportionate, numbers. Similarly, where such measures are absent, women are not (s)elected in significantly greater numbers. This should have been enough to persuade Blair and the other party leaders that something more than exhortation – even by the party's general secretary Margaret McDonagh – would be needed to ensure women's (s)election for Westminster in 2001.[82] In fact, Blair did belatedly in March 2000 undergo a conversion to positive discrimination, although his commitment to introduce legislative change was for 'after the next general election' and was dependent upon party selectorates proving 'reluctant to select women' in the 2001 selection round.[83]

In the run-up to the 2001 election supply was not a significant problem for the Labour Party.[84] There was no mass exodus of the new Labour women MPs, too tired and tearful to return to Parliament, whatever the press might have had the public believe. Statements such as 'a huge number of Blair Babes have dropped out' were simply not true.[85] Of the Labour women MPs first elected in 1997 all but two sought re-(s)election in 2001.[86]

In the absence of positive discrimination the Labour Party's selection procedures for 2001 were limited to exhortation and positive action. The party had a sex quota for candidate shortlists – there were equal numbers of women and men on candidate shortlists, with at least two of each sex on each shortlist. Although this quota – adopted according to Criddle to 'placate' advocates of AWS – was meant to ensure selectorates 'looked' at prospective women candidates, and presumably increase the number of women selected, it did not deliver.[87] The percentage of women selected for vacancies in Labour-held seats (10.3 per cent) in 2001 was below those in 1997, 1992 and 1987.[88]

Moreover, the shortlisting sex quotas may even have made matters worse.[89] They caused resentment among the selectorate who, though obliged to consider women, either shortlisted less qualified women who they knew would not win on merit, and/or had already decided that they were going to choose a man whomever they saw.[90] Studies of women's legislative recruitment for the Labour Party in 2001 suggest that women found it hard to be selected for winnable seats.[91] Indeed, the acknowledgement by Labour party officials that the legal ban on AWS was to blame for the low numbers of women selected implied that 'when not forced to choose women, Labour activists tend to pick men'.[92]

THE NEW LABOUR WOMEN MPs TALK ABOUT WOMEN'S LEGISLATIVE RECRUITMENT FOR THE 2001 PARLIAMENT

The new Labour women MPs' perceptions of the 2001 selection round (gathered in the summer of 2000) support the conclusion that the

Labour Party's lack of a 'demand' mechanism accounts for the failure of the party to (s)elect more women.

The MPs were, almost to a woman, disappointed about the lack of new women selected for the 2001 general election:[93] 'I feel very depressed about it'; 'I don't think much progress if any has been made since 1997'; the selection of women was a 'disaster, disaster, absolute disaster'; 'we are going backwards actually'; 'unless we take that impetus forward at this next general election we will slip back yet again … we are going to have to work very hard next time [2001] to increase those numbers'; 'the signs are that there are likely to be fewer' [women]; 'we are actually … failing to get women in'; 'I am not confident at all that in those seats where members are retiring we will manage to do that [select women]'; 'you may actually see in the next Parliament that there are fewer women than there are now which I think would be a great shame'; 'there is no room for complacency … I will be disappointed if after the next election [2001] we end up with less women on our side'; 'I think we are vulnerable … I am fearful that there isn't actually a mechanism in place'; '[it's a] difficult one'; 'I've got some concerns…chances are we will have less women and that's a great worry'; 'oh I think we could lose quite a few seats'; 'it's the same old story, one step forward and two back'; 'well I'm not confident at all'.[94]

Similar disappointment, if not anger, at the failure of the party to challenge the illegality of AWS or to adopt other forms of positive discrimination was also widely shared:[95]

> Now, my view is that that [Industrial Tribunal Ruling] should have been challenged at the time or, if not then, it should have been challenged as soon as we were in power and no one's done a thing about it so we can't have AWS.
>
> It's a vast problem, much bigger than anyone realized, it's why AWS were the only way through … because it is institutionalized discrimination.
>
> I've always regretted the fact … that the NEC of the Labour Party didn't appeal … we would have won.
>
> What troubles me is that we backed away from the legal standpoint … I think we got [so] scared through the Industrial Tribunal that we let go too soon.[96]

Selectorate discrimination in the Labour Party was widely perceived to exist.[97] As one MP stated: 'We've got some brilliant women candidates but they are not coming through the process ... local parties are not picking them.'[98] A few women MPs emphasized in particular the failure of the party to replace retiring women MPs with women candidates and to select women in winnable seats:[99]

> I just feel that with seats like that coming up [by-election seats] where we know they are safe we just say, 'Right, a woman gets this seat.' I think we should be as definite ... people are not going to willingly give up power.
>
> Jenny Jones's seat [Wolverhampton SW], that's gone to a man and that's a seat a woman already hold[s], never mind making advances within seats where, you know, where male MPs are retiring.[100]

One MP considered 'cosmopolitan areas' less hostile to selecting women,[101] while another MP felt that the problem lay more with the electorate, who were not 'suitably concerned' about women's numerical representation.[102] Interestingly, this woman was the sole MP who considered that there was not 'any form of discrimination within the [Labour] Party'.

The policy of sex quotas for shortlists was also criticized by some of the MPs for being ineffective: women might be shortlisted but they were not necessarily selected. Thus they considered that inexperienced women were being shortlisted so that the party could say that it was taking the issue of women's numerical under-representation seriously without actually increasing the numbers of women elected to the House of Commons.[103]

Nevertheless, in an attempt to improve the chances of the women seeking selection, some of the new Labour women MPs had participated in the party's training and mentoring schemes, providing information and support to women seeking selection,[104] although, as one MP recognized, training and mentoring, while useful, do not ensure that women are selected: '[It] can't deliver the votes.' Another argued that many of the women seeking selection 'don't need any more training'.[105] There was also a regret that perhaps the women MPs had, because of their busy schedules, not been able to do more either individually or collectively through the PLP women's group to ensure that women were selected in vacant Labour seats.[106] Finally, one woman MP felt that there needed to be a greater commitment in the wider party.[107]

Indeed, two MPs concluded that the Labour Party's acceptance of women candidates had only ever occurred in the AWS seats in 1997.[108] Other MPs talked about how there had been a backlash against the selection of women in 2001 as a consequence of AWS: 'The smart young men, I suppose, thought that this is their turn, they lost out last time';[109] 'some men feel that they have waited their turn'.[110] Four women MPs also argued that the situation was worse in Scotland and, particularly, Wales as a result of the positive discrimination measures employed in the elections in 1999 coupled with the trade unions' tendency to support their 'favoured sons'.[111]

There was also a shared sense in which the media's representation of the new Labour women MPs, as being unable to cope with the rigours of the House, dampened down rather than inspired greater numbers of women to be (s)elected in 2001, because it reduced supply and/or increased the negative discrimination against women in the party's selection processes. Such reasoning links women's experiences of being a representative and women's numerical representation in subsequent parliaments (and is discussed more fully in the next chapter).[112]

Unsurprisingly, given the support for AWS among the new Labour women MPs, only a lone woman was adamant that the Labour Party should not return to positive discrimination in the selection of women parliamentary candidates, even if this meant that there would be fewer women MPs (s)elected to Parliament: 'We cannot afford any more to do anything, no matter for what excellent purpose, that may lay us open to vulnerability of [being regarded as] lesser equals.' For this MP the criticism levelled at many of the new Labour women MPs for having been selected on AWS in 1997 had caused her to reject their reintroduction. In her opinion the cost is too high. A second MP was also critical of AWS and maintained that AWS were not 'crucial' in the unprecedented numbers of women MPs returned to Parliament in 1997.[113]

Finally, three MPs suggested that there was a problem of supply, and one of these acknowledged the role that AWS had had in increasing the supply of women seeking selection in 1997.[114] Two Scottish MPs considered that the numbers of women seeking selection for Westminster was reduced because they had been elected to the Scottish Parliament as a result of the positive discrimination.[115]

CONCLUSION

Analysis of the 1997 general election strongly suggested that demand-side explanations of women's legislative recruitment have greater explanatory value than supply-side explanations in accounting for the numbers of women selected for the Labour Party, and elected to Parliament in 1997. Although this poses the question of why there is little demand for women candidates in general, AWS nevertheless artificially created a demand for women candidates and ensured the selection and election of proportional numbers of women candidates to male candidates in key seats. By creating seats in which all prospective parliamentary candidates *had* to be women, the Labour Party ensured that women *were* selected.

The success of 1997 should not, however, be interpreted as indicating that the Labour Party had accepted the selection of women *per se*. The new Labour women MPs' perceptions of their party's selection practices for the 2001 general election indicates a widespread agreement that the party had not been transformed by AWS and/or the election of 101 Labour women MPs in 1997 into a party at ease with the selection of women, the point made by Eagle and Lovenduski in 1998.[116] The Labour Party had not experienced a feminist cultural sea-change regarding women's legislative recruitment: the Rubicon was not crossed in 1997.[117]

Following the 2001 general election there seems to be even greater consensus regarding the explanations for women's disproportional numerical representation in the House of Commons: demand is the key problem for women's (s)election in the Labour Party.[118] Discrimination against women is institutionalized in the parties' procedures, organizations and practices: British political parties are 'institutionally sexist'.[119]

Moreover, both the 1997 and 2001 elections demonstrate that the equalization of women's numerical representation in the House of Commons requires 'long-term policies of positive discrimination'.[120] In response, the Labour government introduced the Sex Discrimination (Election Candidates) Bill in 2001. This legislation permits, though does not prescribe, positive discrimination. Whether and to what extent women's numerical representation is likely to advance in subsequent elections is dependent upon how the political parties respond to the Act. The ineffectiveness of sex quotas for shortlists in 2001 suggests that such mechanisms are unlikely to be sufficient even though they are often deemed more acceptable to parties and individuals who are hostile to the principle of positive discrimination. The parties' responses to the Sex Discrimination (Election Candidates) Act are addressed in the Epilogue.

NOTES

1. Two more women MPs, one Conservative and one Liberal Democrat were subsequently returned at by-elections during the Parliament.
2. One of the newly elected Labour women MPs – Sylvia Heal – had been an MP in 1990–92.
3. J. Squires and M. Wickham-Jones (2001), *Women in Parliament* (Manchester: Equal Opportunities Commission).
4. P. Norris and J. Lovenduski (1995), *Political Recruitment* (Cambridge: Cambridge University Press), p. 183.
5. There is a consensus that the legal framework enables most people to stand as a parliamentary candidate in the UK (Electoral Commission Factsheet 05–02, 'Candidates at a General Election', www.electoralcommission.org.uk [2002]).
6. Proportional systems are more favourable to women's (s)election than majoritarian ones (Norris and Lovenduski, *Political Recruitment*, pp. 193–5; K. Barkman [1995], 'Politics and Gender: the Need for Electoral Reform', *Politics*, 15, 3: 141–6).
7. Norris and Lovenduski, *Political Recruitment*; Squires and Wickham-Jones, *Women in Parliament*, p. 70.
8. Norris and Lovenduski, *Political Recruitment*, pp. 31–2, 183; P. Norris (1997), *Passages to Power* (Cambridge: Cambridge University Press), p. 2.
9. Norris and Lovenduski, *Political Recruitment*, p. 15; V. Randall (1987), *Women and Politics: An International Perspective* (Basingstoke: Macmillan), p. 122; F. Mackay (2001), *Love and Politics* (London: Continuum), p. 196. Lovenduski suggests that the failure of the Conservative Party to introduce measures to signal a demand for women for the 1997 general election negatively impacted upon the rate of supply (J. Lovenduski [1997], 'Gender Politics: a Breakthrough for Women?', *Parliamentary Affairs*, 50, 4: 712; L. Shepherd-Robinson and J. Lovenduski [2002], *Women and Candidate Selection* [London: Fawcett Society], p. 23).
10. Norris and Lovenduski, *Political Recruitment*, pp. 15, 108.
11. Ibid., p. 115. The negative impact of women's domestic responsibilities on women's political participation is widely documented (P. Brookes [1967], *Women at Westminster: An Account of Women in the British Parliament 1918–1966* [London: Peter Davies]; M. Currell [1974], *Political Woman* [London: Croom Helm]; E. Vallance [1979] *Women in the House* [London: The Athlone Press]; M. Stacey and M. Price [1981], *Women, Power and Politics* [London: Tavistock]; J. Rasmussen [1981], 'Female Political Career Patterns and Leadership Disabilities in Britain: the Crucial Role of Gatekeepers in Regulating Entry to the Political Elite', *Polity*, 13, 4: 618; Randall, *Women and Politics*; P. Norris [1987], *Politics and Sexual Equality* [Brighton: Wheatsheaf], p. 123; Hansard Society [1990], *The Report of The Hansard Society Commission on Women at the Top* [London: The Hansard Society for Parliamentary Government]; C. Levy [1992], 'A Woman's Place? The Future Scottish Parliament', in L. Paterson [ed.], *Scottish Government Yearbook 1992* [Edinburgh: Unit for the Study of Government in Scotland], p. 66).
12. Norris and Lovenduski, *Political Recruitment*, pp. 14, 115.
13. M. Duverger (1955), *The Political Role of Women* (Paris: UNESCO); Currell, *Political Woman*; J. Rasmussen (1977), 'The Role of Women in British Parliamentary Elections', *Journal of Politics*, 39: 1044–54.
14. Vallance, *Women in the House*.
15. J. Bochel and D. Denver (1983), 'Candidate Selection in the Labour Party: What the Selectors Seek', *British Journal of Political Science*, 13, January: 54–5.
16. S. Welch and D. T. Studlar (1986), 'British Public Opinion Toward Women in Politics: a Comparative Perspective', *Western Political Quarterly*, 39: 148
17. J. Lovenduski and P. Norris (1989), 'Selecting Women Candidates: Obstacles to the Feminization of the House of Commons', *European Journal of Political Research*, 17: 537.

18. Vallance, *Women in the House*, pp. 48–50; Lovenduski and Norris, 'Selecting Women Candidates', pp. 546–7.
19. Vallance, *Women in the House*, pp. 48–50; P. Norris and J. Lovenduski (1989), 'Pathways to Parliament', *Talking Politics*, 1, 3: 94.
20. Randall. *Women in Politics*, p. 144; Norris and Lovenduski, *Political Recruitment*, p. 109.
21. Norris and Lovenduski, *Political Recruitment*, Chapter 7; Lovenduski, 'Gender Politics', pp. 708–19; Mackay, *Love and Politics*, pp. 27–8. The proportion of women candidates and applicants in the Conservative Party were found to be the same, suggesting that Conservative Party women members, most probably because of their older age, lesser education and more traditional gender roles, are 'reluctant to pursue a Westminster career' (Norris and Lovenduski, *Political Recruitment*, p. 116).
22. S. Perrigo (1986), 'Socialist-Feminism and the Labour Party: Some Experiences from Leeds', *Feminist Review*, 23: 101–8; S. Perrigo (1995), 'Gender Struggles in the British Labour Party from 1979 to 1995', *Party Politics*, 1, 3: 407–17; S. Perrigo (1996), 'Women and Change in the Labour Party 1979–1995', in J. Lovenduski and P. Norris (eds), *Women in Politics* (Oxford: Oxford University Press), pp. 118–31; Lovenduski, 'Gender Politics'; J. Lovenduski (1996), 'Sex, Gender and British Politics', in J. Lovenduski and P. Norris (eds.), *Women in Politics* (Oxford: Oxford University Press), pp. 3–18; J. Lovenduski (1994), 'Will Quotas Make Women More Women-Friendly?', *Renewal*, 2, 1: 9–18; Norris and Lovenduski, *Political Recruitment*; P. Norris and J. Lovenduski (1993), 'Gender and Party Politics in Britain', in J. Lovenduski and P. Norris (eds), *Gender and Party Politics* (London: Sage), pp. 35–59; P. Norris (1995), 'Labour Party Quotas for Women', in D. Broughton, D. M. Farrell, D. Denver and C. Rallings (eds), *British Elections and Parties Yearbook 1994* (London: Frank Cass), pp. 167–80; M. Eagle and J. Lovenduski (1998), *High Time or High Tide for Labour Women* (London: Fabian Society).
23. Lovenduski and Norris, 'Selecting Women Candidates'; 1988 saw the establishment of the Labour Women's Network (to encourage women) and Emily's List (to provide financial support for pro-choice women) (Perrigo, 'Women and Change in the Labour Party', p. 128).
24. Eagle and Lovenduski, *High Time or High Tide*, p. 5; Perrigo, 'Women and Change in the Labour Party', p. 129. There were also internal party quotas (C. Short [1996], 'Women and the Labour Party', in J. Lovenduski and P. Norris [eds], *Women in Politics* [Oxford: Oxford University Press], p. 20).
25. B. Criddle (1997), 'MPs and Candidates', in D. Butler and D. Kavanagh (eds), *The British General Election of 1997* (Basingstoke: Macmillan), p. 190; Short, 'Women in the Labour Party', p. 23.
26. Criddle, 'MPs and Candidates', p. 190.
27. Perrigo, 'Women and Change in the Labour Party', p. 129; Perrigo, 'Socialist-Feminism and the Labour Party', p. 102; Lovenduski and Norris, 'Selecting Women Candidates', pp. 544–5; V. Atkinson and J. Spear (1992), 'The Labour Party and Women: Policies and Practices', in M. J. Smith and J. Spear (eds), *The Changing Labour Party* (London: Routledge), pp. 163–4; Short, 'Women and the Labour Party', pp. 19–20.
28. P. Norris (1985), 'The Gender Gap in Britain and America', *Parliamentary Affairs*, 38, 2: 192–201; P. Norris (1986), 'Conservative Attitudes in Recent British Elections: an Emerging Gender Gap?', *Political Studies*, 34: 120–8; R. Brooks, A. Eagle and C. Short (1990), *Quotas Now: Women in the Labour Party* (London: Fabian Society); P. Norris (1996), 'Women Politicians: Transforming Westminster?', in J. Lovenduski and P. Norris (eds), *Women in Politics* (Oxford: Oxford University Press), pp. 91–104; P. Norris (1999), 'Gender: a Gender–Generation Gap?', in P. Norris and G. Evans (eds), *Critical Elections* (London: Sage), pp. 148–63; Shepherd-Robinson and Lovenduski, *Women and Candidate Selection*; J. Bartle (2002), 'Why Labour Won – Again?', in A. King (ed.), *Britain at the Polls* (London: Chatham House).
29. Short, 'Women in the Labour Party', p. 22. The Conference vote saw AWS enmeshed with the issue of 'one member one vote' (Short, 'Women in the Labour Party', p. 23); Perrigo, 'Women and Change in the Labour Party'. Short also emphasized the importance of John Smith in securing AWS (Short, 'Women in the Labour Party', p. 22), although this interpretation is directly refuted by one of the interviewed MPs (Interview 24 [07–04–97]).
30. Perrigo, 'Women and Change in the Labour Party', pp. 129–30; Short, 'Women in the Labour Party', p. 23; Criddle, 'MPs and Candidates', p. 190; Norris, 'Labour Party Quotas for Women', p. 172; Lovenduski, 'Sex, Gender and the Labour Party', p. 14. Other conflicts centred on the ideological differences between new and old Labour, with old Labour hostile to 'feminism' and inhabiting Labour's safe seats, exactly those seats where AWS were aimed and in constituencies where the previous candidate had been against the policy (ibid.).

31. J. Squires (1996), 'Quotas for Women: Fair Representation?', in J. Lovenduski and P. Norris (eds), *Women in Politics* (Oxford: Oxford University Press), p. 73; Perrigo, 'Women and Change in the Labour Party', p. 130; Lovenduski, 'Gender Politics', p. 711; Criddle, 'MPs and Candidates', p. 191; Norris, 'Labour Party Quotas for Women', p. 167.
32. Squires, 'Quotas for Women', p. 73.
33. M. Russell (2000), *Women's Representation in UK Politics* (London: The Constitution Unit), p. 25. Following the Jepson case an Employment Appeal Tribunal ruled in the Ahsan case in 1999 that selection constituted an 'authorization or qualification' for 'engagement in a particular profession' under Section 12 of the Race Relations Act (equivalent of Section 13 of the SDA) (Russell, *Women's Representation in UK Politics*, p. 27).
34. Private information, Women and Labour Conference, Birkbeck College, 1996.
35. Criddle, 'MPs and Candidates'; Squires and Wickham-Jones, *Women in Parliament.*
36. Eagle and Lovenduski, *High Time or High Tide*, p. 29.
37. Ibid., p. 10.
38. Norris and Lovenduski, *Political Recruitment*, p. 125.
39. See Mackay, *Love and Politics*, pp. 72–3.
40. Such concerns are addressed in Chapters 4–7.
41. Interviews 6 (12–11–97) and 20 (01–08–97).
42. The six respondents advocating either the continuation of AWS and/or alternative mechanisms are interviews 11 (23–07–97), 28 (09–07–97), 7 (09–97), 25 (01–07–97), 29 (06–08–97) and 32 (19–11–97).
43. Interview 34 (19–06–97).
44. Interviews 7 (09–97), 21 (18–06–97), 10 (08–07–97), 17 (05–11–97) and 18 (12–06–97).
45. Interviews 14 (03–07–97), 33 (19–06–97) and 16 (24–11–97).
46. Interviews 8 (12–06–97) and 27 (08–07–97).
47. Interview 28 (09–07–97).
48. Interview 15 (14–10–97).
49. Interview 32 (19–11–97). See also Criddle, 'MPs and Candidates'.
50. Interview 30 (10–06–97).
51. Interview 34 (19–06–97).
52. Interviews 30 (10–06–97) and 18 (12–06–97).
53. Interview 8 (03–07–97).
54. Interview 12 (11–06–98).
55. Interviews 1 (04–12–97), 2 (10–07–97), 3 (18–12–97), 6 (12–11–97), 7 (09–97), 9 (29–10–97), 11 (23–07–97), 12 (11–06–97), 17 (05–11–97), 18 (12–06–97), 26 (30–07–97), 29 (06–08–97), 32 (19–11–97) and 33 (19–06–97).
56. Interviews 1 (14–12–97), 2 (10–07–97), 6 (12–11–97), 9 (03–11–97), 12 (11–06–97), 16 (24–11–97), 17 (05–11–97), 18 (12–06–07) and 32 (19–11–97).
57. Interview 9 (29–10–97).
58. Interview 18 (12–06–97). See also Interviews 1 (14–12–97), 16 (24–11–97) and 17 (05–11–97).
59. Interview 2 (10–07–97).
60. Interview 32 (19–11–97).
61. Interviews 6 (12–11–97), 11 (23–7–97), 15 (14–10–97) and 29 (06–08–97).
62. Interview 18 (12–06–97). See also interview 19 (10–12–97).
63. Interview 32 (19–11–97). See B. Gill (n.d.), *Where is Worcester Woman?* (London: Fawcett Society), p. 16 and J. Lovenduski (2001), 'Women and Politics', in P. Norris (ed.), *Britain Votes 2001* (Oxford: Oxford University Press), p. 189.
64. Interviews 5 (23–06–97), 4 (30–07–97) and 10 (08–07–97).
65. Interviews 29 (06–08–97), 28 (09–07–97), 2 (10–07–97), 15 (14–10–97) and 6 (12–11–97).
66. Interviews 21 (18–06–97), 22 (08–09–97), 27 (08–07–97) and 32 (19–11–97).
67. Interviews 10 (08–07–97) and 25 (01–07–97).
68. Interview 32 (19–11–97).
69. Interview 27 (08–07–97).
70. Eagle and Lovenduski, *High Time or High Tide.*
71. The Labour Party's Women's Office confirmed the logic of this argument (Telephone conversation, August 1998).

72. In this instance there was opposition within the constituency party relating to the ambitions of a particular man and opposition to what was perceived as the imposition of the AWS (Interview 8 [03–07–97]).
73. Interview 28 (09–07–97).
74. The 2001 Parliament was the first since 1970 that Northern Ireland returned any women MPs.
75. Eagle and Lovenduski, *High Time or High Tide*; Lovenduski, 'Women and Politics'; Squires and Wickham-Jones, *Women in Parliament*.
76. Lovenduski, 'Women and Politics', p. 192.
77. Ibid., p. 186; Russell, *Women's Representation in UK Politics*; M. Russell (2001), *The Women's Representation Bill* (London: The Constitution Unit).
78. *Guardian* 8 March 2000; 19 May 2000; 23 July 2000; 3 March 2001.
79. Lovenduski, 'Women and Politics', p. 192.
80. *Guardian* 9 January 2000.
81. Squires and Wickham-Jones, *Women in Parliament*, p. x; B. Gill (n.d.), *Winning Women: Lessons from Scotland and Wales* (London: Fawcett Society). No party zipped in Scotland although both the SNP and Labour placed women in high positions; in Wales Plaid Cymru 'informally' zipped its candidates and Labour did so in four of the five regions (Squires and Wickham-Jones, *Women in Parliament*, p. 63). Squires and Wickham-Jones make it clear that the numbers of women returned is also determined by the distribution of support for the parties and how this impacts on the electoral system, particularly whether a party is more likely to win constituency or list seats: there is no point zipping your lists if you are going to return most of your representatives via the constituency seats and vice versa (Squires and Wickham-Jones, *Women in Parliament*, p. 65).
82. Gill, *Winning Women*; Squires and Wickham-Jones, *Women in Parliament*.
83. *Guardian* 8 March 2000.
84. This should not be taken to assume that there are no problems with the Labour Party's 'supply pool'. As Mackay has suggested, these are likely to be composed of atypical women, namely, those with few caring responsibilities or with resources to pay for their caring work (Mackay, *Love and Politics*, p. 73).
85. *Telegraph* 7 April 2001.
86. Indeed, 85 per cent of the new Labour women MPs who discussed whether they would be seeking re-(s)election for the 2001 general election directly stated that they would be. Interviews 1 (04–12–97), 2 (10–07–97), 3 (18–12–97), 4 (30–07–97), 6 (12–11–97), 7 (09–97), 8 (03–07–97), 9 (03–11–97), 10 (08–07–97), 12 (11–06–97), 13 (02–07–97), 14 (03–07–97), 15 (14–10–97), 16 (24–11–97), 17 (05–11–97), 20 (01–08–97), 22 (08–09–97), 25 (01–07–97), 29 (06–08–97), 30 (10–06–97), 32 (19–11–97), 33 (19–06–97) and 34 (19–06–97). Interviews where the topic did not arise: 7 (07–97), 11 (23–07–97), 19 (10–12–97), 21 (18–06–97), 23 (29–07–97), 24 (07–04–97), 26 (30–07–97) and 27 (08–07–97). Only two MPs provided ambivalent responses, neither ruling in or out a decision to seek (s)election for a second term. One stated: '[I've] no idea, [I'll] see how it goes', the other that she didn't know (Interviews 5 [23–06–97] and 18 [12–06–97].
87. B. Criddle (2002), 'MPs and Candidates', in D. Butler and D. Kavanagh (eds), *The British General Election of 2001* (Basingstoke: Palgrave), p. 187.
88. Squires and Wickham-Jones, *Women in Parliament*, p. xi.
89. Shepherd-Robinson and Lovenduski, *Women and Candidate Selection*, p. 17; Squires and Wickham-Jones, *Women in Parliament*, p. 86. The Liberal Democrats' 30 per cent sex quota for shortlisting also 'demonstrably failed to boost women's selection' (Shepherd-Robinson and Lovenduski, *Women and Candidate Selection*, p. 39).
90. Squires and Wickham-Jones, *Women in Parliament*, pp. xii, 87; Shepherd-Robinson and Lovenduski, *Women and Candidate Selection*, pp. 17–18, 29; Lovenduski, 'Women and Politics', p. 186.
91. Shepherd-Robinson and Lovenduski, *Women and Candidate Selection*, pp. 8–9; Criddle, 'MPs and Candidates' (2002), p. 195.
92. *Guardian* 5 March 2001.
93. In some cases MPs wrongly asserted that women were disproportionately elected in 1997 in Labour's landslide seats – interviews 8 (20–06–00), 15 (23–05–00), 16 (27–07–00), 18 (12–07–00), 27 (17–05–00) and 28 (12–07–00) – although one recognized that this was not the case: 31 (10–07–00).
94. Interviews 13 (13–06–00), 5 (22–05–00), 2 (13–06–00), 7 (13–06–00), 9 (22–06–00), 12 (15–06–00), 14 (08–06–00), 15 (23–05–00), 16 (27–07–00), 18 (12–07–00), 22 (16–05–00), 23 (19–06–00), 24 (10–05–00), 27 (17–05–00), 28 (12–07–00) and 29 (15–05–00).

95. Interviews 5 (22–05–00), 7 (13–06–00), 8 (20–06–00), 16 (27–07–00), 22 (16–05–00) and 24 (10–05–00).
96. Interviews 1 (12–07–00), 8 (20–06–00), 12 (15–06–00), 13 (13–06–00), 14 (08–06–00), 18 (12–07–00), 24 (10–05–00), 25 (21–06–00), 28 (12–07–00) and 29 (15–05–00).
97. Interviews 8 (20–06–00), 9 (22–06–00), 12 (15–06–00), 13 (13–06–00), 14 (08–06–00), 18 (12–07–00), 23 (19–06–00), 27 (17–05–00) and 29 (15–05–00).
98. Interview 4 (21–06–00).
99. Interviews 16 (27–07–00), 18 (12–07–00), 23 (19–06–00), 27 (17–05–00) and 29 (15–05–00).
100. Interviews 29 (15–05–00) and 15 (23–05–00).
101. Interview 23 (19–06–00).
102. Interview 7 (13–06–00).
103. Interviews 13 (13–06–00), 2 (13–06–00) and 24 (10–05–00). This MP's view supports Shepherd-Robinson and Lovenduski's (*Women and Candidate Selection*) and Squires and Wickham-Jones's (*Women in Parliament*) analysis presented earlier (Interview 13 [13–06–00]).
104. Interviews 1 (12–07–00), 2 (13–06–00), 4 (21–06–00), 7 (16–03–00), 8 (20–06–00), 9 (22–06–00), 13 (13–06–00), 14 (08–06–00), 24 (10–05–00), 25 (21–06–00), 27 (17–05–00), 29 (15–05–00), 31 (10–07–00) and 33 (13–06–00). Of the women who did not participate in these schemes either formally or informally one said that it was because of an illness, two that they were willing to be a mentor or to advise other women but had not been approached, a fourth that she had not participated but her friends had, and a fifth that she was too busy, a result of her constituency's marginality (Interviews 3 [14–06–00], 5 [22–06–00], 18 [12–07–00] and 16 [27–07–00]).
105. Interviews 25 (21–06–00) and 4 (21–06–00).
106. Interviews 15 (23–05–00) and 16 (27–07–00).
107. Interview 15 (23–05–00).
108. Interviews 2 (13–06–00) and 4 (21–06–00).
109. Interview 3 (14–06–00).
110. Interview 14 (08–06–00).
111. Interviews 3 (14–06–00), 24 (10–05–00), 25 (21–06–00) and 28 (12–07–00).
112. Lovenduski, 'Gender Politics', p. 712.
113. Interview 31 (10–07–00).
114. Ibid.
115. Interviews 3 (14–06–00) and 28 (12–07–00). Criddle makes a similar point (Criddle [2002], 'MPs and Candidates', p.195), although Squires and Wickham-Jones argues that this does not account for women's selection in England (Squires and Wickham-Jones, *Women in Parliament*, p. 79).
116. Eagle and Lovenduski, *High Time or High Tide.*
117. Mark Wickham-Jones made the same point (*Guardian* 12 March 2001).
118. Squires and Wickham-Jones, *Women in Parliament*, p. xii; Shepherd-Robinson and Lovenduski, *Women and Candidate Selection*, p. 2; Russell, *Women's Representation in UK Politics*; Russell, *The Women's Representation Bill.*
119. Shepherd-Robinson and Lovenduski, *Women and Candidate Selection*, p. 1. The Conservative Party had both a supply and a demand problem while women face difficulties being selected for Liberal Democrat-held and winnable seats (Shepherd-Robinson and Lovenduski, *Women and Candidate Selection*, pp. 23, 33). See also J. Elgood, L. Vinter and R. Williams (2002), *Man Enough for the Job? A Study of Parliamentary Candidates* (Manchester: EOC).
120. Squires and Wickham-Jones, *Women in Parliament*, p. xii; Shepherd-Robinson and Lovenduski, *Women and Candidate Selection*, p. 2; Russell, *Women's Representation in UK Politics*; Russell, *The Women's Representation Bill.*

4

Symbolic and Descriptive Representation

SYMBOLIC REPRESENTATION

Why does women's political presence matter? For the new Labour women MPs it matters for symbolic reasons: more than 80 per cent considered symbolic representation an important dimension of political representation.[1] The presence of 120 women MPs in the 1997 Parliament challenges, and changes, the 'cultural impression' of politics and Parliament. It symbolizes women's equality by demonstrating that women are equally capable of participating in politics. Their presence also confers legitimacy on the House of Commons, engendering 'faith' and 'trust in the democratic process'; preventing Westminster from appearing 'backward-looking'; reducing electorate cynicism in politics; and demonstrating the basic fairness and equity of legislative recruitment.[2]

One of the MPs outlined her understanding of symbolic representation by retelling how she asks school children to close their eyes and imagine a politician.[3] When she then asks the children to put up their hands if their image was male she stated that 99 per cent do so. Symbolic representation, for this MP, is about 'seeing' women in Parliament and about the expectation that women 'are in' politics. Thus cultural change will have been effected only when 'imagining politicians' results in a more proportionate number of 'imagined' women politicians or, perhaps, when it is impossible to imagine *a* politician because they do not come in a singular form.

Another MP put it simply in terms of the importance of people switching on television and seeing women present when and where politics is being discussed.[4] Two others made specific reference to the photograph of the Labour women MPs with Tony Blair. One MP realized its importance even while she had considered it a 'bit of a drag' to pose for.[5]

> Now I can see the significance of that [photograph] to a whole load of people who've told me what that meant to them in terms of the change that represented in the House of Commons ... and you know

> it's not just people like me that say 'oh they're all a bunch of men wearing grey suits in the House of Commons'. I think there is quite a lot of power in that image.

The second MP also thought that it was 'good' that the 'photos came out ... visual images are good ... [it was] wonderful to see at the time', although she had some concerns that such images 'can also be quite trivializing'.[6]

A number of the MPs also emphasized the symbolic value of women's presence in leading positions in society. For example, one MP listed a range of jobs she would like to see women holding: the chairmanship (*sic*) of the CBI; the Governor of the Bank of England and editor of the *Times*, though she acknowledged that the requirements for these jobs are in conflict with accepted notions of femininity and that society 'will have to change' in order for women to be appointed to these positions.[7]

Interestingly, one MP, when talking at length about the importance she placed on seeing women in important places, admitted: 'When I see women in important and leading roles I still am taken aback and there is part of me culturally [which] says I am surprised she's doing that.' Moreover, she acknowledged that she has trouble reconciling her own presence in politics:

> Sometimes I have to admit [to] myself I am surprised that I am here and surprised that these other women are here ... and I think if I delve into myself I'm still not convinced at a deeper level that women have a right to be there, I'm still not convinced, I still feel that I've got through the net.[8]

What is important about this MP's response is that a woman who is in one of the 'leading roles' in society experiences her own presence as illegitimate. Yet, if women who legitimately occupy 'male' spaces feel that they do so illegitimately, this must question the extent to which symbolic cultural change has occurred, even among those who are present. It also reinforces arguments about the importance of symbolic representation in challenging the identification of politics, and the public sphere more generally, with men.

Among many of the new Labour women MPs there is clear support for the notion that women's political presence is important in terms of symbolizing women's equality within society through demonstrating women's inclusion in the political community at the highest level and of women's presence enhancing the legitimacy of our political institutions. In contrast to traditional understandings of symbolic representation, many of the women MPs contended that for women to be symbolically represented women *have* to be present; *there is* a relationship between the represented and the symbol.[9] The apparent arbitrariness of the flag which 'represents' the nation, or the symbols on a map is at odds with the understanding of symbolic representation shared by the Labour women MPs; only women representatives can be the 'symbol' that represents the referent (women). One of the MPs engaged with this directly:

> I think women being in Parliament is much more direct than some abstract representation, it's an actual person, an actual woman, that you can see, who was a little girl ... I think that is very much more direct than something like a flag.[10]

Another woman shared this sentiment: '[The] greatest compliment paid [to] women MPs either individually or collectively is that role models [are] trailblazers, people who *look like them*' (emphasis added).[11] A few of the MPs specifically contended that the Labour women MPs elected in 1997 symbolically represented all women because the 1997 intake was an heterogeneous group.[12]

The role model effect

If the new Labour women MPs saw symbolic value in their presence, many also considered that their presence was more than symbolic. Many argued that there was a direct relationship between their election in 1997 and future levels of women's numerical representation. The role model effect works by the presence of women in politics encouraging more women to participate in politics, in the same way as increased numbers of women judges, doctors or police officers will indicate to young women that these professions are no longer male preserves.

Although it is usually valorized for its positive impact, questions have been raised as to whether the role model effect is inherently positive. It has been claimed that increasing the numbers of women in politics does not necessarily normalize women's presence, especially when women's numerical representation is secured through positive discrimination.[13] A positive effect may also be dependent upon the women representatives being regarded as successful. If, for example, they are not promoted, or do not stand again, might not the role model effect of Labour's women

MPs be negative? Furthermore, is the role model effect limited to those women who share the social characteristics of the women who are present?

There is agreement among approximately one-third of the new women MPs that women politicians act as role models for young women.[14] In the words of one MP:

> I suspect more women who are now in their teens and twenties will participate than women of my age [who] weren't brought up to expect that they would do anything in public life ... unless you happened to come from a high-profile political family ... I never had any role model presented to me other than [the] kind of housewife.[15]

Other MPs talked more generally of 'the need to make girls think'; the fact that it is easier to follow than to lead and that young women 'must now perceive Parliament as a potential workplace'; girls can say ' "she's done it and she's local" ... it gives them the strength to say "yes if I want it I can do it" '; and that 'if there are little girls out there wondering if they can do this sort of job they can see lots of examples of women doing it, some of which may appeal to them, whatever their particular interests'.[16] Yet others perceived that young people will 'think, "oh, we had a woman MP and I could do that" '[17] and that women generally will be encouraged to think about becoming involved in politics.[18] Finally, one MP made reference to the role model effect on older women. She wanted to 'shout out' that 'older women can still go on and do things'.[19]

Another MP retold her experiences of visiting schools and hearing young women talk about the kinds of job they would like to do: 'I want to work in beauty therapy, or I want to be a nursery nurse.' She said that she finds this depressing, and hopes that one day she will find a young woman who wants to be a marine biologist. In the face of what she considered to be young women's 'limited' horizons this MP sees her role as expanding young women's aspirations. In her opinion they will see that she has become an MP and infer that they can do anything they want to do.

It was also apparent that many of the new Labour women MPs considered that women in earlier Parliaments had acted as role models; that their election in 1997 was evidence of the role model effect of previous women MPs. For example, one MP talked about how as a child she was conscious that Barbara Castle was 'virtually' the only woman in politics. She continued: 'She certainly meant a lot to me, one of the things she meant of course, [was that] women can do this.'[20] Another recalled the fact that as a child she had a woman MP representing her constituency and that she had, therefore, never considered it 'odd' to have a woman MP.[21] A third MP mentioned how the women MPs who had represented her constituency and a neighbouring constituency had acted as role models and 'paved the way' for her (s)election.[22] Yet another MP talked more generally about how it had been very important for her to see women 'doing things I could probably do [and] that not seeing them there [is] equally offputting'.[23] Finally, one MP talked about the role model effect of Clare Short and Teresa Gorman (longstanding Labour and Conservative MPs respectively), suggesting that the role model effect of women MPs may not be party-specific.[24]

In contrast to these positive interpretations, two MPs provided less favourable comments. The first MP explicitly rejected the positive valuation of role models, and her assertion stands out from the other responses. She stated: 'It didn't matter to me at all that there weren't women in politics, [I] thought there weren't enough but [it] did not reflect on whether I did it or not.'[25] This assertion was forcefully put and challenges the interpretations of many of the MPs who emphasized the impact their presence in politics will have on the aspirations of young women, in terms of both participation in politics and in terms of their wider participation in public life and paid employment.

The second MP dismissed Barbara Castle as 'too magnificent' to act as a role model.[26] This statement links with wider criticisms of the concept of role model raised by a larger number of MPs, including those who both accepted that symbolic representation is an important dimension of representation and who considered the role model effect important. Such criticism was apparent in approximately one-quarter of the responses. One of the MPs thought that the concept is too demanding for the individual women who are labelled as role models. She spoke of the pressure to be 'perfect' and she was particularly concerned that any behaviour by a woman MP that was deemed inappropriate would be interpreted by others, and experienced by herself, as 'letting the female sex down'.[27] In truth, she didn't 'really like the word'.

However, the most common criticism of the concept of role model was the way in which it constructs the 'role model' as different from, and superior to, other women. One woman's response illustrates this. This MP was adamant in her rejection of the concept and her statement questions the assertion that because some women (the role models) can achieve 'x', *all* women can also achieve 'x'.[28] Another agreed:

> I am trying desperately to avoid the word role model, because I don't think that is what it is ... you are not setting yourself up as someone who should be ... followed as an individual ... [it] doesn't mean that you as an individual are in any way, I think, asking people to follow your own personal achievements, your own morals.[29]

The MP who had previously argued that her presence in the House of Commons acted as a positive role model for older women presented a similar interpretation.[30] She acknowledged that she was, in many ways, different from other women. She considered that she had benefited from advantages in life that other women might not have had; she was in good health and had plenty of stamina. In contrast, the MP acknowledged that other women might have experienced 'confined expectations'. Conscious of these differences, she admitted that it was unfair to suggest that just because she had been able to achieve (s)election to Parliament other women could enter Parliament or 'start a new career' in their late fifties.

This MP's sensitivity to the way in which women's possibilities for participation in politics and in wider society are not homogeneous indicates an important limitation to the positive interpretation of the role model effect. It raises the possibility that the link between women's symbolic and numerical representation may be limited to women who are similar (in terms of their background, experiences and/or resources) to the women who are currently present.

Awareness of the differences between themselves and other women is further evidenced in two other MPs' responses. The first discussed the way in which her participation in politics (she had held an important position in local government) had dominated her life.[31] This MP was concerned that the way in which other women might interpret this would act as an inhibitor to, rather than an encouragement for, women's participation in politics. She felt she had to state that other women did not have to follow the route she had taken to the House of Commons nor participate to the same extent: 'You don't have to do [it] like I do, *all the time*' [emphasis added]. The second MP agreed with these sentiments.[32] She stressed that she 'might be offputting rather than encouraging'. She considered that other women might see that 'she does all these things' and decide 'I'm not sure I want to do that'.

Critical interpretations of the way in which the concept of role model functions to divide women is discussed by two more women who talked about the former Conservative Prime Minister, Lady Thatcher. One felt that Lady Thatcher had created the image of 'superwomen' that raised expectations among women that they should have paid employment and be responsible for domestic and caring responsibilities.[33] The other MP focused upon the way Lady Thatcher had operated within politics and questioned whether she constituted a positive role model. Her comments suggest that the style of politics practised by women MPs may have an impact on whether they act as role models for other women. She considered that Lady Thatcher had acted in a 'very dogmatic', 'hierarchical' and 'male manner', and had failed to appoint greater numbers of women to her Cabinet: '[Lady Thatcher] did us [women] a disservice' and 'led a lot of people, ordinary people, men and women, to think that women in politics are no better than men in politics'.[34]

The MP who talked about Barbara Castle being 'too magnificent' provides a further critical interpretation of the concept of role model. Her comments indicate that role models need to have a link with ordinary people.[35] While this MP treasures her memories of Barbara Castle – '[they] will stay with me for ever' – Castle's 'magnificence' and 'exceptionalness' prevented her from being a role model according to the definition preferred by this MP. Role models, in her opinion, should be accessible, as being and doing something that one can 'dream of *and* achieve' (emphasis added). Castle, in contrast, 'was so alone in all of this, so exceptional' that she was considered a 'pop star': 'when people dream of being [a] pop star, [they] don't really dream that they themselves will be a pop star'. Thus, Castle's role model effect was limited because it seemed 'unreal'. However, on a more positive note, this MP considered that the presence of 120 women MPs in the 1997 Parliament meant that there were now sufficient women to ensure that the women MPs are role models rather than pop stars.

In 1997 three of the new Labour women MPs talked about the media representation of women MPs. While these discussions were brief they intimate a concern with the way in which the new Labour women MPs were being symbolically represented in the media and the negative impact this might have on women's numerical representation in politics, as well as on their own careers. One MP was unhappy about the term 'Blair's babe'. She considered that 'babe' implied 'oh [I'd] like to have sex with her' and is associated with women with breast implants and 'blonde tousled hair'.[36] Another noted how newspaper articles on 'Blair's Babes' concentrated on the 'frivolous side' of women's presence in the House of Commons, particularly on women MPs' clothing.[37] Indeed, a third MP talked about having been invited on to a television programme to discuss what women should wear for the State Opening of Parliament.[38]

How women politicians discussed their experiences as politicians was also identified as a negative factor contributing to the media representation of the new Labour women MPs. Some of the MPs considered that such representations would reduce the numbers of women seeking (s)election to Parliament: 'When [I] read articles about different female politicians who work 54-hour days, [I] really want to ask them what they think [they are] encouraging?'[39] In this MP's opinion, women MPs have a responsibility to present a fair reflection of how politics fits with their wider lives, rather than 'over-egg[ing] the pudding', although she also wondered whether part of the reason for this is that women politicians feel pressurized into stating how hard they work in order to demonstrate women's ability as MPs – a 'catch-22' scenario.

Whether the presence of 101 Labour women MPs in the 1997 Parliament had a positive impact on women seeking (s)election for the 2001 general election is difficult to discern on the basis of this research.[40] Yet, if a positive role model effect is reliant upon the 'success' of the current women MPs, any hope or expectation that the presence of 101 Labour women MPs in the 1997 Parliament might have engendered the selection of greater numbers of women was, arguably, not helped by the British print media. Throughout the 1997 Parliament Labour's new women MPs experienced more than their fair share of critical media coverage, as these headlines, along with those presented in the Introduction, demonstrate:

> Division Belles: Blair's Babes are unhappy. Three are quitting, many more are complaining
>
> Speaker extends ban on breastfeeding
>
> MP mums revolt
>
> 'Blair's Babes' beat a retreat
>
> Six months hard Labour[41]

Such headlines created the impression that the new Labour women MPs were unable to cope with the demands of family life and life in the House of Commons. In an *Observer* article, Tess Kingham, MP for Gloucester (who was first elected to Parliament in 1997 and who decided not to stand for the 2001 general election) stated that Parliament was 'not geared to anybody who had any kind of family life'. But the article's headline, rather than noting Kingham's stress on Parliament's 'family-unfriendly' hours, depicted the problem as one for women MPs: 'Blair Babe to quit over MPs' hours'.

In the 2000 interviews, concerns about the media representation of women MPs were revisited by a few MPs, specifically the stories that claimed that women MPs first elected in 1997 were not seeking reselection *en masse* for gender-related reasons. Even though such stories were untrue the MPs were concerned that such reports had had a negative impact on the supply of women seeking selection in 2001.[42] Some also argued that the representations might have been internalized by the party selectorates who would then chose male candidates with a clear conscience.[43] Why would selectorates select women if they perceive that women MPs cannot cope with the hours of the House, MPs' workload and childcare?

However, a couple of the new Labour women MPs appeared (just as in the 1997 interviews) to lay the blame with those women MPs who had been vocal in their criticism of the practices and norms of the House of Commons. Women MPs, they argued, have a responsibility to keep their criticisms and concerns to themselves. To do otherwise would be to give ammunition to the women MPs' critics in the media and in the party.

> I think some of the reporters who write it are stirring *but only because* they have the ammunition to do so (emphasis added).

> I think the impression that might be given is that somehow women can't cope with doing the job ... and the media have portrayed it as that ... but women who've done that [been critical] see that as a strength, saying 'oh it's women who won't put up with the nonsense'.[44]

The logic of these MPs' arguments may be fair but their conclusions have serious implications. They suggest that women MPs should not – or at least not publicly – articulate their criticisms of the House of Commons because the cost of doing so may well be women's greater numerical representation in future Parliaments. Yet, if they do not voice their concerns, then the House's structures, practices and norms will remain unreformed and an unreformed House of Commons is one determinant of the number of women seeking and being (s)elected as MPs (as discussed in Chapter 3).[45]

DESCRIPTIVE REPRESENTATION

In many of the 1997 interviews the women MPs' discussion of symbolic representation slipped into discussions of, first, descriptive representation and, second, substantive representation. While the arguments for symbolic and descriptive representation do not require that the newly present women representatives make a difference in any substantive sense – there is no attendant presumption that the women representatives will act for women – it appears that many of the women MPs consider that the presence of women will have just such an effect. One MP stated: 'You want your political process and Parliament to be broadly reflective of society as a whole because it is important.'[46] Another hoped that women will see that Parliament is important to them and perceive that it discusses issues that 'reflect their needs'. A third argued: 'The symbolic role about having more women ... isn't enough.' Women need to be able to see that Parliament is 'taking more account of women's issues and women's concerns'. And a fourth talked of the proof of symbolic representation being whether legislation is 'more responsive to women's needs'.[47]

Yet, although the claim that the House of Commons should be descriptively representative in terms of sex is increasingly accepted, concerns remain that emphasis on the composition of political fora draws attention away from the activity of representation.[48] Concerns remain about the assumed relationship between characteristics and actions even though many feminists consider these criticisms unconvincing and argue that securing women's descriptive representation is important.[49] Exploring these assumptions with the new women MPs should help in evaluating whether the feminist case holds in practice.

The new Labour women MPs' reflections upon the concept of descriptive representation resulted in a general agreement that the House of Commons should broadly reflect British society: 23 MPs directly stated this.[50] 'The weight of representation ought to reflect the community as a whole';[51] '[it would] not [be] a representative democracy if there were no women';[52] 'women are 52 per cent of the population ... [but] more than 80 per cent of men are MPs, [the number of women] seems [an] enormous number, [but] when you think of it ... [men are] still 80 per cent';[53] 'I am relatively relaxed whether you have 60/40 or 40/60 ... I am very relaxed if it was 80[/20] women in one particular Parliament'.[54]

A link between a representative's identity and attitudes is also accepted by many of the MPs. For example, one MP talked of there being insufficient people of a 'certain type' present in the Commons; of how the 'House of Commons, even now, and certainly prior to the last election, was heavily dominated by middle-class and upper-class, public-school-educated, predominantly male interests'.[55] She continued: 'There were not enough people whose own life experiences reflected that of probably the majority of their constituents.' A second MP stated: 'It's fairly self-evident that you will have [a] better spread of opinion and [a] more representative spread of opinion within Parliament which is a microcosm of society.'[56]

Four of the new Labour women MPs suggested that the House of Commons should be, in addition to sex, descriptively representative in terms of race and class[57] though Britain's disabled, homosexual and Muslim communities were also identified as requiring descriptive representation.[58]

Nevertheless, the difficulty of determining which particular characteristics should be represented is present in a number of the MPs' responses, although of the six who made such a criticism, four are included in the 23 who indicate a commitment to the broad reflection of the House of Commons.[59] One MP cited victims of domestic violence and asylum seekers as inappropriate for descriptive representation and another mentioned paedophiles.[60] Another recognized the danger in demanding a strict interpretation of descriptive representation, fearing that this makes a mockery of the more limited aims, in her opinion, of women's descriptive representation.[61] The difficulty in securing an accurate reflection of society was also suggested by one MP, who argued that people in these groups do not seek legislative recruitment.[62]

Two other MPs, whose wider discussions did not indicate support for descriptive representation, agreed that women's descriptive representation 'opened up a can of worms' for other groups to demand a presence. They were concerned that moves to include women in proportion to their numbers in the population might serve to reduce the opportunities for the presence of minority groups.[63] The second MP was more forceful. She asked: 'Do we have enough Jewish MPs, Muslim MPs, Catholic MPs? It's how totally representative do you want to be?'[64]

One MP made an even stronger rejection of the appropriateness of descriptive representation.[65] Echoing those writers who dispute a relationship between identity, attitudes and behaviour, she asked: 'Is it important we have women or is it important [to] have a House of Commons [which] genuinely reflects society?' Evidently, this MP considered that a House of Commons that is descriptively representative in terms of sex may not reflect society in terms of other characteristics. Furthermore, she maintained that the representation of women occurs not by representatives 'being the same' but by representatives' actions: acting for is more important than being like the represented.

Descriptive representation: the promise of substantive representation

Just under one-third of the new Labour women MPs directly considered why women's descriptive representation was important.[66] Many linked women's descriptive and substantive representation. As various MPs stated:

> 52 per cent of the population [is] represented by 90 per cent men ... in the past women's concerns, which is on every issue, were seen as irrelevant, I mean, a joke, not taken seriously, not at [the] centre of [the] agenda, childcare has never been at [the] centre of [the] political agenda, but it is very much [on] the agenda of this government and I think that's a reflection of the way in which women both in the party and in Parliament put such a high emphasis on it.[67]

> So it's important to get people, not because they are women, but because they have different life experiences and their priorities for government will be quite different ... there is a difference between the new and old women and we are probably arguing much more clearly for things that the previous women weren't.[68]

> This is why it is important for women to be here not just because they are women, [it is] because they are representative of 50 per cent of the population whose experiences of life are quite different to the experiences of life of the other 50 per cent of the population, so that we are bringing into this place our experiences, and [we] will bring [these] to bear on policies.[69]

> The question is the absence of women [it] means that there is a voice missing ... there's a colour missing from the picture, it's just why the absence?[70]

The above comments demonstrate MPs' reasons for why they think women will make a difference, namely, the experiential differences between women and men. It is the idea that women's voices are missing from politics and of bringing a new colour to the picture that evokes a transformed image. One MP simply stated: 'No man could experience what it is to be a woman and no woman experience what it is to be a man, so we bring those different experiences.'[71] She supported this statement with direct reference to the practical argument that a House of Commons, which had in the past failed in terms of sex representativeness, had failed to represent women substantively.[72] She stated: '[I] came to see that [the] cluster of problems [which] women [are] facing were caused also by their not being politically represented. If [we] are ever going [to] change things [we] had to get women in there.' This viewpoint is reinforced by a comment from a colleague who argued that women's concerns will not be considered significant without women's presence, even if there is some discussion of them.[73]

Another woman MP made an analogy to the substantive representation of black people by black representatives:

> However sympathetic I might be about getting racial harassment, racism eliminated in this country, I have not experienced it. I can't put into the argument the passion, the practical argument, the detail, the necessity which black members of Parliament will. It is the same for women.[74]

Yet another colleague asserted that the presence of women representatives (and black representatives), 'doesn't mean [that] miracles are going to happen',[75] although she acknowledged the likely 'knock-on effects', such as a more engaged electorate and more effective lobbying. More importantly, she also acknowledged that 'women do look at politics [in a] different way [from men]'. A second MP, while arguing that women MPs 'represent women in general, across the country', found it difficult to express what that meant – it is 'a bit nebulous', 'it doesn't translate easily into specific things'.[76]

A few of the MPs' comments echoed a more pessimistic reading of Phillips's 'shot in the dark' thesis.[77] One saw Phillips's 'guarantee' diluted to the extent that she is 'concerned' that 'what you've got now is the appearance of change without the reality of it':[78] '[We've] got women there who for all intents and purposes are men in skirts.' The second MP, while believing that legislation would be better informed as a result of women's presence, held back from stating that this was inevitable. She added that it was too early to draw a conclusion either way.[79]

Interestingly, only one MP, at the point when descriptive representation was discussed, raised the question of differences between women. She said: 'I don't think it would be true to say that female representation in the House of Commons today has meant that working-class women are now represented.'[80] However, this MP's comments are somewhat contradictory. On the one hand she is critical of women's descriptive representation because she considered that if the criterion of women's descriptive representation is sex, then other salient characteristics such as class and race, which cross-cut sex, are ignored. Consequently, her response alludes to the debates in the literature discussed in Chapter 2, which challenged the ease by which women's multiple identities are reduced to their sex.[81] Her comments also support the argument that if the descriptive representation of women is merely a rough approximation of women in society, then it becomes more like symbolic representation.[82] On the other hand, her comments also suggest that she is advocating a more expansive definition of descriptive representation; that different women must be present.[83]

Clearly, there is a great deal of support among the new Labour women MPs for the claim that women's descriptive and substantive representation are related. Yet, if Phillips was right in arguing that there is no empirical or theoretical plausibility to the argument that (women's) 'shared experiences *guarantee* shared beliefs or goals',[84] in what ways did the new Labour women MPs, who felt they acted for women, consider the basis of their substantive representation of women?

A biological basis for women's representation by women is supported by just two MPs, while another mentioned Lady Thatcher as proof that there are exceptions to the assumption that 'women represent women'.[85] One MP regarded the fact that women bear children as something which 'genuinely does matter', although she continued her statement by discussing women's different experiences, a slippage that limits the interpretation of her response as based upon biology.

Another MP began by rejecting any notion that biology is a relevant determinant in political representation: 'that is nonsensical'. But her comments demonstrate the difficulty of employing the terms 'sex' and 'gender'.[86] A prompt that distinguished between biological and gender differences was introduced into the discussion to try to deepen and clarify the analysis. As the extended extract below shows, this MP was using the term 'gender' where 'sex' might have been more appropriate – the addition of the term 'sex' in square brackets demonstrates this. As the discussion continued it became clear that this MP was asserting that gender is the greater determinant of women's and men's experiences because of the way society is structured according to notions of appropriate gender roles.

> I think … looking at society's stereotyping of gender … single parents, we think of women but there are men who are single parents, who suffer the same problems, sometimes more because the benefit system is less geared to them as single parents, so I mean it isn't actually a bodily difference … isn't based on gender [sex] but on his role, now it may well be some roles in society and stereotypes in society have been based in the past upon gender [sex] and expectations of what people have been allowed to do … but they are not specifically determined by biology … many of [the experiences] may have been based upon their expected roles in society because of their gender, but which is not determined by their gender [sex] itself … it just so happens that gender [sex] often coincides with life experiences that make people able to represent those who have had similar life experiences … women are forced by expectations into certain roles because they are women but, as I have said, I mean it's not just gender [sex], because you come across examples, like our male single parent, who fulfils a gender role which is not expected of him … but say there were another group of people who were blue, if they got stereotyped for the same reason, then they would be crowded into the same place, not just because you are a woman, its because that's the way society has oppressed … as I say it's not just biological though [it just happens] to be women who happen to have to look after kids because of the way society works.

The acceptance of a relationship between gender identity (being a woman in a gendered society) and attitudes and behaviour was the striking feature of the new Labour women MPs' responses. It combined with, in many cases, a strong sense of identification with women in society. Nearly one-third of the MPs discussed how they experienced this affinity with women and how they considered that it was underpinned by a consciousness that women share similar experiences, many of which relate directly to the sexual division of labour in society.[87] The MPs articulated this in the following ways:

> I have an understanding of issues that women are concerned about, I mean, I have been [a] working mother and I understand the problems that brings.[88]

> [Women], you know, they are the ones responsible for elderly parents, more often than not, or their husbands' elderly parents or partners … have children, we give birth to them.[89]

> A lot of us have similarities, brought up children, combined working, many [of] them involved [in] caring [for] old relatives.[90]

> Well our experience out there links up with the experience of women who are not now MPs, many of us have had the same experiences as women in the country, we are mothers, partners, you know, we have gone through a lot of other things that other people have lived through.[91]

> [It] doesn't matter how high flown [we] get in our careers [we are] still carers, [we] tend [to be] those [who are] better [at] going to see our ageing relatives ... even in very enlightened relationships women still do the bulk of caring; that aspect does separate men from women.[92]

Other MPs made briefer comments but demonstrated similar sentiments: 'I've got some rapport, some empathy, some links'; 'I think there are common themes which touch upon the lives of many, if not most women'; '[it is] largely my experience that women do have [shared interests]'; 'by and large women's experiences of life are different from men's'; 'we have common interests and common aims, mostly do the same things, mostly all of us have a monthly period, mostly have things in common with each other'.[93]

Interestingly, one MP who considered that her experiences had been atypical of women still perceived a sense of affinity with women. Her statement follows Mansbridge's analysis in arguing that it is not necessary for a representative to have 'lived through' the same experiences and that the substantive representation of women can occur even when the women representatives are different from the women who are being represented:[94] 'I haven't had to fight my way through, when [I've] talked to some other women [who've] experienced violence in the home, [or] had [an] educational experience [which has] told them they are second-class citizens'.[95]

The extensive reproduction of these MPs' comments is not meant to suggest that the MPs were not cognisant of the complexity of women's identities. For example, the last of the MPs quoted above prefixed her statement with the assertion that it was being 'extremely naïve if we think we have a whole collective of 52 per cent identifying with each other, I think that's untrue',[96] while another considered that while gender is cross-cut by other differences, 'women [have] got experiences they can share that on the whole men don't'.[97]

A more critical set of responses from some of the new Labour women MPs included one who was concerned about asserting women's difference from men. While she acknowledged that 'there are experiences shared by women more than men', she stated, 'at same time, I resist seeing women in stereotypical roles'.[98] She also stated how she resists the notion 'that women are there [in politics] to speak about nursery education'. Clearly, this MP is concerned about rigidifying and entrenching women's differences. This interpretation is important in that, while accepting one aspect of the link between descriptive and substantive representation, the notion of women's shared concerns, the MP rejected the normative assumption that this should structure the actions of women representatives at least in terms of acting for women only in respect of the currently accepted, and limited, realm of women's concerns.

However, other MPs were clear about the relationship between gender and attitudes and behaviour:

> On a personal level [I] bring all my baggage as a woman with me, in [a] totally inherent way, you just bring everything you have experienced as a woman, [it] informs you as a person. I … have had my experience as a woman in a mainstream political party, in the workplace, on that … level you know … experience what other women experience in terms of jobs, children … [although] I don't want to create too broad a brush, I represent all women, that's what you've experienced as a woman and it is totally different, I think, personally different to what men experience in the same situation.[99]

> I think I will probably always draw from my own experience of life and the extent to which that has been governed by the fact that I am a woman then that might determine my agenda. It's not an active link, it's only the same sort of link I might expect other people to make with their own experience … [the] individual experience of MPs and what they are bringing to it, and that's why it's very good that people are bringing a very wide range of experiences to the job because it enables you to understand more at first hand, without purely empathizing with people who you are talking to.[100]

> I think it's like everything in life, [we learn] from our experiences, [they] come bubbling to the surface, [it's] fifteen years since, on a daily basis, I went around [the constituency] with a buggy, it has never left me.[101]

> I think most men don't have the variety of life experiences that women do, I don't necessarily have children, but I think that in the way women are reared, and ... men [are] reared, is different.[102]

Only one woman MP was explicit in her assertion that her gender directly informed her actions: 'I do have a gendered perspective.'[103] She went on to intimate that she understands a 'gendered perspective' as a feminist one, although not a 'separatist' or 'radical' feminist perspective.

Other MPs found it harder to conceptualize the relationship: '[It is] very hard to know, [to] disaggregate experience.'[104] A discussion with one MP revealed, quite startlingly, the difficulty in examining the extent to which a representative's identity determines their attitudes and behaviour.[105] The woman asserted that she is influenced by her gender and her religion: 'I am a product of all these things.' When attention was drawn to the possible assumption that as a Catholic she might be presumed to be anti-abortion, this MP stated that she was, in fact, pro-choice. Evidently, a simple reading of this representative's identity and a failure to recognize her competing identities is troubling in terms of considering the basis upon which women MPs substantively represent women; it highlights the complicated relationship between women's descriptive and substantive representation.

The second example begins with the MP acknowledging that characteristics inform attitudes and behaviour: 'whatever [one is] brought up [with] must affect [what you do]'.[106] She asserted that both women of her age and older men are 'very conscious of sexism in society' and that it is this consciousness and empathy that underpin the substantive representation of women.[107]

Three of the MPs more directly challenged the link between identity, attitudes and behaviour:

> I am not [from the constituency]; I am not born and bred there, [there] is [an] argument [that] only people who come from the area fully understand. I don't think [that] is an argument that fully holds water, what they want is somebody who is going to do a good job.[108]

The second MP, while acknowledging that women 'do look at things different[ly]' from men, is concerned about the way in which women present the link between their gender identity and the concerns they articulate.[109] This tension is further apparent when she admitted that she cannot operate 'other than as a woman' because 'that is what I am'. At the same time, however, she argued that women 'mustn't constantly be identifying ourselves' as women. She continued:

> I mean, a man would sound silly if he said, 'as a man I think this, that and the other', it would just sound stupid, so I don't see why women should be saying, 'as a woman it's important for me to say this, that or the other'.

This statement appears to be an appeal to women representatives to distance themselves from women's concerns and to adopt a more 'neutral' way of discussing them. Calling for women MPs to stop drawing attention to their gendered experiences seems, on first consideration, a strange position, and somewhat at odds with the tenor of many of the other MPs' interpretation of the relationship between women's descriptive and substantive representation. However, when this MP argues that a man would sound silly if he stood up and said, 'as a man I think x', her argument is more convincing. It would seem strange, as in different from the norm, if men prefixed their statements in this way. Perhaps the same statement said by a woman needs further unpacking. Maybe the emphasis on women's experiences as the basis for the substantive representation of women is merely accepting the convention that women are more emotional beings, moved by experience rather than reason. Alternatively, this might be a reason for women representatives *to* ground their issues and interests in women's experiences. Nevertheless, for the MP in question, what is clear is that she is concerned that women MPs do not continually make reference to their gender as the source of their concerns.

The third MP's response is more extensive and perhaps more significant in that she is the one woman MP whose identity is deemed to be directly linked with the substantive representation of a certain group.[110] In talking about the substantive representation of disabled people, Ann Begg made direct reference to the substantive representation of women.

> [The] obvious one I am trying not to represent is the disabled lobby, and I don't particularly think I represent women because both of these groups are not homogeneous ... I can't possibly represent them because I have no understanding of what it is like being on benefits because you are disabled, or because you are unemployed, those things are not any different to anyone else, so I've no particular expertise in that ... I can no more speak for disabled people than I can for anyone else ... I think it is very arrogant if you set yourself

> up as some kind of spokesman for disabled people, I have not come up through the disabled rights organization … I come to campaigning through teaching … nobody would expect me to speak on behalf of teachers because all teachers are not the same and they have got all different political views and got all different views on everything, but I can speak knowledgeably about education, I can speak knowledgeably about being a wheelchair user … I shouldn't and daren't represent, and try and represent, people with a multitude of different disabilities, with different needs.

In contrast, one of her colleagues argued that Begg's presence meant that the disabled would be better represented in substantive terms.[111] This is a claim based on the latter MP's perception that Begg is an advocate for disabled people in the House of Commons: Begg can 'speak for' disabled people because she 'know[s] what she is saying' rather than being reliant upon 'what somebody else told her' and because she has 'been' an advocate for disabled people. Yet, all of these points are clearly contradicted by Begg's own comments: the former in terms of the multiplicity of disabilities and the latter because Begg sees herself representing teachers, if she accepts the notion of representing a group at all.

The importance of exploring Begg's response lies, in addition to what it tells us about her own understanding of representation, in what her understanding contributes to the discussion of the relationship between descriptive and substantive representation. In colloquial terms, what Begg is suggesting is that somebody who is an expert on disability might substantively represent disabled people to a greater extent than she does or seeks to even though she 'is' disabled. This position, evidently, distinguishes clearly between substantive and descriptive representation and prioritizes the former over the latter. Nevertheless, her position is a minority one. Many of her colleagues accept the claim in much of the feminist literature that there is a relationship between women's descriptive and substantive representation.

NOTES

1. Interviews 1 (14–12–97), 2 (10–07–97), 4 (30–07–97), 5 (23–06–97), 7 (07–97), 8 (03–07–97), 9 (03–11–97), 10 (08–07–97), 11 (23–07–97), 12 (11–06–97), 13 (02–07–97), 14 (03–07–97), 15 (14–10–97), 16 (24–11–97), 17 (05–11–97), 18 (12–06–97), 19 (10–12–97), 20 (01–08–97), 21 (18–06–97), 22 (08–09–97), 25 (01–07–97), 26 (30–07–97), 28 (09–07–97), 29 (06–08–97), 30 (10–06–97), 31 (08–07–97), 32 (19–011–97), 33 (19–06–97) and 34 (19–06–97).

2. Interviews 32 (19–11–97), 11 (23–07–97), 17 (05–11–97), 18 (12–06–97), 27 (08–07–97) and 14 (03–07–97).
3. Interview 1 (14–12–97).
4. Interview 20 (01–08–97).
5. Interview 32 (19–11–97).
6. Interview 25 (01–07–97).
7. Interview 5 (23–06–97). See also interview 6 (12–11–97).
8. Interview 4 (30–07–97).
9. H. F. Pitkin (1967), *The Concept of Representation* (Berkeley, CA: University of California Press).
10. Interview 11 (23–07–97).
11. Interview 31 (08–07–97).
12. Interviews 31 (08–07–97), 33 (19–06–97), 11 (23–07–97) and 30 (10–06–97). This will be addressed further in the next chapter.
13. R. Voet (1992), 'Political Representation and Quotas', *Acta Politica*, 27, 4: 395. Voet also asks the question of whether feminists want women to be 'acceptable' in politics as this would imply harmlessness (ibid.).
14. Interviews 4 (30–07–97), 7 (09–97), 8 (03–07–97), 11 (23–07–97), 14 (03–03–97), 16 (24–11–97), 29 (06–08–97), 31 (08–07–97) and 34 (19–11–97). The symbolic representation of Asian women is discussed in interview 8 (03–07–97).
15. Interview 17 (05–11–97).
16. Interviews 14 (03–07–97), 7 (09–97), 16 (24–11–97) and 11 (23–07–97).
17. Interview 17 (05–11–97). While, in this instance, the MP uses the term 'young people' it can be surmised that the use of 'I' later in the sentence suggests that the 'young people' she is referring to are 'young women'.
18. Interview 10 (08–07–97).
19. Interview 9 (29–10–97).
20. Interview 11 (23–07–97).
21. Interview 21 (18–06–97).
22. Interview 9 (29–10–97).
23. Interview 15 (14–10–97).
24. Interview 18 (12–06–97).
25. Interview 24 (07–04–97).
26. Interview 26 (30–07–97).
27. Interview 5 (23–06–97).
28. Interview 24 (07–04–97). This MP is the one cited above who dismissed the impact of role models on her own participation.
29. Interview 6 (12–11–97). See also interview 28 (09–07–97).
30. Interview 9 (29–10–97).
31. Interview 12 (11–06–97).
32. Interview 22 (08–09–97).
33. Interview 7 (09–97).
34. Interview 9 (29–10–97). One exception was Baroness Young, who was Lord Privy Seal and Leader of the House of Lords between 1982 and 1983.
35. Interview 26 (30–07–97).
36. Interview 5 (23–06–97).
37. Interview 29 (06–08–97).
38. Interview 33 (19–06–97).
39. Interview 22 (08–09–97).
40. Future research might identify the ways in which women MPs act in order to enhance their 'role model' effect; examine whether women MPs' presence impacts upon levels of women's numerical representation; and consider the views of women, especially young women and women who are different from the elected women MPs.
41. *Sunday Times Magazine* 17 December 2000; *Guardian* 7 April 2000; *Mirror* 30 March 2000; *Telegraph* 14 February 1998; *Observer* 30 November 1997.
42. Interviews 5 (22–05–00) and 14 (08–06–00).
43. Interviews 1 (12–07–00) and 23 (19–06–00).

44. Interviews 31 (10–07–00) and 12 (15–06–00).
45. Women's style of politics is addressed in Chapter 10.
46. Interview 6 (12–11–97).
47. Interviews 10 (08–07–97), 29 (01–08–97) and 25 (01–07–97). The relationship between women's descriptive and substantive representation is the subject of the next chapter.
48. Pitkin, *The Concept of Representation*, p. 72.
49. This is discussed in Chapter 2.
50. Interviews 1 (14–12–97), 3 (18–12–97), 4 (30–07–97), 5 (23–06–07), 6 (12–11–97), 7 (07–97), 8 (03–07–97), 9 (29–10–97), 10 (08–07–97), 11 (23–07–97), 12 (11–06–97), 14 (03–07–97), 15 (14–10–97), 17 (05–11–97), 18 (12–06–97), 19 (10–12–97), 21 (18–06–97), 22 (08–09–97), 23 (29–07–97), 27 (08–07–97), 29 (06–08–97), 30 (10–06–97) and 32 (19–11–97).
51. Interview 4 (30–07–97). See also Interviews 5 (23–06–97) and 7 (07–97).
52. Interview 3 (18–12–97).
53. Interview 29 (06–08–97).
54. Interview 1 (14–12–97).
55. Interview 6 (12–11–97).
56. Interview 11 (23–07–97).
57. Interviews 4 (30–07–97), 6 (12–11–97), 9 (29–10–97) and 11 (23–07–97).
58. Interviews 4 (30–07–97), 6 (12–11–97) and 9 (29–10–97) respectively.
59. Interviews 6 (12–11–97), 10 (08–07–97), 12 (11–06–97) and 23 (29–07–97).
60. Interviews 6 (12–11–97) and 23 (29–07–97) respectively. No judgement is made here concerning the legitimacy of these categories.
61. Interview 12 (11–06–97).
62. Interview 10 (08–07–97).
63. Interview 24 (07–04–97).
64. Interview 33 (19–06–97). This MP also added that attempts to secure such descriptive representation in Europe had failed because the mechanics of the particular electoral systems cannot accommodate descriptive representation (see Chapter 3).
65. Interview 31 (08–07–97).
66. It is arguable on the basis of intimation within the data that others felt it self-evident that women should be present in numbers (approaching) proportionate representation, thereby fulfilling the criterion of descriptive representation. See notes 67–70 below.
67. Interview 1 (14–12–97).
68. Interview 3 (18–12–97).
69. Interview 8 (03–07–97). See also interview 11 (23–07–97).
70. Interview 6 (12–11–97).
71. Interview 14 (03–07–97).
72. See also interview 32 (19–11–97).
73. Interview 22 (08–09–97). The concept of women's issues will be discussed in the next chapter.
74. Interview 9 (29–10–97).
75. Interview 18 (12–06–97).
76. Interview 19 (10–12–97).
77. A. Phillips (1995), *The Politics of Presence* (Oxford: Oxford University Press), pp. 82–3.
78. Interview 20 (01–08–97).
79. Interview 25 (01–07–97).
80. Interview 12 (11–06–97).
81. A. Phillips (1991), *Engendering Democracy* (Cambridge: Polity Press), p. 152.
82. Voet, 'Representation and Quotas', p. 392. Accepting this interpretation would require re-engaging with the above discussion of women's symbolic representation which, as has already been demonstrated, is seen as an inadequate concept of political representation by many of the new Labour women MPs.
83. This will be discussed in the next chapter.
84. Phillips, *The Politics of Presence*, p. 53.
85. Interviews 8 (03–07–97) and 28 (09–07–97). See also interview 10 (08–07–97).
86. Interview 11 (23–07–97).
87. See notes 88–93 below.
88. Interview 2 (10–07–97).

89. Interview 5 (23–06–97).
90. Interview 8 (03–07–97).
91. Interview 19 (10–12–97).
92. Interview 30 (10–06–97).
93. Interviews 4 (30–07–97), 6 (12–11–97), 18 (12–06–97), 24 (07–04–97) and 27 (08–07–97).
94. J. Mansbridge (1999), 'Should Blacks Represent Blacks and Women Represent Women?', *Journal of Politics*, 61, 3: 635. Such an interpretation, arguably, limits criticisms of women's political representation that stress the unrepresentativeness of the women representatives to undermine the case for women's political presence *per se*. This insight is reconsidered in the next chapter.
95. Interview 9 (29–10–97).
96. Interview 24 (07–04–97).
97. Interview 25 (01–07–97).
98. Interview 12 (11–06–97).
99. Interview 13 (02–07–97). See also Interview 14 (03–07–97).
100. Interview 19 (10–12–97).
101. Interview 30 (10–06–97).
102. Interview 2 (10–07–97). Interview 15 (14–10–97) cited biological and 'sex roles' as structuring women's lives and therefore impacting upon an individual's point of view. However, she added that there are 'many things [which] make women different from each other'.
103. Interview 28 (09–07–97).
104. Interviews 14 (03–07–97) and 3 (18–12–97).
105. For reasons of anonymity the interview number is not included.
106. Interview 31 (08–07–97).
107. Her insights point to the importance of exploring how women MPs consider that men represent women. This is addressed in the next chapter.
108. Interview 27 (08–07–97).
109. Interview 17 (05–11–97).
110. Ann Begg agreed that her identity could be revealed in relation to this aspect of her transcript.
111. Interview 5 (23–06–97).

5

Substantive Representation

A useful starting point if we want to establish whether the new Labour women MPs – many of whom accept the link between women's descriptive and substantive representation – would act for women is to identify what and/or whom they perceive they are representing. When asked directly the new Labour women MPs gave the responses listed in Table 5.1.

Table 5.1 shows that the new Labour women MPs' initial conceptions of representation conform to traditional understandings of the concept. While three new Labour women MPs made reference to the concept of descriptive representation, only two of them explicitly identified the representation of women as part of their general understanding of representation. However, when the MPs identified other interests and issues their commitment to act for women became more apparent.

Table 5.2 shows that four of the new Labour women MPs directly identified women as part of what they understand as representation and another five indicated an association with the substantive representation of women when their responses are recategorized as constituting 'women's concerns' (that is, childcare, lone parents, nursery education

TABLE 5.1 THE NEW LABOUR WOMEN MPs: CONCEPTIONS OF POLITICAL REPRESENTATION*

Conceptions of representation	*Number of responses*
The representation of constituency interests	18
Party representation	16
Responding to individual constituents	13
Independence/mandate debate	11
Acting as a conduit to Parliament and government	12
Descriptive representation	3

*In this table the figures refer to the number of new Labour women MPs. Of the 18 responses mentioning party representation, one MP talked of representing those who had voted for her. Four of the 18 MPs whose responses are categorized under the label 'constituency' representation explicitly stated that they only sought to be a representative for their local constituency. Two of the three MPs whose responses are categorized under 'descriptive' representation explicitly mentioned the representation of women. Of the 13 MPs whose responses referred to the mandate/independence debate, five talked about representing their own personal positions on conscience issues.
Some of the women MPs provided multiple responses. N=31.

TABLE 5.2 THE NEW LABOUR WOMEN MPs: ADDITIONAL ISSUES AND INTERESTS

Issues and interests	*Number of responses*
Women	4
Childcare	4
Development	3
Lone parents	2
Nursery education	2
Party	2
Human rights	2
Transport	2
Health	2
Employment	2
Workers' rights	1
Animal rights	1
Housing	1
Pensions	1
Planning	1
Ethnic minorities	1
Disability	1
Social security	1
Criminal justice	1

Note: Some women MPs provided multiple responses. N= 16.

and health). One of the MPs who talked about representing health issues also considered that she represented ethnic minority issues and disability issues; in her opinion she had become conscious of these issues because of her experiences of women's discrimination in society.

A further three MPs indirectly discussed the substantive representation of women. Their responses initially identified broad issues but then the MPs explained how these issues – the minimum wage, part-timers' rights, housing and pensions – specifically, and differentially, impacted upon women. Altogether more than 40 per cent of the new Labour women MPs considered that political representation included acting for women, even if this occurs for most after their primary conceptions, which emphasize more traditional definitions.

Another way to explore whether women MPs are likely to act for women is to consider whether they perceive a responsibility (positive) or obligation (negative) to represent women.[1] Nearly one-third talked about the positive way in which they interpreted the responsibility to represent women.[2] It was, for one MP, a 'natural thing to do'.[3] Another talked about how 'obviously' she would be 'keen' to act for anything 'which is particular to women',[4] while a third considered that there is an expectation that women are 'going to stand up for women'.[5]

Five of the MPs who were happy to accept the responsibility also felt that women MPs could not avoid the responsibility to represent women. They could not do so, first, because of the low number of women MPs historically in the House of Commons;[6] second, until women were equally present in the House,[7] third, because if they did not they ran 'the danger of being compared to Lady Thatcher',[8] and fourth, because it was felt that unless women substantively represented women nobody else (that is, men) would.[9]

Four women MPs who acknowledged the responsibility also considered that sometimes it felt like an obligation.[10] They talked of 'sometimes' being 'expected to fit in a role'[11] and of having some sense of being obliged.[12] Yet others directly rejected the contention that women MPs are obliged to act for women. These responses give greater force to arguments that suggest that women MPs seek to represent women of their own volition, notwithstanding, or in addition to, any perceived expectations or obligations. Two MPs talked about 'not having come across that'.[13] Another, while stating that she had not experienced the obligation to represent women, personally sought to do so. A colleague asserted that if she took up an issue it was because she had chosen to do so.[14]

Some women MPs also accepted that they had a responsibility to act for women over and above their own women constituents (surrogate representation).[15] For example, one MP talked of the shared responsibility among the women MPs because '[we] are women and therefore they have a role to play in speaking up for women generally'.[16] Another stated: 'Clearly the 101 of us have a responsibility to bring about change in this place, in Parliament, which will have implications on bringing around change in the country for women.'[17] A colleague considered that she 'would make more [of an] effort to do things, perhaps, that particularly concern women as a general rule'[18] while a fourth MP discussed how she has been contacted by a women's campaign group not because she was the constituency representative of any particular individual member, but because she was a woman representative.[19] Yet another MP recalled how, after the local paper had carried a story about her signing an Early Day Motion on breast implants, a woman who was from a neighbouring constituency contacted her.[20] She felt that the woman had 'rung me up because I was a woman'.[21] A further example is provided by a MP who linked the substantive representation of women by women to the substantive representation of sexuality. She recalled how, when she was a councillor, she had been identified as sympathetic towards, and contacted by, transsexuals.[22]

An additional interpretation of the link between women's descriptive and substantive representation was voiced by a couple of the MPs who were selected from AWS. One specifically made a link between her selection on an AWS and the responsibility she felt to act for women: to 'represent more broadly those issues which might be seen as of concern to women'.

> I feel it is a duty in a positive sense because the whole point, the whole argument I use to justify … my selection on an all-women shortlist was the need for a voice for women who had not had a voice previously. Now I don't think that is the only reason I am elected as an MP, but I do think it is an important reason, therefore I do feel an obligation to try and use that voice when it's possible for me to do it without coming into conflict with what I would believe to be the views of the people who elected me.[23]

A colleague also selected on an AWS perceived, however, that she was charged by local activists and the media and, more diffusely, by her constituents as being unable to represent adequately her constituency and of only substantively representing women.[24] Thus, rather than women's numerical and descriptive representation being related to women's substantive representation, in this MP's opinion women's substantive representation was the *casualty* of women's descriptive representation. This is because the MP actively sought to deflect the charge that she was only interested in acting for women. She achieved this by playing down her presence as a woman and by not 'acting for women'. The MP talked of having carefully to 'pick' her way through the 'minefield' and of having to 'build' her relationship with her constituents. For this MP her profile as a feminist and the fact that her region had seen very few women MPs and had 'provincial views' compounded the perception of her inability to represent traditional workers in her constituency. As a consequence, she felt that she 'needed … [a] few months to reassure' her constituency that she was able to represent its interests. A second MP, who was not selected on an AWS, agreed with this interpretation. She stated that she had 'tried not to go around saying publicly "oh isn't it wonderful you have got a woman candidate"'.[25]

Thus, it could be suggested that being selected on an AWS forces women MPs to be conscious of possible charges of only representing women and act pre-emptively. Yet the apparent need to deny substantively representing women appears to rupture the link between the institutional mechanisms adopted to achieve women's descriptive representation and women's substantive representation. However, the lasting impact of this perceived criticism remains unclear. It may only be a short-term effect. Once women MPs have *proved* that they can represent their constituencyconstituents, they may be able to articulate women's concerns and substantively represent women. But, if AWS or other forms of positive discrimination are reintroduced in the UK in the future, this point may, once again, take on greater significance.

Only a single MP argued that the increase in the number of women MPs in the 1997 Parliament negated the pressure on women MPs to act for women.[26] Here, rather than the outcome of the greater presence of women MPs engendering the substantive representation of women, the opposite is true: their greater presence removes the need for women MPs to act for women. The MP stated: 'I think as there become more and more of us it does allow individual women who feel, "no, they are not there to represent women" because of their life experiences or for whatever [reason], their political views' they do not have substantively to represent women. This MP's interpretation appears to challenge the association between women's descriptive and substantive representation, although it might point to a future when the political agenda has been thoroughly feminized by the presence of women MPs.

WOMEN'S DIFFERENCES AND THE SUBSTANTIVE REPRESENTATION OF WOMEN

Many of the women MPs appear untroubled in their understanding that experiential differences between women and men in a gendered society constitutes the basis for the representation of women by women representatives. Many also accept the positively interpreted responsibility to represent women. But these two statements raise the question of whether they are able to act for women who are different from them. Acknowledgement of women's heterogeneity challenges the link between women's descriptive and substantive representation. As Phillips suggested, it appears reliant upon a sameness that has no empirical basis.[27] However, if women MPs consider that they substantively represent all women, notwithstanding their differences, then maybe there is no need for the presence of different kinds of women because white, middle-class women can act for all women. Yet, as was made clear in Chapter 2, this conclusion is troubling for those sensitive to women's differences.

Whether the new Labour women MPs perceived that they could act for women despite their differences was explored in a number of the interview conversations. The first point to make is that class was rarely mentioned as a division between women and/or between women and their women MPs.[28] For example, one MP talked about how she considered that women from different classes have a 'lot more life experiences in common … than they actually realize', although she also admitted that some women are economically privileged and therefore in a more advantageous position in society. Another MP highlighted single women on low incomes as a category of women who are different.[29]

Ethnicity was the difference that the new Labour women MPs were most cognisant of. The discussions produced both simple statements – the 'fact [that] you are a woman [is] more of something to get you together than race' – and in some instances more extensive and thoughtful responses:[30]

> I am not like all women, all women are not like all women … particularly with black women, then I find there are lots of things I don't know, that's part of the process of representing people, [I] wouldn't presume because I am a woman therefore I know what you think, because you are going to come from a different angle, background.[31]

This particular MP's statement, which is clear in recognizing the limits to the experiential sameness between women, indicates that the substantive representation of black women requires her to accept that she cannot presume that she 'knows' what black women 'know'.[32] More importantly, because she accepted that experiential differences give rise to different perspectives, this MP felt that she would have to 'do some work' and 'listen more' to women who were different from her.[33] This statement suggests that this MP perceived that acting for black women was qualitatively different from representing white women, although she arguably leaves the category 'white women' unproblematized. Yet, earlier in her interview, when the category woman was undefined, this MP had talked about how women representatives wouldn't need to 'go through all the bits of … finding out who they [women] are, where they come from [and] how they feel' because women representatives have 'empathy' and 'links'. It was only when gender identity was directly problematized that she qualified her statement, as is made clear in the following statement:

> And somebody said to me, 'how can you represent engineers', and I said well I can't say that I have been an engineer, so I can't directly speak for you, what I can do is try [to] learn from you, what your ideas are, how you feel, talk to you, and then do my best to advocate on those terms ... spend quite a lot of time getting those links going and getting that relationship [going] before I am able to represent them.[34]

This particular MP's responses do not elicit a simple reading. On the one hand, the MP recognizes the importance of difference to the practice of representation, particularly in respect of a group of individuals who are different from her, namely, engineers. However, at the same time she considered women to be a homogeneous group whom she already knows and with whom she has some rapport. But she also admits that black women are different and therefore require a similar response to engineers. Yet, this MP's reasoning may not be so surprising. That women may be both the same and different might reflect how gender is one, but only one, identity that an individual acquires and/or adopts.

A second woman demonstrated a similar understanding of women's sameness and difference:

> We are not homogeneous ... but I think there are common themes which touch upon the lives of many, if not most women ... they have different levels of experience, so can I represent them? I can't represent them as well as they represent themselves, can I try to engage in their experiences? Yes I can, but to do that I have to recognize that I am always going to [be] one step away from their own experiences, so I have to listen to them.[35]

This MP acknowledges that acting for different women requires certain kinds of action – namely, listening to different women – in order to act for them: '[I] can't represent them as well as they [could] represent themselves.' Her interpretation suggests that the substantive representation of women by women is subject to a similar critique that feminists have levelled at the substantive representation of women by men. It also suggests that securing the presence of white, well-educated, middle-class women is insufficient. This ambivalence is evident in a subsequent statement:

> I don't think the experience of an asylum-seeking woman is, *it is so far removed from my own experience* that it would be glib of me to say that I could represent them because they are a woman; *on the other hand, there are common experiences, I'm not even sure that is entirely true*. (emphasis added)

Similar sentiments are displayed by a third MP. Of note is the way in which this MP appears to compartmentalize black women's identity, apparently believing that some aspects of black women's experiences are determined solely by their gender and others by their ethnicity.

> Whether or not I can properly represent black women, I don't know, I think I can in the parts of their lives that relate to them being women, but I'm not sure I can in the part of their lives that relates to being black or Asian … [you] realize that you have to actually make a positive effort to ensure that you are listening to what those people are saying.[36]

Another colleague talked in similar terms, although she also highlighted disability as a salient difference:

> I'm not black and I'm not disabled but I like to feel that I am sensitive to issues, yet I mean, it is difficult, and I don't go around telling disabled or black people what they should do, or how their attitudes should be … I think you can share, I think if you are sensitive you can feel for the other person, you can't know what it's like to be that person obviously … say to them, 'OK, tell me what you want me to do', unless you are in someone else's skin you can't know but you can empathize with them.[37]

The difficulty of reconciling women's sameness and difference in the minds of these women MPs is clear. But, the above examples do point to practical strategies that could open up lines of communication through which different women can be substantively represented by the new Labour women MPs (and held to account by women).[38] Importantly, these strategies, which begin with the recognition that acting for women means acting for different women, suggest that if different women are listened to, and their opinions and perspectives addressed, then different women can be substantively represented on the basis of shared gender identity.[39]

Two women MPs also argued that women were more able to act for those who are different from them than men representatives could, with one arguing that women are in a better position to do this because women, in her opinion, have a broader range of experiences and are better able to empathize with people.[40]

This discussion of whether women MPs who are different from the women they seek to act for can act for them also needs to consider the apparent homogeneity of the new Labour women MPs. In objective terms they are a homogeneous group. As one MP admitted, they are entirely unrepresentative of women in society.[41] In terms of ethnicity and education they are largely similar (disproportionately white and well educated) and although in respect of age there is a wider range, most of the women MPs are in the 40–50 age bracket. However, some MPs directly rejected the notion that they were all the same. As one stated: 'We are a very large group, very diverse as a group of women in all sorts of ways, culture, background, creed, age, children, work experience, Labour Party experience.'[42] Two other MPs emphasized their own difference, one by highlighting her lack of higher education and the other by referring to her previous employment.[43]

So, although the new Labour women MPs can be classified as middle-class according to objective criteria (such as education or income), some do not subjectively experience their class identity in this way. Such assertions challenge the way in which the new Labour women MPs have been dismissed as an homogeneous middle-class group who, by dint of 'objective' criteria, cannot represent those who are not like them. For example, a number talked about how they were the first generation in their families to have a university education, while others talked about their families' working-class backgrounds. One stated that the 'values I hold dear' are the 'solid working-class [values] of thrift, of hard work' and 'emphasis on education'.[44] Yet others mentioned their previous employment in the public sector.

Another difference that was identified as disrupting the substantive representation of women by women MPs is political ideology, although only one woman MP identified it.[45] Mentioned almost in passing, the MP stated: 'If they [women] have different political views to me then I don't think that the fact we are of the same gender helps me to represent them at all.'[46] According to this MP, women's descriptive and substantive representation is by no means inevitable. Unfortunately, what remains unclear is what specifically she meant by 'political views'. Does it refer to party identity or feminism? Although these questions cannot be answered it is important to note that while many women MPs considered differences between women in terms of ethnicity as complicating the substantive representation of women by women, differences in terms of ideas rather than identities were hardly part of the new Labour women MPs' terms of reference in considering the substantive representation of women.

NEW MEN

The claim that women's descriptive and substantive representation are linked also raises the question of whether men can act for women.[47] The assumption that men could not represent women because of 'bodily differences' was widely refuted by the Labour women MPs.[48] Moreover many of them were defensive, if not hostile, to the assertion which they seemed to interpret as a critique of any individual representative's ability to represent others. As such it was regarded as a personal attack on their own abilities. Common responses included the inversion of the prompt: the question of whether this meant that women could not substantively represent men was thrown back to the interviewer. Many also articulated their belief in their own ability to act for all constituents: 'Men can represent women in the same way women can represent men, what you need is to ensure … that there is a representative of men and women to encompass all the issues'; 'we all do our best to represent both men and women'; 'many of my male colleagues have done that [representing women] very, very well, raised issues … [it's the] skill of being a representative'; 'if saying [men can't represent women] it opens up all sorts of problems, that women couldn't represent men'.[49]

As the discussions deepened many of the MPs revealed additional and, in some cases, competing analyses of whether men can substantively represent women. Their responses can be categorized into the following: the assertion that men can and do act for women; that men cannot and do not act for women; that 'new men' can act for women while 'old men' cannot; and that men can act for women but they cannot until women perceive that they can.

New men constitute a distinct group of men who are, according to the new Labour women MPs, in a better position to represent women substantively. The distinguishing mark of the new man is his youth. But they are not genetically different from previous generations of male representatives. Rather, they are the generation whose life experiences are less structured by rigid and conventional gender roles. In the words of one MP, new men are those who 'mix with women more', are 'not set in [their] ways', and whose 'discussion [is] more open'.[50] Another woman MP talked about how, because 'roles have changed out of all recognition', 'what is good for women [is] also good for any person'.[51] Another MP agreed. New men would have 'exactly the same views as many of the women over many issues' because of their 'values and attitudes to their life' and because they are 'coming from very much the same place as women are coming from'.[52] Indeed, one MP identified Tony Blair as a new man, although she held back from defining him as the new man *par excellence*.[53] What qualified Blair for inclusion in this category was, in her opinion, that '[he] actually understands the issues because he has got a working wife and family' and 'because he doesn't have a little woman at home looking after the children'.

Such new men contrast starkly with male MPs who have 'gone [to] public school' and whose family lives are more traditional.[54] Political ideology was introduced by another woman MP as a possible mark which distinguishes between new and old men: in her discussion of new men, which reiterates the importance of less rigid gender roles, particularly within the family, she says she 'can't comment' on whether new men exist across the political spectrum.[55] Ultimately, she considered new men to be just 'normal people with family responsibilities' and who are 'caring'.[56]

What is being suggested in these women MPs' responses is the belief that there is a noticeable difference with the men elected in 1997 (although some might have been elected earlier). This difference, according to the new Labour women MPs, derives from the declining rigidity of gender roles in contemporary British society. The new men's similarity to, and greater understanding of, women's experiences in society reflect their less bifurcated experiences which enables them to act more adequately for women. Two MPs even suggested that the presence of new men might have a transformative effect on 'old' men.[57] However, another MP, while agreeing that new men are present, and agreeing that these men will be supportive of women's concerns, felt that they were less likely than women to act for women or, in her own terms, less likely to initiate discussion and/or legislative changes than women representatives.[58]

Another way in which male MPs were considered to be in a better position now to act for women than previously was because of the greater numerical representation of women in the 1997 Parliament. Though the substantive representation of women remains premised, in this example, upon women's political presence, a link was made between women's descriptive representation and the substantive representation of women by women *and* men representatives. To illustrate: one MP considered that women MPs can say to their male colleagues, 'it's actually important and "OK" for you to be involved in these [women's] issues'.[59] The presence of more women MPs therefore enables 'background information' to be passed on to male MPs so that they can act for women 'properly'. In addition, male MPs would be able to 'talk to the women' in their constituencies 'more easily'.

However, there were a couple of women MPs who challenged the phenomenon of the new man. The first argued that she had seen no evidence to support their existence.[60] The second, while accepting the way in which, drawing on her own example, men who are primary carers would be likely to have similar attitudes to women, considered on reflection that the 'vast majority of men don't have that experience'.[61] This conclusion was reached after some consideration. Although she discussed women's and men's experiences of living in the same house, she concluded that their experiences remain, nevertheless, different.[62] Reflecting on her own experience of having lived in a house with no inside toilet, hot water or bathroom, she argued that a man who was out all day at work would not share the same experiences of 'coping' in these circumstances. When it was suggested to her that a male primary carer who would be at home all day might share these experiences, she responded in the following way: 'Yes, to be fair, [I] don't think it's anything in the genes, of course, [I] do know men who are primary carers, and I dare say their attitudes would be very similar to mine, but the truth is the vast majority of men don't have that experience.' Evidently, this particular MP is not refuting the new man thesis *per se*, but is qualifying the extent to which it exists in reality.

Those women MPs who concluded that men have insufficiently acted for women in the past speculated on the more adequate substantive representation of women that they believed would have occurred if more women MPs had been present.[63] For example, although one remarked that she did not think that women's substantive representation is 'inevitably inadequate and doomed to failure' in the absence of women, she also stated: 'If you had gone back and replaced part of the House of Commons in 1945 or 1974 Labour governments with more women in it, I suspect it would have been easier and better', and that positive changes in women's lives 'may not have taken so long'.[64]

Only one woman MP was adamant that men could represent women in the 'acting for' sense of the concept.[65] She provided an example of when she was working for a feminist action group and talked about the way in which she considered that her male MP represented their concerns. This male MP 'raised issues' in the House on the basis of information the feminist action group presented to him and had been 'actually quite supportive'. More importantly, she offered a reminder that one must not presume that women will automatically substantively represent women. In her opinion it was better to have a responsive male MP than a woman MP 'who thinks she knows it all'.

Another of the MP's responses was more ambivalent as to whether men can act for women: 'I represent men and I would expect a man to represent women, [but it] depends on the issues, if [it's a] gender issue, [say] on childcare, although [I] don't think [there are] exclusively male/ female issues either, they could get a fair deal with male MP.'[66] This MP appears, initially at least, to reject the assertion that men inadequately act for women. However, she then suggested that, in respect of women's concerns, men might be less able to represent women substantively, before concluding that maybe this is not the case after all and that the sex of the representative does not really impact upon the adequacy of representation. Her discussion continued with the rejoinder that 'there are women MPs who are anti-abortion'. The totality of this particular woman MP's analysis indicates that, ultimately, she rejects the notion that men cannot substantively represent women and, in line with the woman MP cited above, is critical of an assumed direct relationship between women's descriptive and substantive representation. In her opinion it is being conscious of women's concerns that is the key to women's substantive representation.

Yet, another MP was concerned that women constituents might not trust men to represent them, although she added that 'acting for' is part of ensuring that women feel adequately represented: 'I think it partly depends on what they do ... ensure male MPs take on board issues that they [women] want to raise.'[67] Elaborating further, this MP, drawing on the experience of a male family member who was also an MP, suggested that it was his wife that 'sort of represented him' to women and women's groups in his constituency. Moreover, the assertion that men's abilities to represent women are determined by the perception of the women who are said to be 'represented' seems to take the discussion back to the realm of symbolic representation: one is represented if one feels represented.

A second woman MP was similarly concerned about 'whether women perceive that they [men] can represent [women]'.[68] In her opinion, if women do not perceive that men can act for them this has the negative effect of reducing the likelihood of men being able to represent women substantively. This, she considered, is because women must access male MPs and provide them with the opportunity and means to act for them. However, this MP also noted that in the past women's concerns have not been well represented by men: 'unless you [are] actually faced with them [women's issues] you don't consider them'. In light of this statement, it is possible to suggest that the link between symbolic and substantive representation, which this woman MP identified as important to ensure that men could represent women, was broken.

GENDER IDENTITY: 'ATTITUDINALLY FEMINIST'

As was made clear in the Introduction, counting the numbers of biological women present in any given political forum will not tell us enough about the probability of women representatives acting for women. One way of establishing the attitudes of the new Labour women MPs (and therefore the nature of the change they are seeking when they act for women) is to identify whether they are 'attitudinally feminist'.[69] Moreover, establishing whether the new Labour women MPs are attitudinally feminist provides one indication of whether they would seek to be behaviourally feminist.[70]

Seventy-three per cent of the new Labour women MPs identified themselves as feminists.[71] A further three MPs, less than 10 per cent, provided responses which were sufficiently ambiguous that they could not easily be quantified, though it will be suggested that they too might be reclassified as attitudinally feminist.[72] In contrast, only five (18 per cent) of the new Labour women MPs chose not to identify themselves as feminists.[73] In a similar fashion to the way in which the 'ambivalent' responses were reclassified, these women MPs' responses required further investigation. This suggested that only two of these women MPs reject feminist analysis.

Definitions of feminism provided by the MPs ranged widely, although unifying themes reflected beliefs in women's autonomy and equality. Examples included: the importance of recognizing the role of women and that women 'are equal to men';[74] that girls and women should have choice in their lives, including the ability to have opportunities to do what they want;[75] that feminism 'is to be personally free to make my own choices, to play my part in society in a way that I believe is right, to have the right to equal pay for work of equal value';[76] that one should 'actively promote women's greater role in society, take an interest in women's issues [and] give them serious consideration';[77] and that a person's gender is not in any way relevant to what they can achieve in any area at all be it work or public life, or anything.[78] Another respondent referred to Rebecca West's quotation: 'I myself have never been able to find out precisely what feminism is: I only know that people call me a feminist whenever I express sentiments that differentiate me from a doormat.'[79] The question of women's traditional gender roles, and women's choices to either follow or reject them, was present in one woman MP's response: 'Of course [I] don't think people should [be] told to look after [the] kids, [but] if that's what they want to do, I don't have a problem with that.'[80]

Other MPs were more specific and employed terminology similar to academic feminism. One MP defined feminism as: 'A recognition that, both institutionally and in many people's attitudes, women ... are oppressed and that therefore there needs to be some positive action that recognizes women as women, in order to right that imbalance.'[81] A second talked about her recognition that 'there is a gender dimension to life ... that women traditionally, even now, experience barriers and disadvantages because of the nature of their gender' and that feminism is 'fundamentally [a] belief in that there is almost equality or should be between [the] genders and there isn't'.[82]

More than one-third of the new Labour women MPs also indicated that those who identified themselves as feminists and who articulate feminist perspectives face an inhospitable climate.[83] One MP added mid-sentence: 'I wouldn't necessarily say this [about being a feminist] publicly.'[84] Other examples include those who asserted that feminism is seen as a 'dirty', 'pejorative' and 'emotive' word, which is 'misunderstood ... a bit harsh' and has 'negative connotations'.[85] Indeed, the one woman MP whose response can be categorized unambiguously as 'strongly feminist' acknowledged that she is reticent about using the term 'feminist' not because she is 'ashamed of it', but because it is 'so easily misinterpreted'.[86] Another MP sought to distance herself from 'radical' feminists by stating that she 'had never been a strident feminist', that there are 'degrees of being a feminist', and that she 'always looked at what is practical' and how one 'can improve [women's] daily lives'.[87] Perhaps even more revealing is the assertion that she has 'worked quite hard over the years [to] avoid being stereotyped' as a feminist.

Another of the MPs stated that she would be concerned if her local paper ran a story highlighting her feminism because she was worried that being labelled a feminist might alienate her from women constituents.[88] A colleague also resigned herself to the fact that so few young women identify themselves as feminists because feminists are negatively stereotyped as women in 'dungarees' with 'dangly earrings' and 'spiky hair'.[89] Lastly, one woman MP was highly critical of the way in which feminist analysis has been reframed as a 'ridiculous argument about keeping doors open', a reframing that had handed feminism to 'men who wanted to ridicule it'.[90] Together these statements suggest that many women MPs actively try to avoid being labelled as a feminist because of the negative perceptions of feminists and feminism.

Indeed, the one strongly feminist MP considered that there was only a limited space for women MPs to act for women in a feminist way in British politics. She indicated that her involvement in party politics – of becoming part of the 'establishment' – limited the extent to which she could effect 'feminist' change.[91] She stated, 'I have to watch that I don't compromise too much.' Nevertheless, in her opinion women MPs' actions, even when limited, were 'still worth doing'.

The MPs' responses that were categorized as 'ambivalent' further demonstrate the contested nature and negative perception of the term 'feminism'. One woman MP stated that she finds it rather difficult to answer the question of whether she considers herself a feminist.[92] On the one hand, she stated that if she had been asked the question twenty years ago, she would have said 'yes'. More importantly, she added that her views are not any different now. Arguably, this would place her in the category of self-identification as a feminist, and would increase the percentage of new Labour women MPs who consider themselves feminists. However, she went on to say that she was not really 'sure what it means to be a feminist now', and that she did not 'really want to be described as a feminist'. She would, in contrast, rather see herself as 'working productively with people on things we all ought to be achieving for society'. The motive for this change in her self-perception is that 'people want the same sort of things, men want to be involved in fathering more and women want to have careers as well as being mothers'. Perhaps, as she admitted, her feminist views about women's autonomy have not changed, but society has. It has changed, in her opinion, to one in which women's autonomy is no longer contested: 'we don't have to choose whether we are a parent or not', where women are treated with the same 'respect', and have 'the same safeguards against violence'.

The second new Labour women MP's response was difficult to categorize because she introduced a ten-point feminist scale and positioned herself at point three on it. This would suggest that she did not identify herself as strongly feminist.[93]

The final ambivalent response came from a woman MP who stated that she wanted women to be equal with men, to be able to live their own lives, and to be able to do what they want to do.[94] Again this response could be categorized as indicating identification with feminist views of women's autonomy. However, the MP prefixed this statement with the assertion that whether she defines herself as a feminist depends on 'what you mean by it'. In addition, she asserted that she was not anti-men, a characteristic she perceived as associated with feminism and one with which she did not want to be identified. Moreover, her subsequent comments that she was never active in the Women's Liberation Movement in the 1960s, despite her involvement in many other campaigning groups and activities at that time, suggested that she does not consider herself as a feminist. She stated: 'I have always thought of myself as, well, you know, "I am me" and I can make my way in life.' This response intimates a perspective in which women are perceived as being able to participate fully in society. Overall, while there is no direct rejection of feminism, this woman MP's response *may* place her in the 'no' camp.

In discussing the five new Labour women MPs who did not identify themselves as feminists, it is important to distinguish between those women who, while they rejected the feminist label, subscribed to feminist views and those women who rejected feminism *per se*. Those in the former category demonstrate an aversion to being labelled as feminist, which is a feature, in a weaker form, of many of those women MPs' responses who identified themselves as feminists. One MP considered that she was not radical enough to consider herself a feminist, particularly in relation to the notion of separatism and in terms of sexuality.[95] When she was asked about how she might explain her apparent interest in women's concerns, which was clearly evident in her interview, she was happier to accept that she was 'gender-conscious' rather than feminist. Second, is a colleague who talked about how her involvement in equal opportunities at the local council level had increased her awareness,[96] although she perceived that feminism 'sometimes ... put women ahead of everything else'. Another MP admitted that while she 'supported many feminist causes', she refused to identify herself as a feminist because of her dislike of labels, and because feminism had had a 'very strident voice' when she was younger. This she had found 'less than helpful'.[97]

The remaining 'nos' are also critical of labels, but they also appear critical of feminism. The first MP said that she wanted a society in which people are recognized as individuals, and judged on merit rather than 'gender', 'place of birth' or 'accent'.[98] The second MP, echoing these sentiments, stated that she had never had to battle for gender issues, had experienced society as meritocratic and, 'just want[ed] to see fairness for all'.[99] When asked whether feminism precluded that, she replied that it 'puts greater emphasis for women', and pointed to the lack of opportunities for men, which she considered 'just as limiting'.

On the basis of their own perceptions of feminism a majority of the new Labour women MPs identify with, and support, feminist concerns. While this definition of feminism – a shared appreciation of women's right to autonomy and equality – is 'loose', the fact that more than 70 per cent of the new Labour women MPs identified themselves as feminists, and even greater numbers of them subscribed to general principles of feminism, is important. However, this finding should not be overstated: it is one, but only one, indicator that these women representatives are predisposed to seek a feminist substantive representation of women. Moreover, even among those women MPs who are attitudinally feminist and might therefore be expected to be behaviourally feminist, some feel that they are unable to act fully for women because the environment in which they represent them (the House and wider British society) is not conducive to women representatives seeking to represent women substantively in a feminist way.

PARTY IDENTITY

If the relationship between women's descriptive and substantive representation is affected by women representatives' gender identity, it is also affected by their party identity. Indeed, the prioritization of party representation by many of the new Labour women MPs when they discussed their understanding of the concept of representation suggests that party is a key factor in explaining their attitudes and behaviour.

In order to explore how party impacts upon women representatives' substantive representation of women, the women MPs were asked to consider, in general terms, the adequacy of women's substantive representation by women MPs in the other main parties. One strong theme coming out of the data is that the new Labour women MPs considered that conservative/right-wing politics (as defined by the women MPs themselves) are not compatible with the substantive representation of women.[100] This is because, in their opinion, 'acting for' women requires the political principles and premises of left-inspired political analysis. Although all the MPs in this study were by definition Labour MPs, the anonymity guaranteed to them should have tempered the likelihood of their responses being influenced by 'party politics'. Indeed, the categorization of the 'left' by two of the new Labour women MPs as inclusive of the Liberal Democrats is suggestive that some women MPs were prepared to step beyond their party identity.[101]

For many of the new Labour women MPs conservatism was regarded as antithetical to the substantive representation of women. Examples included MPs who considered that conservatism is premised upon an 'ethos which sees women as totally peripheral'[102] and that the policies of right-wing governments 'tend [to] buttress and reinforce [the] powers of [the] existing powerful class', which this MP considered excludes most women. Another MP considered that the Conservative Party's class interest is 'against the interest of women',[103] while a colleague argued that equality is 'not fundamentally a right-wing concept'.[104]

These interpretations are supported by other new Labour woman MPs, one of whom stated, 'justice and fairness, equality and opportunity ... [are] real philosophical principles' which the right refute. A second MP talked about the 'free for all' of the right.[105] Another highlighted the right's belief that 'people can thrive [and] help themselves in a minimal framework',[106] while a third talked more generally of the Conservative Party having more traditional attitudes towards gender roles in society.[107] In less abstract terms, one of the new Labour women MPs noted that the necessary collective provision of childcare means that it is 'unlikely that that would be a policy solution put forward by a right-wing party'.[108] Finally, one woman MP concluded: 'I can't imagine a Conservative Party position that would ever be appropriate to the needs of people anyway.'[109]

A smaller group of women, while accepting that the Labour Party is more likely to substantively represent women than any of the other political parties (one of the new Labour women stated that parties of the left and centre 'actually make efforts' to go beyond 'warm words')[110] were not uncritical about the adequacy of their own party's substantive representation of women,[111] although others simply endorsed their party.

Analysis of how gender and party identities affect the relationship between women's descriptive and substantive representation was deepened with a consideration of whether women representatives share perspectives regarding women's concerns. One of the new Labour women MPs argued that women MPs' shared gender encourages the articulation of a feminized agenda within politics. A second MP identified childcare, wages, who does the housework, peace, justice, international co-operation and other 'more prosaic kind of things' as women's concerns, around which women can unite.[112] Other MPs identified drugs, unemployment, domestic violence and women's health issues.[113]

However, one MP made the important distinction between a shared appreciation of and desire to articulate women's concerns in politics – the feminized agenda – and party political divisions in terms of how one responds to this agenda. She stated: 'It's when you come to the next stage about proposed policy and solutions then [you] get the divergence.'[114] In her opinion, the 'proposed solutions ... probably in the majority of cases, throw up different approaches'.

Nevertheless, abortion was mentioned by six of the new Labour women MPs as a cross-party women's concern.[115] The discussion of abortion often involved comments about a particular Conservative woman MP.[116] Of note is the way in which initially the MPs considered this particular Conservative MP an ally, at least on women's concerns:

> [She made probably one of the] ... most radical speeches on abortion, rights to control [one's own fertility] ... she happened to be saying a lot of things that people on our side would have agreed with absolutely about abortion rights.
>
> If [you] look at [the] issue of abortion ... [she is] incredible, she said women [should] tell judges [to] mind [their] own business.
>
> I think she's quite good on abortion, isn't she?
>
> I'm with her on abortion.[117]

However, in a couple of cases, and when the comments are analysed within the context of the sections of conversation from which they have been removed, a different insight into how the new Labour women MPs conceptualized women's concerns, and the impact of party identity on these, becomes apparent. Important is the way in which the MPs seem to separate off women's concerns from political issues. One of the MPs quoted above began her statement with the assertion that there are some Tory women who are 'strongly feminist' before stating that the named Conservative woman MP is a 'dreadful woman', notwithstanding her support for abortion.[118] More importantly, this MP recognized a difference between this Conservative woman MP and herself in respect of economic policy. However, she also mentioned childcare as a policy on which she perceived that she and the Conservative woman MP would be in agreement. When it was suggested to her that this particular Conservative woman MP's notion of childcare might be familial and unregulated and that this would probably contrast with the new Labour woman MP's perception of acceptable childcare, the MP retorted: 'But I say again, it's a question about employment and the economy rather than childcare *per se*' and went on to assert that she believed strongly in regulation to prevent sweatshops. Evidently, there is some confusion here as to whether this MP considered that a shared concern with childcare provision results in a corresponding shared solution, in respect of its provision, between herself and this particular Conservative woman MP.

The second example is provided by one of her colleagues who, despite the fact that she perceived the named Conservative woman MP as 'quite good' on abortion, considered that 'politically I wouldn't have a great deal in common with her'. Again, an unproblematic opposition between women's and political issues is made.[119]

Further examples, which combined discussions of this particular Conservative woman MP and women's concerns more generally, also demonstrate the difficulty women MPs seem to have in articulating the way in which party identity impacts upon the substantive representation of women. Another MP stated: '[I] couldn't disagree with any politician more on political issues', although not 'when it comes to women's issues'.[120] In this instance, this MP was asked to explain the basis upon which she distinguished between women's and political issues. Her response suggested that women's concerns could be cross-party. The MP also referred to the aforementioned Conservative woman MP's proposals for childcare. She asserted that 'at least [we would have] had the argument in public'. Consequently, women's concerns would no longer be marginalized but brought to the centre of political decision-making even if the solutions to women's concerns might reflect party differences. Another MP said that she had signed the Conservative woman MP's Early Day

Motion relating to women's concerns, even though she 'probably' does not agree 'one jot' with her in terms of the economy.[121] The explanation of this apparent ability to agree with the Conservative woman MP on women's concerns and yet be critical of her economic perspectives is, in the Labour MP's opinion, to do with being sufficiently 'grown up' to state that 'we differ on this, but on this we agree'. Yet, another MP drew this distinction between women's and political issues in which the former would more likely reflect a consensus among women and the latter is bifurcated by party.[122]

The apparent ease with which some of the new Labour women MPs distinguish between women's concerns and political issues and which, in turn, corresponds to a shared women's perspective and party-specific perspective is interesting, and open to differing interpretations. On the one hand it seems to suggest that the MPs consider that women's concerns have a singular solution to which all women representatives can agree. In contrast, solutions to political issues were felt to be clearly demarcated according to political party. Yet it can also be suggested that the MPs perceive that women representatives share a desire to see a feminized agenda articulated and that this is what they mean when they identify themselves with the Conservative woman MP discussed above and, by implication, other women representatives from different parties.

It would be mistaken therefore to conclude that the new Labour women MPs consider that all women substantively represent women in the same way. What many do seem to accept is that women from other political parties are interested in centring women's concerns. Once women's concerns are on the political agenda, however, in most instances the new Labour women MPs consider that party identity comes into play. Further evidence for this interpretation derives from the fact that they considered that 'the right' in general and women representatives from right-wing parties are unable to act for women on the basis that they consider that solutions to women's concerns require left-inspired solutions. Importantly, however, this insight does not preclude cross-party co-operation in feminizing the political agenda.

CONCLUSION

This and the preceding chapter have explored the ways in which the new Labour women MPs understand the concept of descriptive representation and how it relates to substantive representation. Support for a descriptively representative House of Commons in terms of sex is strong among the MPs. The assumption of a link between an individual representative's gender, attitudes and behaviour is considered by many of the new Labour women MPs to be a reasonable one. This is not to say that they are unaware of how an acknowledgement of women's differences challenges the certainty of the relationship. But many emphasized listening and empathizing across women's differences, strategies that might counter, at least to some extent, the concern that women's substantive representation is wrongly premised upon essentialism. In this way, and following Mansbridge, many of the women MPs considered that they could act for women who were different from them.[123]

The overriding finding, then, is the belief on behalf of many of the new Labour women MPs that women must be present in politics because women have a different set of experiences from men, that these experiences are relevant to politics and that women are more likely to be substantively represented when women are 'acting for' women. Whether a particular woman MP acts for women is, however, best understood as being dependent upon both her gender and party identity (along with an appreciation of the gendered environments in which women representatives represent). That more than 70 per cent of the new Labour women MPs were attitudinally feminist provides one indication of the form and content of the likely substantive representation of women by these women MPs. Though evidence to support these conclusions has been, in this and the previous chapter, rather abstract, in the following chapters the focus shifts to the ways in which these women MPs consider that women MPs act for women in terms of the representative roles of a British MP, namely in the constituency, in Parliament and in government.

NOTES

1. The MPs' responses came from the part of their interview conversations where the notion of women representatives having a responsibility to represent women arose or was introduced as a probe. Responses were recategorized when women MPs used either terms in such a way as to imply the opposite of the meaning adopted in the analytic framework. For example, a representative might assert that she considered the responsibility to represent women as a burden for her. Such a statement would be recategorized as an obligation.
2. Interviews 1 (14–12–97), 4 (20–07–97), 7 (09–97), 8 (03–07–97), 9 (29–10–97), 17 (05–11–97), 18 (12–06–97), 19 (10–12–97), 20 (01–08–97), 26 (30–07–97) and 32 (19–11–97).
3. Interview 26 (30–07–97).
4. Interview 17 (05–11–97). See also interviews 18 (12–06–97) and 19 (10–12–97).

5. Interview 20 (01–08–97). See also interview 31 (08–07–97), although this MP raised the question of whether women MPs are 'sick to death of childcare'.
6. Interview 19 (10–12–97).
7. Interview 18 (12–06–97).
8. Interview 24 (07–04–97).
9. Interview 12 (11–06–97).
10. Interviews 6 (12–11–97), 12 (11–06–97), 17 (05–11–97) and 31 (08–07–97).
11. Interview 12 (11–06–97).
12. Interviews 6 (12–11–97) and 31 (08–07–97).
13. Interview 34 (19–06–97). See also interview 15 (14–10–97).
14. Interview 5 (23–06–97). See also interview 27 (08–07–97).
15. J. Mansbridge (1999), 'Should Blacks Represent Blacks and Women Represent Women?', *Journal of Politics*, 6, 3: 642.
16. Interview 4 (30–07–97).
17. Interview 1 (14–12–97). See also interview 19 (10–12–97).
18. Interview 19 (10–12–97). See also interview 32 (19–11–97).
19. Interview 6 (12–11–97).
20. Interview 10 (08–07–97).
21. In line with parliamentary practice the MP made it clear that if the woman had a personal issue she must contact her local MP. See also interview 11 (23–07–97).
22. Interview 9 (03–11–97).
23. Interview 32 (19–11–97). Her statement also intimates that there may be a conflict between substantively representing women and representing her Labour voting constituents (although she may be referring to her constituents *in toto*). She speculated that gay rights would probably be one area where conflict would arise.
24. Interview 1 (04–12–97).
25. Interview 30 (10–06–97).
26. Interview 11 (23–07–97).
27. A. Phillips (1995), *The Politics of Presence* (Oxford: Oxford University Press), pp. 53–5.
28. Interview 12 (11–06–97). See also interviews 28 (09–07–97), 32 (19–11–97) and 9 (29–10–97). See C. Hoskyns and S. M. Rai (1998), 'Gender, Class and Representation: India and the European Union', *The European Journal of Women's Studies*, 5: 345–65.
29. Interviews 28 (09–07–97) and 9 (29–10–97).
30. Interview 29 (06–08–97). Examples of the former include interviews 9 (29–10–97), 15 (14–10–97), 19 (10–12–97), 24 (07–04–97) and 28 (09–07–97).
31. Interview 4 (30–07–97).
32. See also interview 6 (12–11–97). See Mansbridge, 'Should Blacks Represent Blacks and Women Represent Women?'.
33. Another MP argued that they would need to 'stand back', an approach that she considered that men 'usually won't do' (interview 20 [01–08–97]).
34. Inteview 4 (30–07–97).
35. Interview 6 (12–11–97).
36. Interview 32 (19–11–97).
37. Interview 16 (24–11–97).
38. Examples of the substantive representation of different women will be outlined in the following chapters that consider constituency, parliamentary and governmental representation.
39. See Mansbridge's point that women representatives share experiences with women (Mansbridge, 'Should Blacks Represent Blacks and Women Represent Women?', p. 629).
40. Interviews 19 (10–12–97) (directly cited) and 30 (10–06–97). It is also worth reconsidering note 33 above where the MP perceives that men 'usually won't do that [listen and stand back] for women'.
41. Interviews 12 (11–06–97) and 5 (23–06–97). The latter also accepted that women and women MPs have shared experiences. Interview 19 (10–12–97) indicated that there might be differences between the 1997 cohort of women MPs and 'old' Labour women MPs based upon the 'roles that they want to occupy'.
42. Interview 13 (02–07–97). See also interview 21 (18–06–97) in terms of age.
43. Interviews 8 (03–07–97) and 21 (18–06–97).

44. Interview 3 (18–12–97). See also interview 4 (30–07–97).
45. The way in which party impacts on the representation of women is discussed by a greater number of women MPs at the stage in the interview when the topic of party representation is introduced. This is discussed later in this chapter.
46. Interview 32 (19–11–97). A second MP made a comment that might be interpreted as supporting this interpretation: 'We shouldn't have more women in Parliament if they were there to restrict other women's rights to choose' (interview 1 [14–12–97]).
47. In the interviews a prompt was introduced where the discussion needed some guidance and which drew upon the notion that men cannot represent women because of the bodily differences between men and women (A. Phillips [1991], *Engendering Democracy* [Cambridge: Polity Press], p. 36).
48. 46 Interviews 1 (04–12–97), 4 (30–07–97), 12 (11–06–97), 14 (03–07–97), 17 (05–11–97), 19 (10–12–97), 20 (01–08–97), 21 (18–06–97), 22 (08–09–97), 23 (29–07–97), 24 (07–04–97), 27 (08–07–97), 29 (06–08–97), 30 (10–06–97), 31 (08–07–97), 32 (19–011–97), 33 (19–06–97) and 34 (19–06–97).
49. Interviews 1 (14–12–97), 4 (30–07–97), 21 (18–06–97) and 29 (06–08–97). See also interviews 12 (11–06–97), 14 (03–07–97), 30 (06–08–97) and 32 (19–11–97).
50. Interview 4 (30–07–97). See also interviews 7 (07–97) and 18 (12–06–97).
51. Interview 15 (14–10–97).
52. Interview 19 (10–12–97).
53. Interview 3 (18–12–97).
54. Here private education – arguably a metaphor for class – is introduced as another characteristic that distinguishes between new and old men.
55. Interview 7 (07–97).
56. See also interview 9 (29–10–97).
57. Interviews 19 (19–12–97) and 32 (19–11–97).
58. Interview 20 (01–08–97).
59. Interview 32 (19–11–97). However, this MP found existing male representatives wanting in terms of representing women's concerns in Parliament and in their acting for women at the constituency level.
60. Interview 5 (23–06–97).
61. Interview 8 (03–07–97).
62. The assertion that women and men have different experiences in the same situation is supported by other MPs (Interviews 13 [02–07–97] and 14 [03–07–97]).
63. Interviews 6 (12–11–97) and 32 (19–11–97).
64. Interview 6 (12–11–97). The first part of the statement may be considered another example of where MPs responded aggressively to the notion that men cannot represent women and vice versa. The importance of gender and party in this example should also be noted. See also interview 16 (24–11–97).
65. Interview 28 (09–07–97).
66. Interview 31 (08–07–97). See also interview 23 (29–07–97).
67. Interview 2 (10–07–97).
68. Interview 10 (08–07–97). See also interview 12 (11–06–97).
69. Because the term 'feminism' covers a wide range of different definitions and is an identity that few women seek to claim because of its associated negative connotations, the term was left purposefully undefined and the discussion was introduced only towards the end of the interviews. However, a number of the women MPs discussed the feminism spontaneously, and in their own terms, at other points in the interview conversations.
70. S. Carroll (1984), 'Women Candidates and Support for Feminist Concerns', *Western Political Quarterly*, 37: 319.
71. Interviews 2 (10–07–97), 3 (18–12–97), 4 (30–07–97), 5 (23–06–97), 6 (12–11–97), 7 (09–97), 8 (03–07–97), 11 (23–07–97), 12 (11–06–97), 13 (02–07–97), 14 (03–07–97), 17 (05–11–97), 18 (12–06–97), 21 (01–08–97), 22 (08–09–97), 23 (29–07–97), 24 (07–04–97), 25 (01–07–97), 26 (30–07–97), 28 (09–07–97), 29 (06–08–97), 31 (08–07–97), 32 (19–11–97) and 34 (19–06–97). Interview 8 (03–07–97) considered herself a 'fainthearted feminist', and added that women's rights should not be exercised 'at the expense of children's rights', although she also recognized that 'you shouldn't have to make those choices'. One MP, early in the interview conversation, stated that she is a feminist (interview 1 [14–12–97]).
72. Interviews 15 (14–10–97), 16 (24–11–97) and 19 (10–12–97).

73. Interviews 9 (03–11–97), 10 (08–07–97), 20 (01–08–97), 27 (08–07–97) and 33 (19–06–97).
74. Interview 29 (06–08–97).
75. Interview 11 (23–07–97). This MP stated a number of times that she had not read academic feminist theory and therefore did not 'know' what feminism meant.
76. Interview 24 (07–04–97). Similar sentiments are displayed in interviews 3 (18–12–97), 4 (30–07–97) and 5 (23–06–97).
77. Interview 18 (12–06–97). See also interview 2 (10–07–97).
78. Interview 17 (05–11–97).
79. Interview 7 (09–97). The quote is reproduced from C. McKenzie (1992), *Quotable Woman* (Edinburgh: Mainstream Publishing), p. 75.
80. Interview 34 (19–06–97).
81. Interview 32 (19–11–97). This response also appears to suggest that the MP is not trying to judge or prescribe for other women.
82. Interview 6 (12–11–97).
83. See notes 84–9 below.
84. Interview 32 (19–11–97).
85. Interviews 24 (07–04–97) and 11 (23–07–97), 23 (29–07–97) 34 (19–06–97) and 22 (08–09–97) respectively.
86. Interview 28 (09–07–97). The categorization of this MP as 'strongly feminist' derives from responses in the interview in which she asserted that she has a gendered perspective, had worked in women's groups and remarked that she had been involved in the women's movement before she became involved in the Labour Party.
87. Interview 30 (10–06–97). See also interviews 26 (30–07–97) and 3 (18–12–97). The latter stated that she was happier to be identified as a feminist now than she would have been twenty years ago because of the association of radicalism with feminism in the past. She prefers the 'quiet', 'calm', 'rational and reasonable' approach to change. As an afterthought, she added that women would probably have had to wait longer for suffrage if it had not been for Emmeline Pankhurst.
88. Interview 12 (11–06–97).
89. Interview 31 (08–07–97).
90. Interview 24 (07–04–97).
91. Interview 28 (06–08–97).
92. Interview 19 (10–12–97).
93. Interview 15 (24–11–97).
94. Interview 16 (24–11–97).
95. Interview 20 (01–08–97).
96. Interview 10 (08–07–97).
97. Interview 9 (03–11–97).
98. Interview 33 (19–06–97).
99. Interview 27 (08–07–97).
100. Hoskyns and Rai argue that increases in women's presence 'without economic redistribution' will succeed only in symbolic representation (Hoskyns and Rai, 'Gender, Class and Representation: India and the European Union', p. 357).
101. Interviews 10 (08–07–97) and 29 (06–08–97). This argument is reinforced by the recognition that this does not prevent critical comments about the Liberal Democrats' inability to secure the (s)election of more than three MPs in 1997 and their refusal to support Labour's AWS.
102. Interview 1 (14–12–97).
103. Interviews 4 (30–07–97) and 20 (01–08–97).
104. Interview 6 (12–11–97).
105. Interviews 27 (08–07–97) and 10 (08–07–97).
106. Interview 15 (14–10–97). See also interviews 16 (24–22–97) and 22 (08–09–97) that draw attention to the state provision of social security, education and health services as fundamental to women's ability to participate in society. Interview 16 (24–22–97) was critical of the way in which the previous Conservative government had 'foisted' community care on to women.
107. See also interviews 9 (03–11–97), 11 (23–07–97), 12 (11–06–97), 14 (03–07–97) and 26 (30–07–97).
108. Interview 32 (19–11–97).
109. Interview 17 (05–11–97).

110. Interview 16 (24–11–97). See also interviews 18 (12–06–97) and 10 (08–08–97). Interview 10 (08–08–97) considered that the general philosophy of the Labour Party 'must be of benefit to women and children'.
111. Interviews 25 (01–07–97), 28 (09–07–97) and 32 (19–11–97).
112. Interview 4 (30–07–97).
113. Interviews 13 (02–07–97) and 32 (19–11–97).
114. Interview 4 (30–07–97). This interpretation is also supported in interviews 11 (23–07–97), 13 (02–07–97) and 29 (06–08–97).
115. Interviews 8 (03–07–97), 10 (08–08–97), 11 (23–07–97), 17 (05–11–97), 25 (01–07–97) and 34 (19–06–97). It should be noted that one MP (interview 34 [19–06–97]) acknowledged that there are some Conservative women who are anti-abortion. Another MP recalled her recent experience on a trip to Cairo with Labour and Liberal Democrat women MPs. Among the women, she argued, there was a shared 'base point' that women had the right to abortion and contraception (interview 1 [14–12–97]).
116. Interviews 8 (03–07–97), 11 (23–07–97), 17 (05–11–97) and 34 (19–06–97). The identity of the Conservative woman MP, while cited by the new Labour women MPs, is not revealed to protect her anonymity.
117. Interviews 8 (03–07–97), 11 (23–07–97), 17 (05–11–97) and 34 (19–06–97).
118. Interview 17 (05–11–97).
119. Interview 8 (03–07–97). See also interview 11 (23–07–97).
120. Interview 33 (19–06–97).
121. Interview 14 (03–07–97).
122. Interview 32 (19–11–97).
123. Mansbridge, 'Should Blacks Represent Blacks and Women Represent Women?'.

6

Women's Substantive Representation in the Constituency

Most analyses of whether women make a difference in politics fail to consider what MPs do in their constituencies. Yet responding to and representing their constituents is a significant, albeit unsung, part of a British MP's representative role.[1] Moreover, if party identity and discipline is less important in the constituency, then the sex of the representative might make a significant difference in the constituency as women MPs act for women.[2]

IDENTITY, AFFINITY AND ACCESS IN THE CONSTITUENCY

According to the 1997 data, more than one-third of the new Labour women MPs thought that women in their constituencies were contacting them in greater numbers as a result of their shared gender, while only two MPs considered that their sex and/or gender did not determine the make up of their surgeries.[3] Of the 14 MPs who perceived an increase, five specifically considered that their formal constituency surgeries were drawing in greater numbers of women, and eight, including two who felt there was an increase in this formal channel, perceived that women constituents were also contacting them more informally,[4] for example, at 'supermarket surgeries' (where MPs hold surgeries in supermarkets), at the school gates and at the bus stop.[5]

A small number of women MPs also suggested that the presence of women representatives in the constituency might result in greater numbers of both women and men going to see their representative. This assumption was underpinned by a perception that women representatives are considered, because of stereotypical notions of gender, to be good at 'listening' and especially at listening to 'personal problems'.[6] One MP considered party identification as part of the reason that accounted for her perception that greater numbers of people were coming to her surgeries,[7] although a colleague stated that although her constituency had previously been represented by a male Labour MP, her women constituents still 'feel that you understand more about what life is like for them and what their concerns are'.[8]

The issues which women raise with their women MPs is another way of evaluating the substantive representation of women by women representatives in the constituencies. Nearly one-third of the new Labour women MPs considered that women constituents were voicing women's concerns with them.[9]

> From [my] mailbag [and] surgeries women [are] coming forward, excited [by the] prospect [of] discussing issues that affect them as women ... [I] had one on breast feeding the other day.[10]

> I've had a couple of cases where women had complaints against the police, where they have actually said to me [that] they would have felt reluctant in sharing some personal information with a man ... because of the nature of what she had been through [she] probably couldn't talk to a man about it.[11]

> For example this lady came to see me about her daughter who [had] been very violently raped, [she had] strong criticism, not of the police, but of [the] legal system, I felt she found it easier to talk to me than she may have a male MP.[12]

According to the women MPs women constituents were voicing their concerns with them because of their shared gender. One MP's response explicitly demonstrated these links:

> [I'm] absolutely convinced ... [I] don't want to give away too much of confidences, [I'll] summarize one particular incident ... [a woman had the] sort of problem [that she] may not [have] been able to talk [to a] man about at all, involving some abuse, not only could she tell me everything in some detail, detail [I] probably needed to know to help her properly, [but] at the end of the conversation we could hug each other [and] she needed to be hugged ... [it was] almost a privilege to have been asked to help someone like that and to be intimate about it.[13]

One of the ways in which some of the MPs explained the affinity between women MPs and their women constituents was to discuss it in terms analogous to that of women's claimed preference for women doctors. Of the eight MPs who discussed the 'doctor analogy', five considered the analogy appropriate:[14]

> A lot of the constituents I have find it easier to talk through … their problems about perhaps the way they feel about their problems rather than just the factual content of it because I am a woman, in a way that a lot of women prefer having a woman doctor.[15]

> It's a bit like doctors, women should really have [the] choice whether they see a woman doctor or a male doctor and I suppose, at least now, with so many women in the House we have opened the choice a bit.[16]

Another colleague accepted too that 'it's a bit like going to the doctor's', noting that some women have told her that they did not want to raise a particular issue with the previous MP, although this MP did acknowledge that this was only the case for a small number of constituents.[17]

However, the doctor analogy was not universally accepted by all of the MPs who mentioned it. One of the new Labour women MPs questioned the extent to which any MP should be dealing with constituents' personal problems. In this MP's opinion, the substantive representation of women is not the same thing as enabling women constituents to access their women MPs to talk about women's concerns.

> Let's be clear what [it] is we have select[ed], it is not my choice of gynaecologist … there are areas where it is important whether it is a man or a woman [but if this is the case] then [I] seriously suggest to you that your Member of Parliament is not the right person to go and see, [they've] got a confusion of what we are here to do, not [to] listen [to] women's experiences of child abuse.[18]

A second MP, while accepting the legitimacy of women's right to see a woman doctor on the basis that some medical issues are 'intimate', rejected the notion that intimacy has a role in political representation. Another colleague agreed and questioned whether the additional letters she claimed she receives from women – 'I get quite long chatty letters usually from elderly women' – reflected her gender and thought that they might be from 'people who just fancied writing to me'.[19] Implicit here is a critical judgement that what these elderly women are writing to her about are not the kinds of concern about which MPs should be addressed.

Two other MPs were also ambivalent about the appropriateness of the doctor analogy. The first asserted:

> Well, if you were going along for a gynaecological examination you might feel that you want a woman doctor, if you were going for an

> ear examination you might be less bothered ... if there was a woman who had been assaulted she might rather come and talk to a woman MP. I think that does happen on occasion, that women MPs pick up issues like that, [women] who would rather talk to a woman, but if it's a problem about ... local school provision then a good sympathetic listening local MP would be good, be it male or female.[20]

The second MP, on the one hand, said that she considered more women were accessing her but then rejected the notion that the women were bringing with them a feminized agenda. However, she then went on to state: 'Ideally [there should be] women MPs for women, women engage with other women, where [they have the] opportunity, for example, [a] doctor or solicitor, if available [women will] go to women.'[21] She then added that this is the case specifically for issues such as childcare, the Child Support Agency, divorce issues, equal opportunities and education.

Some of the new Labour women MPs appear to be subscribing to a division between women's concerns and political issues, the former that require women representatives and the latter which do not. Yet, one of their colleagues forcefully contested this interpretation:

> I think that is what it [representation] is about, isn't it? I think that is what it is about ... if women come to me. I have had women come to me who have lost, who are damaged by radiation treatment for cancer ... Who come to me and talk to me about their experience of having radioactive [therapy], they have actually been bombarded with radiation vaginally and lost their breasts, and who I think would find that very difficult to talk to men about ... That is a political issue because it is actually to do with the way in which [the] battle for compensation [and the] medical establishment provided treatment to women without making them aware of the risks, and there are political issues that are within it.[22]

According to this MP women's concerns *are* political. She considered that the effect of cancer and cancer treatment on women is political because women's experiences of medical conditions, and in more general terms women's concerns *per se*, are determined by the decisions (and non-decisions) of political actors.

Interestingly, another MP stated that she felt that the issues that had been brought before her in constituency surgeries, like 'the importance of childcare for women in getting women back to work or into education', had 'hardened up the things I believe [in]'.[23] Although this point is raised by only one of the new Labour women MPs, it does suggest that for this particular MP such reinforcement may enable the MP to articulate women's concerns in Parliament safe in the knowledge that it reflects her constituents' concerns. This might also go some way to deflect the criticism of women MPs that was identified as operating in some constituencies in the previous chapter and which constrains women representatives' substantive representation of women.

WOMEN'S DIFFERENCES AND THE SUBSTANTIVE REPRESENTATION OF WOMEN IN THE CONSTITUENCY

Of the six new Labour women MPs who discussed the substantive representation of different women in the constituency, five considered that ethnic differences are not insurmountable obstacles to the substantive representation of women. More importantly, the MPs were conscious of the need to open and maintain communication links with these women at both the individual and group level within the constituency. Asian women, in particular, were identified as coming to the women MPs' constituency surgeries. They came both to introduce themselves to their women MPs and to raise their concerns.[24] One of the new Labour women MPs claimed that because she had met Asian and Caribbean women during the election campaign they would 'in the future ... have better representation'.[25] Because these women had already accessed her they would continue to do so even though she was a white women representative. Furthermore, she believed that Asian women would find it culturally difficult to contact male MPs. Another colleague agreed. She considered that Asian women were more comfortable coming to a woman than a man.[26] Yet another MP, while admitting that she does not 'understand Asian women's problems', also stated that Asian women had accessed her and articulated their concerns. She felt that she had got to get 'alongside' Asian women and that 'they need encouragement to solve their own problems'.[27] This woman MP's reflection suggests a consciousness of the existence of women's differently experienced problems, demonstrates her commitment to engaging with women from different communities in her constituency and her support for community-specific actions.

Another MP told, with evident pride, of a meeting she had held with Asian women in her constituency. In the meeting she broached the issue of differences of ethnicity, class and status between herself and the women who were present:

> On the face of it I probably look a great deal different from you, middle class, you probably think I am wealthy, and live in a nice house, white, and I've been to school which many of them haven't, but really at the basis of it my life has been very much like your life, bringing up children, looking after older parents, and I said, this morning I did my washing, put my washing on the line, then I went for [my grandchild], took him to the nursery, picked up [another grandchild] who's here, he has come with me, then I will take him back, give him lunch, so I said for many of you grandmas here it won't be all that different from what you have done, so I was able to break the ice, they were a bit resistant, I think they were just a bit shy of me to start with but I kept it going and Shamin was translating for the older women and we were able to do a lot of questions and answers, and it was very interesting, I really enjoyed it.[28]

To be sure, the above statement could be interpreted as asserting a perspective that might be said to reject differences between women and reasserts women's sameness. In contrast, the episode can, and *should*, be interpreted as an attempt not to discount differences but to build bridges between women. Again, although it might be claimed that this MP was 'seeking out' Asian women to garner their votes, it is my contention that this MP is honestly seeking to act for the Asian women in her constituency rather than being engaged in electoral opportunism. The interview with this MP took place in the MP's Westminster office where a small photograph of four sisters sent by a young Asian girl was on display. It was revealed by the MP that the accompanying letter had stated how happy the young girl was to have a woman MP.

In contrast to these examples, which suggest that the new Labour women MPs seek to act for women who are different from themselves, a couple of other MPs, including one who also subscribed to the view that women MPs will enable the substantive representation of ethnic minority women, pointed out that notions of identity, affinity and access between women and women MPs might be replaced in minority ethnic communities by minority ethnic MPs, such as Keith Vaz and Diane Abbott.[29] Indeed, one MP asked whether white constituents might find it difficult to contact Keith Vaz.[30]

Overall, many of the women MPs who discussed the issue of the substantive representation of different women agreed that while the homogeneity of new Labour women is problematic at some levels (namely, symbolic and/or numerical representation), their presence nevertheless engenders women's substantive representation. Admittedly, this interpretation is based upon the perceptions of the MPs and may not reflect the perceptions of minority ethnic women, but it demonstrates that women MPs seek to act for women who are different from them.

Moreover, and as a counter-charge to the small absolute numbers who addressed the substantive representation of different women, there is the fact that four out of these five MPs represent constituencies with non-white populations higher than the mean for the participating new Labour women MPs.[31] The example of the MP who holds special meetings with minority ethnic women also points to one way in which accountability can be explicit between women representatives and their women constituents who may be obviously (in this instance regarding ethnicity), or more obliquely, different.

WOMEN MPs AND THE SUBSTANTIVE REPRESENTATION OF MEN

During the interview discussions just under one-third of the MPs brought up the question of how men might react to a woman MP representing their constituency.[32] Two themes came out of these discussions: first, there was a concern that men might not be accessing women representatives in the same numbers as when they had had a male representative; and, second, there was the contention that men might find it difficult to accept that women can fulfil the role of an MP.

Only one MP asserted that she did not believe that men would find it more difficult coming to see a woman MP,[33] while eight MPs concluded that 'it might be that men are staying away' and that, consequently, they might have 'problems' that would not be on the political agenda.[34] One MP, for example, who was indignant at the suggestion that her sex and/or gender might prevent men coming to see her and who articulated her offence at the suggestion, nevertheless stated that she had been alerted to the possibility of men staying away: 'There may be some situations, surgeries where I may take [a] male councillor with me.'[35] This qualification seems to suggest that, notwithstanding her initial response, she did consider that her sex and/or gender might be perceived by men as preventing a shared sense of identity, affinity and access between themselves and their woman representative.

Interestingly, another two MPs thought that even if men were not accessing their women MPs, this was less of a problem than is the case when women do not have woman MPs.[36] The MPs' reasoning was that because there are fewer women MPs overall, a woman is more likely to find herself surrounded by constituencies represented by male MPs. In contrast, she argued that even if a man is represented by a woman MP, they would be more likely to find neighbouring constituencies with male MPs whom they could access.[37]

Another MP took the view that she and her neighbouring male MP 'together ... make a better representation'.[38] The male MP is, in her opinion, 'much nearer to the male workers in the factory and understands their concerns about losing their jobs' whereas she 'perhaps better understands their wives or the women workers'. She concluded, in light of this, that 'you need both slants' and admits her preference for multi-member constituencies. This interpretation is, however, different from one of her colleagues, who at this stage of the interview was joined in her shared office by her neighbouring male MP.[39] Their conversation discussed whether twinned constituencies (where a larger area is represented by both a male and female MP) might engender more adequate substantive representation through the woman MP acting for the women and the man MP acting for men. Both MPs rejected this interpretation:

> Male MP: Well, it's not a gender issue.
> Woman MP: No, it isn't.
> Male MP: [The] cross over [she] gets, cases from [my constituency] and I get cases from [her constituency] because [she] has represented the ward on the edge of [my constituency] and I represented a ward on the council ... and it's one bloody town and most people don't know what constituency they live in and we are not territorial.
> Woman MP: No, it's got nothing to do with gender, I don't think.
> Male MP: I don't get blokes coming to me because they are shy of going to [the woman MP] ... I get loads of women coming to my surgeries.

If there was some concern that male constituents might not access women MPs, three MPs thought that male constituents were unable to accept women as competent representatives. As one MP stated:

> [I] sometimes get the impression they [men constituents] feel as though they ought to put me right on a thing or two, I do get this impression [from] a lot of men: 'She's a woman, does she really understand about all of this or should I correct her?'[40]

Interpreting this statement is not easy. Perhaps this woman MP's perception of why the male constituents want to 'correct her' is because of her inability to empathize or understand men's concerns, because of the experiential differences between women and men. This is a similar argument to that advocated in respect of men's inability to act for women. Alternatively, her statement may be interpreted as an example which suggests that men have problems accepting women's authority, an interpretation supported by two other woman MPs. The first MP claimed that 'a few [men] have come in and tried to be the kind of male role and sort of say, "do this and do that"',[41] while the second perceived that whether she could act for the 300 traditional male workers who had been made redundant was being 'judged'.[42]

ACTING FOR WOMEN IN THE CONSTITUENCY, 1997–2000

Just after their election in 1997 many of the new Labour women MPs considered that an initial politics of transformation was occurring within the MP–constituent relationship as a result of women's political presence. More women were accessing them and raising women's concerns with them. Moreover, some considered that they had acted as surrogate representatives for women outside their own constituencies and had acted for women who were different from them.[43] Though some acknowledged that their presence might have reduced the access between men constituents, most of the MPs did not appear to be too disturbed by this.

Yet, these conclusions were based on the MPs' limited experience of office. At the time of the interviews many had been elected for only a couple of months or so. By 2000 the MPs would have a much greater set of experiences to draw on. Would they still hold the view that women's presence in the constituency means that women were being substantively represented?

There was, once again, a shared perception among the reinterviewed new Labour women MPs that their presence had engendered access by women in the constituency. This had two dimensions: first, individual access between women constituents; and, second, increased access between women's organizations and women MPs. Moreover, the women MPs also considered that their presence had made a difference through the articulation of a feminized agenda.

In 2000 more than half of the MPs considered that women constituents were accessing them in greater numbers, especially in terms of their constituency surgeries.[44] Five women MPs felt that women from ethnic minority communities were similarly accessing them and voicing women's concerns and three MPs added that male MPs' women constituents had also contacted them.[45] This perception, that women constituents are more likely to access women MPs, implies that some women constituents neither identify with nor seek out male MPs (irrespective of party). Rather, they seek out either the nearest woman MP or a specific woman MP[46] because she is identified as associated with women's concerns.[47]

In contrast, only two women MPs rejected outright the claim that the presence of women MPs had engendered increased access by women,[48] one because she was not sure which of her characteristics might account for women accessing her. Was it because she was a woman, local or had an approachable image?[49] Similarly, the other MP felt that it was the fact that she was both a woman and a Labour MP that accounted for the greater propensity of women and women's organizations to access her.[50] In addition, five MPs considered that any increase reflected women's greater propensity to be responsible for the concerns that require MPs' assistance and because women are at the centre of the family and inner-city communities.[51] Nevertheless, in the opinion of nearly one-third of the new Labour women MPs women constituents' propensity to access women MPs is because women 'prefer to come and talk to a woman MP'.[52]

The MPs talked, once again, about their women constituents' desire to discuss women's concerns:[53] 'The issues they want to talk about they only want to talk about with a woman.'[54] Another MP stated that 'some [women] actually do say "oh I wouldn't have gone to see a man about that, I would never have sat down and told a man that"'.[55] She added, accompanied with laughter, that her previous occupation might also explain this 'because I think they think you've seen everything'.

Women constituents, when they access their women MPs, according to the MPs, voice women's concerns. They talk about childcare,[56] domestic violence (including forced marriages),[57] education,[58] the Child Support Agency (CSA),[59] health,[60] women's employment,[61] housing,[62] caring,[63] the environment,[64] young people,[65] or 'things [they] might not want to say to a man'.[66] One MP argued, in line with the comments made above concerning women's tendency to be community activists, that women bring community issues: 'If you're a mum you are going to be concerned about where your kids go to school.'[67]

In contrast, the women MPs considered that men constituents wanted to talk about economic issues,[68] 'have an issue or a principle they want to explore with you'[69] and are more 'self-centred' and have less 'genuine' problems.[70] However, there was some recognition that this division between women and men and their concerns is not absolute: 'Some men obviously write on family issues but there is a higher tendency among women.'[71] Two MPs stated that both women and men had brought the issue of the CSA to them, while another asserted that she did not think there was any sex stereotyping, although she added, rather contradictorily, 'outside those areas which are clearly differentiated as a male preserve'.[72]

As in the 1997 research, support for the contention that women are more likely to discuss women's concerns with women MPs is susceptible to the criticism that these concerns are not really what constituency representation should be about. One MP, for example, suggested that some of her constituents, who she does not think would have 'talked to a man', came to see her about 'intimate issues, medical problems' and other 'emotional things'.[73] However, this MP seemed to reject this separation between women's concerns and what is political when she added: 'Lots of the emotional stuff [has] a practical side to sort out.'

Perhaps more significant than the perception on behalf of the new Labour women MPs that individual women constituents are accessing them and raising women's concerns is the finding that more than three-quarters of the women MPs considered that their presence has engendered contact between themselves and women's organizations in their constituencies.[74] Some women MPs claimed to have sought out women's organizations while others that they have been contacted by them. Where women's organizations are accessing women MPs it could be said that they are accessing them in the same way that they would any MP. But, there is a perception that women's organizations are accessing women MPs because they perceive that the women MPs will identify with their concerns and 'in anticipation' that they 'might have been more understanding'.[75] There is also a strong sense coming out of the data that women MPs accept a (positively interpreted) responsibility to act for women. The basis for this relationship is, once again, a shared sense of identity and affinity based on gender.

> It's been useful to be able to use that position as a woman MP to highlight that [domestic violence] and I'm glad to say I've done so ... I knew those issues were there and were relevant and I wanted them to make sure that their woman MP was there with them.[76]

> I look at my women and say if you need me for anything I will always be here to serve you and to help you the best way that I can.[77]

> I mean, I have tried particularly to reach women ... women who represented organizations that had a particular interest in women.[78]

> I'm more likely to turn up to them, I think that's maybe the difference ... if you get an invite from the rape crisis centre then I'm more likely to go than they [male MPs] are.[79]

The types of women's organization most frequently identified by the women MPs were those associated with domestic violence,[80] those involved with caring, pre-school childcare and voluntary work more generally.[81] Contact between Asian women's groups and women MPs was also identified by five women MPs.[82]

While these perceptions suggest that new Labour women MPs are acting for women's organizations in their constituencies, it could be argued that this finding is limited because the research does not explore whether male representatives similarly act for women. However, what the data can show is the opinions of the women MPs regarding whether and which men might be acting for individual women and/or women's organizations at the constituency level. On reflection, the MPs who discussed this did not consider that this was the case. One MP recognized that some individual men MPs did act for women, although the particular MP she identified was, she admitted, characterized by, and she implied that his behaviour was similarly influenced by, his association with a Labour woman MP. Another MP recalled that when women from outside her constituency contacted her she always asked them whether they had already tried their own male MP. But she then stated that she felt a responsibility to take up the cases 'if they say "yes" and he's not interested'.[83] Moreover, she considered that the previous male MP had failed to act for the Asian women in her constituency.

Other MPs explained that the greater likelihood of women representatives acting for women was determined by their ability to 'go into situations that I think you know, male predecessors wouldn't'.[84] A second woman stated that she might 'pop into a school' and recognized that she was very comfortable 'in those sorts of environments', whereas she considered men wouldn't feel 'quite so comfortable'.[85] Another considered that 'male MPs in [her] area get very little casework on domestic violence'. One MP explained further why she contends that women representatives act for women:

> I think women tend to get involved much more in issues facing women because you just, you know, you ... empathize, take a very different view on child support ... some men [will say] 'how dreadful, fancy taking all that money off you' ... we'll probably [be] much more likely to see the women who are suffering because they are not getting the child support for their children, so I think there is a completely different perspective there.[86]

This interpretation is reinforced by a colleague who talked about how as a woman MP 'you get points of reference that a man couldn't have' concerning domestic violence and that 'that's sparked off more of an interest'.[87]

CONCLUSION

At the constituency level, many of the new Labour women MPs contended that their presence in the constituency has made a difference. The 1997 data established that nearly one-third of them considered that women were accessing them in greater numbers and that a feminized agenda was being articulated. By 2000, the women MPs were more confident that their presence in the constituencies was making a difference for women. There was strong support for the claim of a link between women's descriptive and substantive representation. More than one-half considered that their presence engendered greater access between themselves and their women constituents and more than two-thirds stressed their relationships with women's organizations. Evidently women's concerns, whether articulated by individual women constituents or by women's organizations, are being discussed with women MPs. According to many of the new Labour women MPs, women representatives do act for women in their constituencies.

Support for the claim that women representatives can act for women who are different from them was forthcoming in both sets of interviews. The MPs' perception that women were accessing them in greater numbers was not limited to white women. In 1997 a number of the women MPs talked about how they had had contact with Asian women in their constituencies, and three years on some women MPs again included ethnic minority women and women's organizations when they were discussing whether women were accessing them in greater numbers because of their shared gender identity. Admittedly these examples, which suggest that women's differences do not necessarily prevent the substantive representation of women who are different, are based on the opinions of the women MPs. One cannot therefore suppose that women from minority ethnic communities would necessarily agree with the women MPs' analysis. Notwithstanding this qualification, the data suggest that a transformation may have occurred within the MP–constituent relationship as a result of women's political presence and that this was not limited to women who shared the class, ethnic or educational backgrounds of the women MPs. This conclusion supports Mansbridge's argument that women representatives do not have to have shared, identical experiences with the women they seek to represent.[88] Furthermore, if the presence of women MPs has engendered enhanced contact between women, women's organizations and women MPs, then it is possible that the concerns and experiences that women constituents have brought to their MPs will inform the MPs' attitudes and actions in Parliament as well. In this way, acting for women in the constituency may have an effect beyond the constituency.

NOTES

1. D. D. Searing (1985), 'The Role of the Good Constituency Member and the Practice of Representation in Great Britain', *Journal of Politics*, 47: 348–81; P. Norton and D. Wood (1993), *Back from Westminster* (Lexington, KY: University of Kentucky Press).
2. D. Beetham (1992), 'The Plant Report and the Theory of Political Representation', *Political Quarterly*, 63, 4: 462; A. Reeve and A. Ware (1992), *Electoral Systems* (London: Routledge), p. 82.
3. Interviews 34 (19–06–97) and 19 (10–12–97).
4. Interviews 7 (07–97), 9 (29–10–97), 15 (14–10–97), 22 (08–09–97) and 18 (12–06–97) for the former, and 1 (14–12–97), 6 (12–11–97), 9 (29–10–97), 13 (02–07–97), 16 (24–11–97), 17 (05–11–97), 20 (01–08–97), 25 (01–07–97), 26 (30–07–97) and 32 (19–11–97) for the latter.
5. Interviews 13 (02–07–97) and 17 (05–11–97), 32 (19–11–97) and 9 (03–11–97), respectively.
6. Interview 3 (18–12–97). See also interviews 15 (14–10–97), 17 (05–11–97) and 19 (10–12–97).
7. Interview 9 (03–11–97). Interview 19 (10–12–97) rejected the 'feminized agenda' thesis but considered that women find it 'easier' to talk to and approach women.
8. Interview 11 (23–07–97).
9. Interviews 1 (14–12–97), 4 (30–07–97), 10 (08–07–97), 13 (02–07–97), 20 (01–08–97), 22 (08–09–97), 26 (30–07–97), 29 (06–08–97), 30 (10–06–97) and 32 (19–11–97).
10. Interview 13 (02–07–97).
11. Interview 4 (30–07–97).
12. Interview 22 (08–09–97).

13. Interview 26 (30–07–97).
14. Interviews 1 (04–12–97), 6 (12–11–97), 7 (09–97), 16 (24–11–97) and 29 (06–08–97).
15. Interview 6 (12–11–97).
16. Interview 16 (24–11–97).
17. Interview 1 (04–12–97).
18. Interview 24 (07–04–97).
19. Interview 17 (05–11–97).
20. Interview 19 (10–12–97). It is acknowledged that this extract demonstrates some acceptance of the 'doctor' analogy.
21. Interview 7 (09–97).
22. Interview 6 (12–11–97).
23. Interview 3 (18–12–97).
24. Interviews 22 (08–09–97), 10 (08–07–97), 18 (12–06–97) and 9 (03–11–97).
25. Interview 10 (08–07–97).
26. Interview 18 (12–06–97).
27. Interview 9 (03–11–97).
28. Interview 8 (03–07–97).
29. Interview 9 (03–11–97).
30. Interview 29 (06–08–97).
31. The constituencies have 21.3 per cent, 19.9 per cent, 7.5 per cent, 7.1 per cent and 4.3 per cent (R. Waller and B. Criddle [1996], *The Almanac of British Politics* [London: Routledge]. Of the MPs who participated in this research, the mean of non-white populations is 6.2 per cent. This compares with a mean of 6.9 per cent of non-participating new Labour women MPs. Participating women MPs with higher than mean non-white populations who did not discuss the impact of women's differences in respect of constituency-level representation are interviews 6 (12–11–97), 12 (11–06–97), 17 (05–11–97), 21 (18–06–97), 29 (06–08–97) and 33 (19–06–97). None of these, or any of the constituencies represented by new women MPs, is a constituency in the top 20 seats with the highest proportion of non-white voters.
32. Interviews 4 (30–07–97), 6 (12–11–97), 10 (08–07–97), 17 (05–11–97), 22 (08–09–97), 26 (30–07–97), 32 (19–11–97) and 33 (19–06–97).
33. Interview 15 (14–10–97).
34. Interviews 4 (30–07–97), 6 (12–11–97), 10 (08–07–97), 17 (05–11–97), 22 (08–09–97), 26 (30–07–97), 32 (19–11–97) and 33 (19–06–97).
35. Interview 33 (19–06–97).
36. Interviews 26 (30–07–97) and 10 (08–07–97).
37. This interpretation might be considered to contradict the convention that MPs only represent their constituents.
38. Interview 9 (03–11–97).
39. Interview 17 (05–11–97).
40. Interview 8 (03–07–97).
41. Interview 16 (24–11–97).
42. Interview 28 (09–07–97). This MP added that she perceived that she had to 'prove' herself against a neighbouring Labour male MP who, she considered, was competing against her. This seems to suggest that rather than supporting her, her male colleague was trying to undermine her position as a competent MP.
43. The research data do not lead to a strong conclusion to be made here regarding whether it is gender and/or party identity that prevents women from identifying and accessing men MPs.
44. Interviews 1 (12–07–00), 3 (14–06–00), 16 (26–07–00), 18 (12–07–00), 22 (16–05–00), 23 (19–06–00), 24 (10–05–00), 25 (21–06–00) and 29 (15–5–00).
45. Interviews 8 (20–06–00), 18 (12–07–00), 22 (16–05–00), 24 (10–05–00) and 29 (15–05–00).
46. Interviews 3 (14–06–00) and 23 (19–06–00).
47. Interview 8 (20–06–00).
48. Interviews 5 (22–05–00) and 7 (13–06–00). Two other MPs were ambivalent (interviews 16 [26–07–00] and 31 [10–07–00]).
49. Interview 31 (10–07–00).
50. Interview 9 (22–06–00).

51. Interviews 16 (26–07–00), 2 (13–06–00) and 4 (21–06–00) respectively, and 13 (13–06–00) and 12 (15–06–00).
52. Interviews 18 (12–07–00), 25 (21–06–00), 12 (15–06–00), 13 (13–06–00), 16 (27–7–00), 18 (12–07–00) and 23 (19–06–00).
53. Many also considered that both women and men are more likely to access women MPs because they prefer to talk to women. See interviews 1 (12–07–00), 3 (14–06–00), 18 (12–07–00), 22 (16–05–00), 27 (17–05–00), 28 (12–07–00) and 31 (10–07–00).
54. Interview 18 (12–07–00). This MP also suggested that part of the explanation is that women are perceived to be more likely to 'get things done'.
55. Interview 24 (10–05–00).
56. Interviews 1 (12–07–00), 4 (21–06–00), 15 (23–05–00), 25 (21–06–00) and 29 (15–05–00).
57. Interviews 3 (14–06–00), 8 (20–06–00), 23 (19–06–00) and 24 (10–05–00).
58. Interviews 1 (12–07–00), 16 (26–07–00) and 29 (15–05–00).
59. Interviews 13 (13–06–00), 23 (19–06–00) and 24 (10–05–00).
60. Interviews 1 (12–07–00), 4 (21–06–00) and 23 (19–06–00).
61. Interview 13 (13–06–00).
62. Interview 16 (26–07–00).
63. Interview 25 (21–06–00).
64. Interview 1 (12–07–00).
65. Interview 2 (13–06–00).
66. Interviews 12 (15–06–00) and 18 (12–07–00).
67. Interview 4 (21–06–00).
68. Interview 1 (12–07–00).
69. Interview 24 (10–05–00).
70. Interviews 16 (26–07–00) and 24 (10–05–00).
71. Interviews 1 (12–07–00) and 15 (23–05–00).
72. Interviews 13 (13–06–00), 5 (22–05–00) and 7 (13–06–00).
73. Interview 31 (10–07–00).
74. Interviews 2 (13–06–00), 3 (14–06–00), 4 (22–06–00), 5 (22–05–00), 7 (13–06–00), 8 (20–06–00), 9 (22–06–00), 13 (13–06–00), 14 (08–06–00), 15 (23–05–00), 16 (26–07–00), 18 (12–07–00), 23 (19–06–00), 24 (10–05–00), 25 (21–06–00), 27 (17–05–00), 29 (15–05–00) and 31 (10–07–00).
75. Interview 9 (22–06–00).
76. Interview 5 (22–05–00).
77. Interview 7 (13–06–00).
78. Interview 25 (21–06–00).
79. Interview 2 (13–06–00).
80. Interviews 5 (22–05–00), 7 (13–06–00), 13 (13–06–00) and 31 (10–07–00).
81. Interviews 7 (13–06–00), 16 (26–07–00), 23 (19–0–00), 27 (17–0–00), 29 (15–5–00) and 31 (10–07–00).
82. Interviews 8 (20–06–00), 18 (12–07–00), 24 (10–05–00), 25 (21–06–00) and 29 (15–05–00).
83. Interview 8 (20–06–00).
84. Interview 2 (13–06–00).
85. Interview 13 (13–06–00)
86. Interview 24 (10–05–00).
87. Interview 31 (10–07–00).
88. J. Mansbridge (1999), 'Should Blacks Represent Blacks and Women Represent Women?', *The Journal of Politics*, 61, 3: 628–57.

7

Substantively Representing Women in Parliament

What difference Labour's 101 women MPs made in Parliament following their election in 1997 is the question that everybody wanted answered. If it could be shown that the women MPs had acted for women in Parliament, then the relationship between women's descriptive and substantive representation would be confirmed. To establish whether the new Labour women MPs acted for women in the House of Commons substantive change needs to be documented.[1] But prior to that, whether the new Labour women MPs actually sought to act for women needs to be demonstrated: women representatives may seek to act for women but have no discernible effect because they act in environments that are not conducive to the substantive representation of women. Thus, it is important to determine first whether the new Labour women MPs actually sought to articulate women's concerns in the House. By drawing on data from 1997 and 2000 it is possible to establish their perceptions when they first arrived in Parliament (what they wanted to do and thought they would achieve) and after having operated in the House for three years (where they considered what effect they had had).

WOMEN'S CONCERNS, WOMEN'S ISSUES

Thus far the concept of women's issues has assiduously been avoided in favour of the less pregnant term 'women's concerns'. But it is now important to clarify what the new Labour women MPs mean when they claim they act for women: what concerns do they consider constitute 'women's issues'; what concerns do they voice?

Many MPs find the concept of 'women's issues' complex.[2] They qualify their initial statements and use the term in ways different from its everyday use. Of particular interest is the way in which many of the MPs reject the way in which women's issues are often seen as a limited group of issues for which women have sole responsibility and which are currently devalued. In contrast, they seek to redefine the concept and introduce a more expansive definition.[3]

Nevertheless, most agree that there are issues that constitute 'women's issues'. As one MP stated: '[I] think [there are] some issues [which] specifically affect women.'[4] Indeed, only two of the MPs rejected the concept of 'women's issues', with one MP citing research that she argued 'comprehensively proved [that] there are not women's issues'.[5] However, she then identified feminine hygiene as an 'esoteric' women's issue.

A good illustration of the difficulty women MPs have with using the term 'women's issues', because of the 'baggage' it brings with it, is provided by one MP. When talking about the impact of the greater presence of Labour women MPs she stated: 'It means that a much higher percentage of women's concerns, issues, *not as in women's issues, but issues which impact on women*, are brought up day after day and [are] changing policies' (emphasis added).[6] This MP appears to be trying very hard to ensure that women's issues are not interpreted in the words' everyday and negative sense. In her opinion, women's issues are all 'those issues which impact on women'.

The strongest advocate of the concept of women's issues was the MP who acknowledged that her gender directly informed her perspectives in politics (as discussed in the previous chapter). For this MP, women's issues are those issues which men do not articulate, are not on the political agenda and, more positively, are those issues which women articulate: 'I still think there are women's issues, I don't see men lining up to talk about childcare, never had, [I] don't see men lining up to talk about women's rights to abortion, never had.'[7]

A number of the MPs identified issues which they felt are currently understood as constituting women's issues. These included: the family, domestic violence, rape, childcare, and abortion.[8] One MP talked about an Early Day Motion which reviewed current rape laws, and particularly the cross-examination of the woman, as a practical example of a women's issue that had already been raised in the 1997 Parliament.[9] Another MP believed that women are more interested in issues that are derived from women's domestic responsibilities, citing education, youth, health and caring issues, although she added that this should not be interpreted as implying that all women 'have the same views'.[10] A third MP, after stating that too much is made of women's issues and arguing that women are interested in similar things to men, admitted that women's issues are derived from the gendered structure of society and that it was this that explains women's greater interest in women's issues.[11]

The desire to challenge the accepted definition of 'women's issues' as a limited group of issues, only of relevance to women, is apparent among a number of the new Labour women MPs. One MP prefixed her definition of women's issues with the statement: 'I'm not happy with the term women's issues'. She then added: 'I think you may talk about abortion or childcare [as women's issues] but those are *issues for everybody*' (emphasis added).[12] This way of redefining women's issues is shared by colleagues:

> *Childcare is not a woman's issue, it is a parenting issue* … [that] need[s] to be addressed by both sexes … [they are] *issues for parents or for society* and it is the fact that they are perceived as women's issues and therefore less important that they have been relegated to something in the second division. (emphasis added)[13]

Another stated: '*There is no issue which is not a person issue, no issue that is specifically a woman's issue*, [the] question of defence priorities, that affects women and the family, everything does' (emphasis added).[14]

Redefining women's issues is clearly something the MPs were keen to do. In a further example, one MP declared: 'I have an interest in industry; [this] is not usually seen as a women's issue, but of course it is a women's issue, very much so.'[15] However, her subsequent comments seem to suggest that the 'women's part' of industry lies less with the mechanics of the industry, or even women's rights to work in it, but resides with the effect of industry in paying for the services which, in her opinion, more directly impact on women's lives:

> [If] you don't have a good solid industry with investments, [you] don't have money [to] pay [for] things [which] make so much difference [to] women's lives, good childcare, nursery education, health service, all those follow on from the successes.[16]

Arguably this statement, while appearing to redefine women's issues in a radical way, entrenches notions of women's and men's separate spheres. Thus, industry is a women's issue in a particularly feminine way. In contrast, another MP placed greater emphasis on the need for women's economic independence, achieved through women's employment as the bedrock of women's wider freedoms.[17]

An appreciation that women's issues are regarded as unimportant and those who voice them as marginal is also evident in many of the new Labour women MPs' comments. Even the MP who strongly asserted that there are women's issues believed that many women are hesitant about associating themselves with women's issues: 'Some women almost want to distance themselves from these issues because [they] don't want [to] see them as women's issues.' This hesitancy is caused by an appreciation of the way in which they will be perceived by others if they are associated with women's issues: 'It's as *if you've got to prove that you are also interested in real issues* in order to be accepted and regarded as having any depth' (emphasis added). A colleague agreed. She considered that if a woman MP 'give[s] the impression' of being interested in women's issues, this could be negatively interpreted by men as the woman representative being '*only* interested in women's issues' (emphasis added).[18]

Another MP believed that women MPs 'do identify with women's interests' but she was concerned that women will be 'pigeon-holed' if they associate themselves with women's issues and argued that 'women representatives who see themselves as MPs for women [are] causing a lot of women to turn off'.[19] This statement, which contradicts her earlier point, implies that women MPs need to distance themselves from women's issues because women MPs who voice women's issues face criticism for doing so, that the women MPs are operating in an inhospitable environment, one where acting for women has accompanying costs.

A number of other MPs supported this interpretation. They noted how political commentators perpetuate the idea that women are only interested in (conventionally defined) women's issues,[20] and one MP revealed how she had overheard MPs saying: 'Oh I don't want anything to do with education or health, they are women's issues.' Her response to hearing this was to think: 'Good heavens, am I still hearing this?'[21] Another colleague reinforced this sentiment:

> I think there is a little bit of a tendency [for women to be interested in women's issues, but] much less than there was ... I don't think you will find so many women battling it out on the defence issues as men, but how much of that is interest, how much of that is expectation? I don't know ... the only issues which are absolutely specific to women are a small cluster of issues to [do] with the physical nature of our bodies and childbearing processes, you know.[22]

An alternative interpretation that exacerbates the above concerns about the public perception of women's issues is raised by another MP. She is concerned that if women claim women's issues as their own (and she acknowledged that there are 'clearly things' which women are more interested in than men), this implies, or rather might be interpreted by men as implying, that these are issues that men 'don't have to worry about'.[23] What troubles this MP is the implication that in the absence of women MPs male MPs would have to act on these issues (and thereby act for women) and that women's presence absolves them of this responsibility.[24]

Yet another example provided by one of the new Labour women MPs illustrates the ways in which the negative perception of women's issues and women MPs' response to this perception impacts directly on the substantive representation of women at the parliamentary level.[25] The MP talked about the expectation that women will be members of the Social Services Select Committee. Yet, she 'want[s] women to break the stereotypes and be on [the] Industry and Employment [Committee]'. However, when it was pointed out to the MP that she was herself a member of the Social Services Select Committee the MP admitted that she was personally interested in 'battling away on those issues' because they are 'critical to people's lives' and especially critical to those 'who don't get a very good deal'. Moreover, she rejected the implicit elision between women's issues and 'soft issues'. In an attempt to reconcile her interest in women's issues and her concern that women break out from the women's issue enclave in which they are put, she concluded: '[It] is very important that when we look at it in the round we make sure that you don't end up with all the women on the Social Services Committees.' Thus, women's interest in women's issues must, in this MP's opinion, be supplemented with women's interest in all areas of politics.

The new Labour women MPs' consideration of the concept of women's issues supports theories of women's political representation that suggest that women representatives seek to represent women substantively. While the concept of women's issues, as it is traditionally defined, has been demonstrated to have been tainted in the eyes of the new Labour women MPs, many are happy to continue using it once they have redefined it. Moreover, their definitions expand its content. In its common usage it is regarded by the women MPs as referring to a limited and devalued set of issues that are considered the sole responsibility of women. In contrast, the women MPs' redefinitions can be summarized in the following way: women's issues are no longer issues in which women are solely interested, but refer to all issues seen from women's perspectives. At the same time, there remains a commitment to traditional notions of women's issues, in the sense that women MPs associate themselves with these issues (as currently defined) and seek to act on this basis.

Notwithstanding this, there are clearly concerns on behalf of the new Labour women MPs that they are not free to 'act for' women; doing so has costs, both in terms of their own careers, the future numerical representation of women, and a more general 'pigeon-holing' of women. The appreciation of the costs associated with being identified as an advocate of women's issues suggests that women's issues are not part of the mainstream, but rather are marginal to it. This marginal position also implies that women's issues are not being articulated by men, which demonstrates, albeit circuitously, that 'women's issues', as a distinct group of issues, exist. Moreover, acknowledgement of the ways in which women MPs distance themselves from women's issues apparently undermines an automatic link between women's descriptive and substantive representation. If women MPs are conscious that they will be negatively judged if they articulate women's issues, then it would seem likely that fewer of them would behave in this way.[26]

FEMINIZING THE PARLIAMENTARY POLITICAL AGENDA

There was widespread support among the new Labour women MPs in 1997 for the contention that their presence enables the articulation of women's issues within Parliament. Half of all the interviewed MPs articulated this effect.[27] Future debates would be 'better informed' and 'more appropriate for the community'.[28] More importantly, there would be the 'setting [of] a new sort of agenda', one with 'different priorities' and which sees the introduction 'of policies which we can see would have helped us [women] in years gone by'.[29] This new agenda is variously defined as encompassing 'women's concerns', 'women's issues', 'our experiences', the 'women's agenda', the 'cluster of problems facing women' and the 'issues [that] specifically affect women'.[30] Of those MPs who defined the feminized agenda, three identified violence against women[31] and women's health,[32] and two each identified childcare,[33] education, equal opportunities and employment.[34] A substantial number of new Labour women MPs considered, then, the articulation of women's concerns as the minimum outcome of women's political presence.

The voicing of women's concerns, which has the potential to transform the parliamentary political agenda, derives from the presence of women who have different experiences from the male MPs in the House.

Women MPs' consciousness of their women constituents' 'experiences of life', in which they have to 'run homes', informs their involvement in policy development.[35] Or, as another MP put it: 'Unless you [are] actually faced with them [women's issues, you] don't consider them.' Indeed, another MP said that her passionate interest in transport was informed by her awareness that half of all women 'do not have a driving licence'. Such insights, she considered, demonstrate that women will be 'putting [a] different perspective'.[36]

In contrast, male politicians were identified as failing to articulate and prioritize women's concerns. However, another MP challenged the link between women's descriptive and substantive representation. She argued that, in the absence of women, the same ends could be achieved because there is 'more than one way to skin a cat',[37] although she added the contradictory qualification that achieving this would be 'much more difficult'; women representatives will act for women as a natural consequence of women talking about issues and experiences that 'touch on their lives'.

Another example supports the claim that women's concerns are marginal to the current political agenda and that the presence of women representatives is necessary to articulate them. One MP talked about 'some brave men' [MPs] who 'wanted' to talk about breast cancer.[38] What is interesting about this short statement is the use of the adjective 'brave'. Why does this MP consider that it is 'brave' for a male MP to introduce the issue of breast cancer? Suggesting that male MPs need courage to discuss breast cancer is qualitatively different from saying that male MPs cannot articulate women's concerns because they do not have the same experiences as women MPs.

Another of the MPs also implies that some men do consider women's concerns as important but that they are unsure about how to demonstrate their support for such concerns and thereby do not seek to 'act for' women.[39] Notwithstanding this, her response suggests, once again, that women's concerns are absent from the political agenda when only men are present.

Clearly, many of the new Labour women MPs considered that part of their representative role in Parliament was to raise women's concerns. However, at the time of the 1997 interviews, the women MPs could only draw on their limited experience since the election or speculate on their likely impact. As one of the new Labour women MPs put it: 'I agree with that argument … [but] I have not been in Parliament long enough to experience the relationship in the Commons.'[40] Six of the MPs did, however, discuss their perceptions of the likely impact:[41] five were optimistic, with one arguing confidently that women's presence in committees would hold the government 'to account from the experiences of women themselves'.[42] Another MP said that legislation will just be 'better informed', 'more appropriate for the community' and produce more all-rounded policies and legislation because of women representatives articulating women's concerns.[43] Finally, three MPs perceived that ministers were already responding to the pressure emanating from women. They argued that issues previously classified as 'women's issues', such as education and the welfare state, have been prioritized as central issues for the current government:[44] 'I think there is a change of emphasis and priorities of government and I keep coming back to that; childcare, minimum wages will affect more women than men ... the issue of reform of the welfare state.'[45] And one MP recalled how, on the day before her interview, a woman MP had introduced an Early Day Motion regarding rape. She did not think 'a man would do' this.[46]

The lone, pessimistic MP felt that, because most of the Labour women MPs, especially the 1997 intake, would be confined to the backbenches, their effect in the 1997 Parliament would be limited. Interestingly, she also argued that any transformation would be determined by the behaviour of the women themselves, in particular, whether or not they actively 'pursue changes' and make politics 'more gender-conscious [and] more gender-sensitive'. She contrasted this with the action of women MPs who seek to 'further their own careers'.[47] This MP's statements indicate a perceived tension between a feminized transformation of politics and a successful parliamentary career for individual women MPs. It points to a perception that women MPs are not free to advocate women's concerns and 'act for' women. This statement also undermines this MP's earlier assertion that it is up to individual women MPs actively to seek to transform the political agenda because she acknowledged that women MPs operate in unfavourable institutional places which may proscribe the extent to which women representatives act for women.

The notion that women representatives may be unable to act for women is highlighted in other MPs' responses too. A consciousness of the pressure to reject an overt identification with women's concerns, if not her gender identity, is made by one MP:

> All of the things I've done in my personal life [and] in my political life, [have] in a way, been denying I am a woman, because in order to make progress in politics, such is the terrible state of affairs, [you] have to almost be asexual, you'll never be a man … [and] you can't be too much one of the girls either.[48]

In this MP's opinion the requirement not to be 'one of the girls' means that women seeking legislative recruitment are cut off from the 'support mechanisms' among women that would have been 'very, very helpful'. Furthermore, the pressure to be 'de-gendered' also means that women are not able substantively to represent women because being perceived as 'acting for women' is unhelpful: 'Being overtly supportive of other women' means 'you get categorized, [you] get put in a box, labelled as a woman's person'. However, the MP added that once (s)elected women have 'certain freedom' to represent women.

Further insights into the relationship between women MPs' experiences of the legislative recruitment process and the substantive representation of women are also forthcoming. Two MPs drew a distinction between themselves and the re-elected Labour women MPs. In their opinion the newly elected women have different views on policy. One of these MPs considered that the previously elected women MPs had entered Parliament 'through the old system'.[49] In order for these women to have succeeded in the legislative recruitment process they would, in this woman MP's opinion, 'probably' have had to 'battle' through and become more 'masculine' in orientation.[50] In contrast, the new Labour women MPs were considered more likely substantively to represent women than women representatives had done in the past because their legislative recruitment had been eased by AWS.[51]

Another example where the space for women MPs to act for women is seen to be limited comes from one woman MP's experience of a meeting of the Commonwealth Parliamentary Association (CPA).[52] According to this MP, a male member of its Executive Committee kept saying that what the women MPs were suggesting would not be 'allowed'. The MP was critical of this attitude, which meant that 'women have to have permission if they want to do something'. Clearly, women cannot, in this woman MP's opinion, (adequately) act for women in these conditions.

A more worrying perspective, at least for those who link women's presence to a feminization of politics, is made by a single MP.[53] Her response to a question concerning the effect of the greater numbers of

Labour women MPs indicated that she felt that it was important for the women MPs not to be 'too strident' or to 'rub all our male colleagues up the wrong way'. She considered that if they were 'too demanding' the men in the Labour Party would report back unfavourably to constituency parties. What she wanted to see happen, in contrast, was an evolutionary approach to ensure that the message to the constituencies would be that women representatives are a 'really good crowd'. This MP considered that acting for women is negatively associated with women's numerical representation because if women are 'too demanding' party selectorates will not select women for Parliament – a highly problematic interpretation for those who argue the link between women's presence in politics and the substantive representation of women.

Yet nearly one-third of the new Labour women MPs considered that the 1997 general election had returned sufficient numbers of women MPs to enable them to act for women;[54] critical mass, they argued, had been established.[55] These MPs' opinions may go some way to counter the more critical perspectives of colleagues who see little space for women representatives to act for women. Nevertheless, some added qualifications: for example, one hoped that there 'were enough of us', a second merely asked whether there were enough women to change things, and a third 'didn't think' there were enough women in powerful enough positions as yet.[56] Indeed, securing critical mass is identified by one woman MP as necessary for women MPs to do more than 'survive' in House.

In contrast, one MP suggested that when greater numbers of women are present women representatives are freer to articulate any issues rather than be confined to articulating women's concerns.[57] Evidently, this woman MP perceives this as a positive, although it throws into relief the link between women's descriptive and substantive representation. Furthermore, she backed up her interpretation by discussing a conversation she had had with a woman who had been elected to Parliament in 1974. This woman MP recalled a shared responsibility among the nine women MPs to act for women in the abortion debates of the 1970s in the face of 'all these Catholic men' who wished to criminalize abortion, even though, when she had been first elected to the House, she had not considered herself to be representing women.[58]

On balance, the women MPs' perceptions of their presence in 1997 pointed to a future in which women's concerns would be articulated and the political agenda feminized. A couple of MPs considered how one might qualify or quantify the effect of women's political presence. One

MP rejected as outdated the desire to see 'gender-based legislation', comparable to that of the 1970s,[59] while a second asked women to resist the temptation of expecting the new Labour women MPs to deliver 'some sort of landmark policy' for women.[60] However, it is possible that these responses constituted a strategy to pre-empt the critical analysis of women representatives' feminized impact on legislation: women, according to the second of the women MPs, must trust them to represent them 'behind [the] scenes'.[61]

ACTING FOR WOMEN IN PARLIAMENT, 1997–2000

The 1997 interview data answered the question of women MPs' attitudes towards the substantive representation of women favourably; more than one-third of the new Labour women MPs felt a responsibility to represent women substantively and half considered that their presence in Parliament enabled the articulation of women's concerns. There were grounds, therefore, to be confident that the presence of Labour women in the 1997 Parliament, or at least the presence of 65 new Labour women MPs, had the potential to make a difference. But, to what extent did the women MPs act for women in practice? And to what effect?

There was widespread support in the 2000 data for the claim that Labour women MPs had articulated women's concerns in the House since their election in 1997. Nearly two-thirds of the MPs argued that they had done this.[62] Women's concerns included violence against women (including forced marriages and sexual harassment),[63] childcare,[64] caring,[65] breast cancer[66] and emergency contraception.[67] Some women MPs specifically named Ruth Kelly's work on paternity leave, Harriet Harman's general concern with women (notwithstanding her dismissal as Secretary of State for Social Security and Minister for Women in July 1998) and Christine McCafferty's campaign to remove VAT on sanitary products.[68] Other women MPs drew attention to the Fabian Pamphlet by Fiona Mactaggart that documented women MPs' contributions.[69]

Acceptance of the link between the presence of women and the substantive representation of women was made explicit by nearly half of the women. The MPs talked about how women's concerns would not have been raised, or would not have been raised in the same form, in their absence:

> I've become increasingly aware that there are issues that affect women disproportionately and that unless women pursue them nobody else will.[70]

> I think … [women's presence] created a discussion and a debate … I think women have shown that they are prepared to take up issues.[71]

> Just by being there we have sort of highlighted issues which affect women.[72]

> The issue of Ann Cryer taking up this issue of forced marriages … we would not have got a change [without women] … none of the men in this place, I think, would have actually taken that up the way we did.[73]

One MP provided a more extensive discussion. She talked of how she had tried to encourage male Labour MPs to participate in a debate on a particular women's concern; she had been 'almost begging them to speak in the debate', but she 'couldn't get any men from our side to speak'.[74] A second recognized that women lead on women's concerns, 'because it's an issue close to our hearts and I think we probably understand it better than men'. While a third stated that 'in any political setting I've ever been in it's never been a man who's taken a lead on childcare'.[75]

The use by Labour women MPs of Early Day Motions (EDMs) to raise women's concerns was raised by six MPs, three of whom mentioned specifically Christine McCafferty's motion on VAT on sanitary products.[76] The perception that 'women's EDMs' are collectively and disproportionately signed by women was also mentioned by four women MPs.[77]

A few MPs also considered that women MPs would articulate women's concerns on an increasing number of occasions in the future. One stated that, although daunted at first, they had 'started to get … organized before the last budget' and were now 'more organized'.[78] Another said that if government policy was not reflecting women's concerns women MPs 'would be more vocal about it'. And a third stated that 'if a number of us … get back in next time we'll see far more assertiveness among the women'. This MP also considered that the expectation that women MPs would be able to come into Parliament and transform the agenda overnight was itself gendered: 'Anybody going into a new job has to take time to build up experience, we have never been tolerated in that respect.'[79] She added that she felt that she was not able to act for women in the 1997 Parliament because of her known association with women's concerns in her pre-parliamentary career: she had 'better not be seen to be just identified with' women's concerns. A colleague also mentioned that her constituency casework had prevented her fully acting for women thus far.[80]

Some of the MPs also made a direct link between the presence of the women MPs and the government's responsiveness regarding women's concerns.[81] One stated: 'If we hadn't had all these women here … I don't think this childcare strategy … would have had all the money it's had, I think that [women's presence] has been very important.'[82] Another highlighted the fact that this Parliament had seen a debate on domestic violence, and she stated that her 'understanding is that [this has] never happened before'.[83] A colleague, discussing family-friendly policies, asked whether the government's policies would have happened 'without the 101 women'. She answered by stating, 'well possibly not, because the imperative wouldn't have been there'.[84] Other women MPs acknowledged the importance of women's activism in the Labour Party in the previous years which had 'got us to this stage'.[85]

Three MPs did, however, acknowledge their disappointment regarding the extent to which they had been able to act for women.[86] One considered that this was because women MPs remained an 'endangered species' and could not afford to act collectively without threatening their political careers.[87] Change would come about only when women MPs were no longer 'threatened' or 'endangered'. Another MP perceived that women 'have failed completely', although she indicated that the women had been trying to introduce feminized change.[88]

Select committees

One area where backbenchers can perhaps have greater influence is within select committees. Although there are only a small number of cases, the seven MPs who discussed their work in select committees *all* perceived that their presence re-gendered their committees' agendas.[89] Illustrative examples included:

> I think that what you find [is] that … women working on select committees will have a different perspective.
>
> We are able to perhaps approach things in a more inclusive way, to think about family a little more, mainly because I can understand as a woman.

> [Women are articulating women's concerns] absolutely, especially on the select committees.[90]

A couple of the MPs were or had been on the Education Select Committee. One emphasized how the committee, notwithstanding male colleagues' suspicions ('[it] wasn't something which won [a] tremendous amount of favour with male colleagues') had undertaken an investigation into school meals and 'early years' education.[91] 'Women', argued the MP, 'will look at education but may look at it slightly differently.' In her opinion examining school meals was about 'how effective children will be in school if they are starving'. She added: 'Men are not quite so interested.' A colleague emphasized how important it had been that the Education Select Committee had and continued to have a strong Labour women's presence.[92] This meant, in her opinion, that the rest of the committee 'now anticipated that it [the women's perspective] will come in regularly ... it's no longer seen as, "oh she would wouldn't she", this is now mainstream', although she added that 'it could well be forgotten' if women's presence was not maintained.

The two other women MPs who talked about their presence on select committees offered slightly more ambivalent responses. Though both women MPs made statements that indicated that they had brought feminized perspectives to their committees and both provided examples where they had articulated women's concerns, they were concerned that by taking up women's concerns they would be stereotyped and marginalized as only interested in women's concerns.[93]

Nevertheless, these discussions suggest that select committees constitute an important site for women MPs to articulate women's concerns. Moreover, select committees appeared to be a place where women MPs were able to act for women, as the women were confident that they had re-gendered their committees' agendas.

The Parliamentary Labour Party Women's Group

In the interviews the role of the Parliamentary Labour Party Women's Group was discussed by some of the women MPs. Those who discussed this fell into three categories: regular attendees, of whom there were five,[94] infrequent attendees, who also numbered five,[95] and non-attendees, who numbered eight.[96] An estimate by one of the attendees puts the number of regular attendees at approximately twenty.[97]

Unsurprisingly, regular attendees considered the group an important site for the substantive representation of women. Yet, seven of the irregular or non-attendees similarly supported it and recognized its effectiveness.[98] Supporters argued that the group constitutes a space within the House in which women MPs can discuss women's concerns in the absence of men.[99] But the group was not merely regarded as a space to voice women's concerns.[100] It aimed to feed into government decision-making. One MP argued that the group should be regarded as working with the government 'to try to get women's issues on the agenda' prior to policy formation and development. This, she considered, was a powerful position to be in.

The Chancellor's decision to reduce VAT on sanitary products was identified as a concrete example of where the group had had an effect on government policy,[101] although one MP lamented that 'Gordon sort of glossed over it' in his Budget speech.[102] Others talked more generally about how they had had meetings with government ministers, including the Chancellor and the Home Secretary.[103] One MP mentioned how the PLP Women's Group had spoken with Jack Straw about rape laws and the granting of a visa to Mike Tyson.[104]

Nevertheless, a few MPs were critical of the effectiveness of the PLP Women's Group. For example, one MP considered that the group was not regarded as 'serious': it had 'no teeth whatsoever'.[105] She felt that ministers regarded the group as an opportunity to explain government policy rather than constituting a proactive body. In her opinion it acts 'as a platform to get various ministers to come along and be massaged'. Another MP, while acknowledging that cynicism may have coloured her view, also felt that executive dominance in the House meant it had 'minimal influence'.[106] And yet another that she felt it was 'too scared'.[107] One of these MPs also considered that the executives of the group were 'career-minded', which she regarded as limiting the extent to which they and the group would seek to act for women. Moreover, she stated that they had not suggested that she hold a meeting on a women's concern with which she is closely associated.

However, only one of the MPs' responses could be interpreted as suggesting that the PLP Women's Group was problematic *per se*. She asserted:

> There are members who feel that there are things we can do … as a women's group … there is a feeling that we … have clout as a

> group and that we should use it but it's not something that I'm really comfortable with … perhaps I'm the wrong person to talk to about the the women's agenda.[108]

Of note too is the reason why some MPs only attended infrequently or did not attend at all. The most frequently cited reason was that the PLP Women's Group meetings clashed with other events.[109] Yet this explanation needs to be unpacked, as one MP's response indicates:

> I keep missing it, the next question is why do I miss that and not miss these other things? So, I think somewhere in my mind the others are doing more than the women's group … somewhere in my mind I think that isn't important, I'm doing other things … I wouldn't like to have justify that [laughter] … there has to be a reason why I keep missing that and not missing the thing it clashes with [laughter].[110]

However, another woman's explanation was that she did not find it a 'congenial group'.[111] And a second that she was not sure the extent to which she considered that it was 'coming from a feminist perspective'.[112]

CONCLUSION

From the perspective of the 1997 data it looked as though the new women MPs would act for women in Parliament. Many of the MPs sought to act for women by voicing women's issues (and they held more expansive definitions of what constitutes women's issues) in Parliament. By 2000 many of the MPs were sure that they had acted for women. Two-thirds argued that Labour women MPs had raised women's concerns in Parliament. In particular, they have focused upon violence against women, childcare and equal opportunities. One-half also acknowledged the link between the presence of women and the substantive representation of women.

Quantifying the effect of the Labour women MPs in the 1997 Parliament is not easy. As one MP said: 'You can't say we have changed that but you can say we've worked six weeks on that and … change has come about.'[113] Nevertheless, many are confident in their claims that the theoretical link between women's descriptive and substantive representation holds in practice.

This is not to say that they considered that their efforts were always rewarded. Their comments suggest that there may well be costs in voicing women's concerns in the House of Commons (or at least in parts of it). The women MPs' perceptions of the conditions in which they seek to act for women are particularly interesting because they link with arguments regarding whether women representatives practise a feminized style of politics, the subject of Chapter 10.

NOTES

1. J. Lovenduski (1997), 'Gender Politics: A Breakthrough for Women?', *Parliamentary Affairs*, 50, 4: 718.
2. This reinforces the case for avoiding the concept so far.
3. See F. Mackay (2001), *Love and Politics* (London: Continuum), p. 113.
4. Interview 18 (12–06–97).
5. Interviews 7 (09–07–97) and 14 (03–07–97) respectively.
6. Interview 1 (14–12–97).
7. Interview 28 (09–07–97).
8. Interview 18 (12–06–97), 21 (18–06–97) and 28 (09–07–97). Interview 24 (07–04–97) identifies childcare as a women's issue before criticizing the concept and outlining the dangers of ghettoizing women's issues. Childcare and abortion were also identified as women's issues.
9. Interview 18 (12–06–97). Interestingly, and in contrast to the MP cited above who categorized feminine hygiene as 'esoteric', this woman MP considered VAT on sanitary towels as a political *and* woman's issue.
10. Interview 12 (11–06–97).
11. Interview 23 (29–07–97).
12. Interview 17 (05–11–97). See also interviews 29 (06–08–97) and 33 (19–06–97).
13. Interview 3 (18–12–97).
14. Interview 5 (23–06–97).
15. Interview 8 (03–07–97).
16. Interview 8 (03–07–97).
17. Interview 21 (18–06–97).
18. Interviews 10 (08–07–97) and 29 (06–08–97).
19. Interview 22 (08–09–97).
20. Interviews 23 (29–07–97) and 29 (06–08–97).
21. Interview 17 (10–06–97). Unfortunately the sex of the politician who made the response cited in the quotation is not apparent from the interview transcript.
22. Interview 6 (12–11–97).
23. Interview 24 (07–04–97).
24. There is little support for this interpretation in the analysis of the data upon which this book is based (see Chapter 5).
25. For reasons of anonymity, this MP's interview number is not included here.
26. Each of these perceptions warrants further research into how women who are perceived as representing women fare in British politics.
27. Interviews 1 (14–12–97), 3 (18–12–97), 5 (23–06–97), 6 (12–11–97), 7 (09–97), 8 (03–07–97), 9 (29–10–97), 10 (08–07–97), 11 (23–07–97), 12 (11–06–97), 14 (03–07–97), 16 (24–11–97), 18 (12–06–97), 19 (10–12–97), 23 (29–07–97), 25 (01–07–97) and 32 (19–11–97). These interviews are those in which the MPs talked about the parliamentary agenda being transformed by women's presence. As a consequence, these figures, arguably, underplay the feminized effect, which women representatives consider will be the outcome of women's political presence.
28. Interview 25 (01–07–97).
29. Interview 8 (03–07–97).

30. Interviews 1 (14–12–97), 8 (03–07–97), 14 (03–07–97) and 18 (12–06–97).
31. Interviews 12 (11–06–97), 18 (12–06–97) and 32 (19–11–97).
32. Interviews 9 (03–11–97), 10 (08–07–97) and 32 (19–11–97).
33. Interviews 7 (09–97) and 12 (11–06–97).
34. Interviews 23 (29–07–97) and 12 (11–06–97).
35. Interview 18 (12–06–97).
36. Interview 30 (10–06–97).
37. Interview 15 (14–10–97).
38. Interview 9 (03–11–97).
39. Interview 32 (19–11–97).
40. Interview 7 (09–97).
41. Interviews 1 (04–12–97), 3 (18–12–97), 6 (12–11–97), 12 (11–06–97) and 20 (01–08–97).
42. Interviews 1 (04–12–97), 3 (18–12–97), 6 (12–11–97) and 12 (11–06–97).
43. However, it is important to 'unpack' these statements. In particular, the MP appears to elide the term 'community' with women. The employment of de-gendered language to talk about the effect of women's political presence, arguably, hides its feminized potential.
44. Interviews 1 (04–12–97) and 32 (19–11–97). No specific examples to substantiate this claim were provided.
45. Interview 3 (18–12–97).
46. Interview 12 (11–06–97).
47. Interview 20 (01–08–97).
48. Interview 4 (30–07–97).
49. Interviews 19 (10–12–97) and 3 (18–12–97).
50. Interview 3 (18–12–97). The view that women in politics are forced to adopt the dominant masculinized style is discussed in Chapter 10.
51. See Chapter 3.
52. Interview 17 (05–11–97).
53. Interview 30 (10–06–97).
54. Another interpretation was that these women were elected together and therefore supported each other. See interview 29 (06–08–97).
55. Interview 19 (10–12–97).
56. Interviews 15 (14–10–97), 25 (01–07–97) and 20 (01–08–97).
57. Interview 11 (23–07–97).
58. In this example, the woman MP is eliding acting for women with a feminist substantive representation of women.
59. Interview 6 (12–11–97).
60. Interview 19 (10–12–97).
61. Other Labour women MPs were also articulating similar arguments. For example, a minister stated to a meeting of women academics in June 1998 that expectations of Labour women MPs were too high. The suggestion was that women academics and women in society were expecting too much and that we (both groups) were unaware of the reality of the changes that women representatives were making. Such sentiments are troubling as they appear to suspend accountability in favour of trust – we are having an effect, you just can't see it, but trust me. See A. Phillips (1995), *A Politics of Presence* (Oxford: Oxford University Press).
62. Interviews 2 (13–06–00), 4 (21–06–00), 5 (22–05–00), 1 (12–07–00), 12 (15–06–00), 15 (23–05–00) and 22 (16–05–00).
63. Interviews 7 (13–06–00), 8 (20–06–00), 13 (13–06–00), 18 (12–07–00), 22 (16–05–00), 5 (22–05–00) and 12 (15–06–00).
64. Interviews 13 (13–06–00), 18 (12–07–00) and 22 (16–05–00).
65. Interview 22 (16–05–00).
66. Interview 23 (19–06–00).
67. Ibid.
68. Interviews 3 (14–06–00), 23 (10–05–00) and 24 (10–05–00).
69. Interviews 2 (13–06–00), 4 (21–06–00) and 29 (15–05–00). F. Mactaggart (2000), 'Women in Parliament: Their Contribution to Labour's First 1,000 Days', research paper prepared for the Fabian Society (London: Fabian Society).

70. Interview 12 (15–06–00).
71. Interview 13 (13–06–00).
72. Interview 16 (26–07–00).
73. Interview 18 (12–07–00). See also interviews 8 (20–06–00), 5 (22–05–00), 3 (14–06–00), 9 (22–06–00), 22 (16–05–00), 25 (21–06–00), 27 (12–07–00) and 31 (10–07–00).
74. Interview 8 (20–06–00).
75. Interviews 25 (21–06–00) and 13 (13–06–00).
76. Interviews 1 (12–07–00), 3 (14–06–00), 16 (26–07–00), 25 (21–06–00), 27 (17–05–00) and 29 (15–05–00).
77. Interviews 3 (14–06–00), 25 (21–06–00), 27 (17–05–00) and 29 (15–05–00). Early Day Motion 89 (24.11.99): 'That this House believes that sanitary products should be classed in the category of essential to the family budget, just as food, children's clothing and books already are, and that, like such products, they should be classed as VAT-free under the EC sixth Directive.' Two hundred and forty-nine MPs signed the motion and despite constituting only 15 per cent of the House, Labour women constituted 23 per cent of all signatures. See S. Childs and J. Withey (2003), 'Signing for Women', paper presented at PSA Annual Conference, University of Leicester, April 2003.
78. Interview 24 (10–05–00).
79. Interview 28 (12–07–00).
80. Interview 1 (12–07–00).
81. Women's substantive representation in government is discussed in Chapter 9.
82. Interview 25 (21–06–00).
83. In fact, in addition to the discussion of the Family Home and Domestic Violence Bill and the Family Law Bill in the 1992 Parliament, there was also an adjournment debate, initiated by Jeff Rooker, on 29 March 1995.
84. Interview 3 (14–06–00).
85. Interview 27 (12–07–00). See also interviews 3 (14–06–00), 12 (15–06–00), 15 (23–05–00) and 18 (12–07–00).
86. Interviews 1 (12–07–00), 12 (15–06–00) and 5 (22–05–00).
87. Interview 5 (22–05–00).
88. Interview 14 (08–06–00).
89. Interviews 2 (13–0–00), 24 (10–05–00), 13 (13–06–00), 14 (08–06–00), 9 (22–06–00), 16 (26–07–00) and 29 (15–05–00).
90. Interviews 2 (13–06–00), 24 (10–05–00) and 14 (08–06–00).
91. For reasons of anonymity the interview number is not included here.
92. Labour women members of the Education and Employment Select Committee: Candy Atherton, Charlotte Atkins, Yvette Cooper (discharged 1999), Valerie Davey, Caroline Flint (discharged 1999), Margaret Hodge (discharged 1998), Helen Jones (added 1999) and Judy Mallaber.
93. Interviews 16 (26–07–00) and 29 (15–05–00).
94. Interviews 2 (13–6–00), 4 (21–06–00), 13 (13–06–00), 15 (23–05–00) and 25 (21–06–00).
95. Interviews 7 (13–06–00), 8 (20–06–00), 9 (22–06–00), 16 (26–07–00) and 33 (13–06–00).
96. Interviews 1 (12–07–00), 3 (14–06–00), 5 (22–05–00), 12 (15–06–00), 18 (12–07–00), 28 (12–07–00), 29 (15–05–00) and 31 (10–07–00).
97. Interview 13 (13–06–00).
98. Interviews 1 (12–07–00), 3 (14–06–00), 5 (22–05–00), 7 (13–06–00), 9 (22–06–00), 18 (12–07–00) and 24 (10–05–00).
99. Interviews 13 (13–06–00) and 2 (13–06–00).
100. Interview 13 (13–06–00).
101. Interview 3 (14–06–00).
102. Interview 23 (19–06–00). The budget in March 2000 announced that from 1 January 2001, the rate of VAT on women's sanitary products would be reduced from 17.5 per cent to 5 per cent.
103. Interview 4 (21–06–00).
104. However, the effectiveness of the group was, arguably, limited in this case because Tyson was allowed into Scotland to box.
105. Interview 5 (22–05–00).
106. Interview 12 (15–06–00).
107. Interview 14 (08–06–00).

108. Interview 29 (15–05–00).
109. Interviews 1 (12–07–00), 3 (14–06–00), 7 (13–06–00), 8 (20–06–00), 9 (22–06–00), 12 (15–06–00), 16 (26–07–00), 31 (15–05–00) and 33 (13–06–00).
110. Interview 12 (15–06–00).
111. Interview 5 (22–05–00).
112. Interview 28 (12–07–00).
113. Interview 2 (13–06–00).

The New Labour Women MPs' Loyalty

(WITH PHILIP COWLEY)

During the passage of the Social Security Bill in December 1997, there was only one new Labour woman MP – Ann Cryer – among the 47 Labour MPs who voted against the cut in lone parent benefit.[1] For some, the new Labour women MPs' loyalty seemed to disprove the link between women's descriptive and substantive representation: if the sex of our representatives matters, then a Bill that would disproportionately – and, arguably, negatively – affect women was where we might expect to see women MPs making a difference.

The new Labour women MPs' apparent failure to 'act for' women brought extensive criticism in the media and from among their Labour colleagues. They were charged with being simply too spineless to rebel. One woman political commentator saw it as a sign that the new Labour women MPs would sacrifice the substantive representation of women on the altar of their own political advancement: the women were derided 'as centrally-programmed automatons ... reviled for failing to rebel, condemned as careerists'. They were considered, in short, 'one great fuschia-suited failure'.[2]

Yet several of the new Labour women MPs doubted whether it was true that they were less likely to rebel. They argued that the media, driven by misogyny, only picked up on those occasions when it was true and ignored those when it was not: 'There are some rebellions they haven't even spotted 'cause I think they are so locked into this Blair's babes thing [that] some of them can't even think straight if they tried now.'[3] Others argued that even if there were fewer women in any rebellion that was merely because there were fewer women in general: 'I'm not sure that's true statistically'; 'there are just as many nodding ... male dogs on [the] government benches ... in fact, actually, percentage-wise more, because there are more of them than women'.[4]

It is important therefore to establish whether the new Labour women MPs voted differently from their male colleagues in the 1997 Parliament.

And if they were more loyal, we need to consider how this is explained. How did the women MPs explain their behaviour?

DATA

This chapter draws on three main sources in addition to the interview data from the new Labour women MPs. First, it utilizes the complete voting records of the 1997 Parliament, around 1,300 divisions, as well as occasionally drawing on data from previous Parliaments. Second, it draws on two surveys of British MPs (the 1997 British Representation Survey [BRS] and the Study of Parliament Group Survey [SPG]). Third, it uses data from approximately 90 interviews with male and female MPs between 1997 and 2001.[5]

The focus here is on those occasions when MPs voted against their own party whip or the apparently clear wishes (sometimes implicit) of their own frontbench.[6] Matters of private legislation, private members' bills, matters internal to the House of Commons and other free votes are excluded. The votes of MPs who act as 'tellers' – that is, the MPs who count those voting – are included.

Because MPs who are in government cannot vote against their whips without first resigning their position, inclusion of government MPs in any statistical analysis has the potential to skew the results. For the purposes of the following analysis, therefore, the PLP is split into three groups. First, there are those MPs – 87 in number – who were in government for the entire period.[7] They have to be excluded from any analysis of rebellions. Second, there are those (191) MPs who were in government for some, but not all, of the period, either because they were promoted to, and/or ejected from, government during the course of the Parliament.[8] And third, there are those (151) MPs who were on the backbenches for the entire Parliament. Any analysis of the characteristics of the PLP as a whole – looking at, say, how many women there were in the PLP – utilizes all three groups (that is, an N of 429). But, except where stated to the contrary, any analysis of the characteristics of rebels and loyalists is conducted with just the second and third groups; that is, it excludes those MPs who were in government for the entire period and uses all MPs who would have been able to vote against the government at some point in the Parliament (so the N = 342). Lest it be thought that the results are being distorted by including those MPs who were on the backbenches for only some of the period, all the analysis was also rerun using just the 151 permanent backbenchers; all differences – and there are very few – are reported in notes.

NEW LABOUR WOMEN AND THE PROPENSITY TO REBEL

There were 96 separate rebellions by Labour MPs in the 1997 Parliament, with 19 issues (broadly defined) seeing individual rebellions consisting of at least ten MPs.[9] These 19 rebellions are listed in Table 8.1, together with the total number of MPs to have voted against the government. The two right-hand columns of the table show the number of new Labour

TABLE 8.1 NEW LABOUR WOMEN MPs' PARTICIPATION IN LARGE LABOUR REBELLIONS, 1997–2001

Issue	*Total number of rebels*	*New women rebels*	*As % of total number of rebels*
Access to Justice Bill	21	0	0
Child Support, Pensions & Social Security Bill	41	2	5
Competition Bill	25	0	0
Criminal Justice (Mode of Trial) Bill	37	2	5
Criminal Justice (Terrorism and Conspiracy) Bill	37	2	5
Defence White Paper	10	0	0
Draft Terrorism Bill	12	1	8
Football (Disorder) Bill	11	0	0
Freedom of Information Bill	41	3	7
House of Lords Bill	35	2	6
Immigration and Asylum Bill	17	0	0
Immigration appeals	17	2	12
Iraq	22	0	0
Kosovo	13	0	0
Social Security Bill	47	1	2
Teaching and Higher Education Bill	34	1	3
Terrorism Bill	14	1	7
Transport Bill	65	7	11
Welfare Reform and Pensions Bill	74	6	8

Note: In cases where there were multiple revolts on an issue, the total number to have rebelled may be larger than the largest single revolt on that issue.

women MPs who rebelled on each issue, together with that figure as a percentage of the total number of rebels. This last figure varies from the seven issues that saw no new Labour women MPs rebel to the revolt over the immigration appeals process on 20 November 2000, when 12 per cent of the rebels were new Labour women. Yet even at its peak, this percentage is below what might be expected. New Labour women MPs constituted 16 per cent of the PLP. Not one of the rebellions consisted of 16 per cent of the new Labour women MPs.[10]

In total, taking all 96 revolts together, just 11 new Labour women Labour MPs voted against their party whip. That constitutes 17 per cent of the 65 new Labour women MPs and compares to a figure of 44 per cent for the rest of the PLP, a difference that is statistically significant.

Moreover, even when they did rebel, the new Labour women MPs did not rebel frequently. Table 8.2 lists the 11 new Labour women MPs who voted against their whips. The most rebellious were Ann Cryer and Betty Williams, both of whom voted against their whips on 16 occasions. While considerable when compared to other new Labour women MPs, 16 dissenting votes makes Cryer and Williams only the (joint) 30th most rebellious Labour MPs. In total, the new women who voted against the party line did so on an average of six occasions. The comparable figure for the rest of the PLP is 11.

In the whole of the first session of the Parliament just two of the new Labour women MPs (3 per cent) voted against their whips (the other being Christine Butler), compared to 27 per cent of the rest of the PLP.[11]

TABLE 8.2 THE 11 'REBELIOUS' NEW LABOUR WOMEN MPs, 1997–2001

Name	*Number of dissenting votes*
Ann Cryer	16
Betty Williams	16
Julie Morgan	14
Jenny Jones	6
Eileen Gordon	5
Christine McCafferty	4
Janet Dean	3
Christine Butler	2
Tess Kingham	2
Oona King	1
Geraldine Smith	1

Other Labour MPs were, then, *nine* times more likely to have rebelled than were the new Labour women MPs. As the number of rebellions increased, the difference between the new Labour women MPs and the rest of the PLP did narrow – from nine times after the first session, to a three-fold difference after the second – but the differences did not disappear over time. Similarly, as the Parliament progressed, the percentage of new Labour women MPs in any rebellion increased – rising from a high of 5 per cent in the first session, to 8 per cent in the second, to 12 per cent in the third – but even this new high remained lower than the proportion in the PLP as a whole.

The new Labour women MPs were, then, less than half as likely to rebel against the party whip as the rest of the PLP; and even those that did rebel did so around half as often. There was, therefore, a genuine difference in legislative behaviour between the new Labour women and the rest of the PLP.[12]

EXPLAINING AWAY THE DIFFERENCE

Explanations for this differential cohesion consist of two different types. The first group of explanations argue that any apparent differences between the new women and the rest of the PLP are spurious, that any differences are in fact caused by the types of MP under examination rather than being genuine differences between the new women MPs and the rest of the PLP. And that once we control for other characteristics or factors, then any apparent differences will disappear.

Rebellion is not a random act. There is clear evidence linking rebellion to an MP's *ideology or beliefs*, the extent to which they may disagree with the government (with left-wing Labour MPs being more likely to rebel than right-wing ones). Rebellion is also related to MPs' *legislative roles*, the extent to which they see their role in Parliament as including rebellion (with delegates being less likely to rebel than those who see themselves as trustees). Explanations that attempt to link parliamentary behaviour with *self-interest* are also successful, although the self-interest of the MP within Parliament (where the young, the newly elected and the ambitious are all less likely to rebel) is more important than any external forces (the marginality of an MP's constituency, for example, appears to play little role, nor does the ideology of his or her constituency party). And lastly, *other characteristics of the MP* are also important. Specific individual characteristics that explain the MP's ability to withstand, or succumb to, the pressures placed upon them (the less educated, those with council experience, and those who are in the Campaign Group all appear more likely to rebel).[13] If the women first elected in 1997 had more (or less) of these characteristics, then we should not be surprised if they were more (or less) rebellious.

By contrast, the second group of explanations do not deny that a difference existed, but explain it – if not celebrate it – by highlighting the way that women MPs behave, seeing this as evidence of a different style of political behaviour.

But we start by examining attempts to explain the difference away, beginning with the three most obvious explanations: sex, newness, and the role of AWS.

Three obvious (but unconvincing) explanations

Sex. The most obvious explanation of all was that the cohesion of the new Labour women MPs resulted from nothing more than the fact that they were women. Many Labour women MPs – along with many of their male colleagues – argued that the apparent differences in the behaviour of the new Labour women were effectively sex differences.

But there are some obvious empirical problems with this argument. It is not the case that women MPs have been more cohesive than male MPs in previous Parliaments. If anything, in previous Parliaments women MPs were more rebellious than their male counterparts. In every Parliament between 1979 and 1997, women MPs were (slightly) more likely to have rebelled than male MPs.[14] And as Table 8.3 shows, the longer-serving Labour women in the 1997 Parliament were in fact *more* rebellious than their longer-serving male colleagues. Some 63 per cent of the longer-serving women rebelled compared to just 17 per cent of those elected in 1997.[15] And just as in previous Parliaments, the more established women MPs – admittedly a small group – were actually more likely to

TABLE 8.3 PROPENSITY TO REBEL, BY SEX AND INTAKE (PER CENT)

	Women	*Men*
Elected before 1997	63	53
Elected in 1997	17	34

vote against the party line than the men (although the difference was not statistically significant).[16] So it was not that women MPs in general were any more cohesive than the men; rather, it was just that the newly elected women were significantly less likely to have rebelled than other Labour MPs.

This suggests that sex can be rejected as an explanation for the differential rate of cohesion. Any explanation must look at the new Labour women MPs in particular rather than at women *qua* women. This may be an occasion when the distinction between sex and gender is important, a point to which we return below.

New intake. Table 8.3 also allows us quickly to reject the other obvious explanation for the difference: that the new women are behaving differently simply because they are new MPs. This explanation trips over almost identical empirical hurdles to the argument (made above) about sex. If it were valid, then we would expect the new male MPs to be similarly less likely to rebel.

While it was true that new MPs were less likely to have rebelled than other MPs (although once we control for all other variables, any differences ceased to be significant), there was still a clear difference between the new Labour women MPs and their male peers. As Table 8.3 shows, some 17 per cent of the new Labour women MPs had rebelled compared to 34 per cent of the new men. So once we control for the cohort of entry the difference narrows somewhat, but it does not go away. The new women were still half as likely to have rebelled as the new men, a statistically significant difference in behaviour.[17]

All-women shortlists. Critics of AWS have argued that this process brought into Parliament MPs who were simply not up to the job.[18] As Ann Widdecombe MP regularly claimed, AWS 'led to a very sub-standard intake of women MPs'.[19] There is, however, an obvious empirical problem with this argument: there was no difference in behaviour between those women selected on AWS and those selected on 'open' shortlists. Of those selected on open lists, five (17 per cent) broke ranks; the figure for those selected on AWS is six (also 17 per cent). Moreover, the three most rebellious of the new women – Ann Cryer, Betty Williams and Julie Morgan – were all selected on AWS. There is, then, little evidence that AWS brought into Parliament less rebellious MPs. With a few exceptions, the new Labour women MPs were not rebelling, no matter how they were selected.

Other (also largely unconvincing) explanations

As well as these three obvious (if ultimately unconvincing) explanations for the differences, many of the new Labour women MPs attempted to explain away the differences in their behaviour by reference to other socio-economic or political characteristics. For example, one argued that the reason they were not rebelling was *ideological*: it 'may be because we happen to agree with the policies and understand the policies'.[20] (It was for this reason that one male Labour MP described the new women MPs as 'true believers'.)[21] Others explained it with reference to their *ambition*, and the belief that ambitious politicians have to vote with the government.[22] As one said: 'Younger women who want to make a career out of this ... know ... [that] in the long term they will not make their voice heard at the level which is needed unless they do incorporate.'[23] She added that she thought they had 'been quite sensible really'.[24] Another put it in terms of their *age*:

> Some of the men who were selected to fight safe seats are people who are in their late fifties who, you know, hold some pretty traditional views, and ... [it's those] men who tend to vote against the government, whereas the new Labour women in many cases are, you know, going to be here for a much longer period of time.[25]

Several others thought the differences resulted from the differing *electoral situations* of the new Labour women MPs ('it may be because we are in more marginal seats'; 'most of us come from key seats, they are marginal seats and to be frank we are not stupid').[26] As another put it: 'I think if you compared the men in target marginal seats who are newly elected with the women in target marginal seats who are newly elected I think you'd find a ... real similarity in their voting experiences.'[27] Another MP thought the difference lay in the *previous political history* of the MPs: 'It would be interesting to see how many of us came from local council backgrounds because my view is that if you have been on a local Labour group in a council your loyalty to the party whip is instilled.'[28]

There are two potential empirical problems with many of these suggestions and with other attempts to explain away the differences between the new women MPs and other MPs. The first is that not all of these variables exert a strong or necessarily significant effect on the propensity to rebel; and, even if they do, they may do so in a different direction from that suggested by the MPs.[29] For example, the effect of marginality on an MP's propensity to rebel is extremely limited once we control for the MPs' intake cohort. And, *pace* the MP quoted above, experience on a local council does not help to instil loyalty to the party whip. Quite the reverse: experience on a local council appears to make MPs more likely to rebel.[30]

The second potential problem is that for these factors to explain the differential behaviour we also need to show that the new Labour women MPs have more (or less) of this factor than other MPs. For example, if the age of the women MPs is a valid explanation, it is not enough for an MP's age to influence their behaviour (as it does), we also need to show that the new Labour women are younger than some comparison group. Since we showed (above) that the differences between the new men and new women are less dramatic (though still clear) than between the new women and the rest of the PLP, in what follows we compare the new women with the new men. Using the categories outlined above, we start by examining the MPs' ideology or beliefs.

IDEOLOGY AND BELIEFS

One of the key issues in studies of legislative voting is the extent to which legislative cohesion is artificial (the result of disciplinary pressures) or natural (resulting from agreement).[31] For if MPs agree, why should they rebel? It could be, for example, that the new women MPs were noticeably more 'Blairite' than their colleagues. If they were, then it should not be surprising that they did not rebel.

As part of the 1997 British Representation Survey (BRS), MPs were asked a series of questions about their ideological positions, including some basic scalar questions designed to tap their underlying political values. The scales measure their left–right self-placement, as well as the trade-offs between inflation and unemployment, taxation and public spending, nationalization and privatization, integration within the European Union, and the issue of sex equality. Table 8.4 shows the responses to these questions in the BRS, split between the new women and the new men.[32] As the table shows, there were few noticeable differences between the new Labour women MPs and their male colleagues. On three of the scales, the women were more to the right (although not by much). On the other three they were more to the left (although again not by much).[33] But none of these differences was of a scale sufficient to be statistically significant. The only difference that approached statistical significance was the question on the government's economic priorities (employment/prices), where the new women were slightly more to the left than their male peers.[34]

Similarly, if we look at their scores on the standard socialist/laissez faire scale, or the libertarian/authoritarian scale, we find few significant differences.[35] On the two overall scale scores there are no significant differences between the new men and the new women.[36] Of the 12 questions that make up the scales, there were differences on just two, both on the libertarian/authoritarian scale. The new women were somewhat less tolerant of homosexuality than the new men and (more broadly) less tolerant of those with unconventional lifestyles (with in both cases the difference being statistically significant).[37] But the liberal/authoritarian scale was a very poor predictor of voting behaviour. On the variables that better explained voting during the Parliament – such as the tax/spend scale or the socialist/laissez faire scale – there are no noticeable differences between the new women and their male colleagues.

There is thus little evidence that the new women constituted a Blairite praetorian guard within the PLP. It is difficult to argue that the new Labour women MPs constitute an ideologically distinct grouping within the PLP, yet alone 'true believers' for Blairism.

ROLES

The idea that MPs' roles influence behaviour is a longstanding one.[38] How MPs behave can be influenced by how they see their role in

TABLE 8.4 NEW LABOUR MPs' POLITICAL ATTITUDES (MEAN SCORES), BY SEX

	New women	*New men*	*Difference*
Left/right	3.97	3.65	+0.32
Employment/prices	2.23	2.97	–0.74
Taxes/spending	4.19	3.98	+0.21
Nationalize/privatize	5.26	4.97	+0.29
Integrate with EU/remain independent	3.87	3.97	–0.10
Women equal/in home	1.00	1.23	–0.23

Note: The significance of the difference is tested by ANOVA: * 0.05; **0.01. The difference is the percentage of new women minus percentage of new men, but none of the items reached the required level of significance.

Parliament. MPs who see their role as being to represent their party are less likely to have voted against it than those who believe that they are in Parliament to represent their constituents or to voice their own opinions.[39] Here we find more mixed evidence. Table 8.5 shows the responses to the questions about party discipline contained in the BRS. If anything, the new women MPs claim to be *more* willing to vote against the party line than the new men (although the differences are not statistically significant). The Study of Parliament Group (SPG) survey, on the other hand, produced slightly different results. While there was almost no difference in the proportion of new men and new women who thought that representing the party was their most important task (16 per cent of women, compared to 14 per cent of men), there was a slightly larger difference in the proportions who said that they relied on the party whips when voting. A majority of the new women (57 per cent) said that they relied on the party whips 'nearly always' when voting, compared to 46 per cent of the new men.

SELF-INTEREST

So far we have looked at what could be termed creditable (or in parliamentary terms, honourable) reasons for the cohesion of MPs. If MPs agree with the party, or see their role at Westminster as a delegate of the party, then why should they rebel? But the most commonly discussed reasons for MPs sticking to the party line are usually less creditable or honourable: that MPs are somehow pressurized into voting with their party, and that they capitulate in order to further their own interests. In addition to newness (examined above), here we investigate four surrogate variables for self-interest: self-declared ambition, age, marginality, and the influence of MPs' local party.

TABLE 8.5 VIEWS ON PARTY DISCIPLINE, BY SEX

	New women	*New men*	*Difference*
MPs should vote with their party, regardless of their conscience	14	20	–6
MPs should vote with their party, regardless of the national interest	7	9	–2

Note: The figures show the proportion that agree, or agree strongly, with each of the statements. The difference is the percentage of new women minus the percentage of new men.

MPs who harbour little or no ambition for ministerial office, and who therefore have less to fear from the removal of patronage, are more likely to vote against the party line.[40] However, the BRS revealed almost no difference between the future ambitions of the new women and those of the new men. Some 61 per cent of the new women wanted to be a government minister in ten years' time, compared to 64 per cent of the new men, a difference that was not statistically significant. Differing levels of ambition in themselves do not, therefore, appear to be behind the differing levels of cohesion.

Age is also an excellent indicator of an MP's propensity to rebel. This relationship is strikingly clear from Table 8.6, which shows the ages (when elected) of the 11 rebellious new Labour women, along with the number of times they rebelled. All but three of the 11 rebels are older than the average age of women of the 1997 intake (43) – and these three are near the bottom of the league table of rebels (having cast just four dissenting votes between them). Of the top six rebels, all but one is aged 50 or more (with the one who is not, Jenny Jones, aged 49 when elected).

Yet, although this is interesting as an explanation for rebellion, it appears to do little to explain the differential rates of rebellion between new women and the new men because there is no evidence that the new women are especially young. The average age of a woman MP elected for the first time in 1997 was 43.2 years, almost identical to the average for a new male MP (43.5).[41] So, although age is important when explaining the propensity to rebel in general, it does not appear to be a plausible

TABLE 8.6 'REBELLIOUS' NEW LABOUR WOMEN MPs AND AGE

Name	*Number of dissenting votes*	*Age when elected*
Ann Cryer	16	57
Betty Williams	16	52
Julie Morgan	14	52
Jenny Jones	6	49
Eileen Gordon	5	50
Christine McCafferty	4	51
Janet Dean	3	48
Christine Butler	2	53
Tess Kingham	2	33
Oona King	1	29
Geraldine Smith	1	35

explanation of why the new women are not rebelling when compared to the new men.

MPs also face two important forces external to the Commons: their local constituency party (which has the power to deselect them) and their electorate (which enjoys the ultimate power to eject them from Parliament altogether). In practice, neither appears to influence behaviour within the Commons.

Despite some academic folklore – and the desire of the Labour leadership – there is little evidence that local parties exerted much influence on an MP's propensity to rebel.[42] Moreover, there are no differences between the new men and the new women when it comes to the attitudes of their constituency parties. Using the left/right scale from the BRS, the new men had constituency parties that were, on average, 0.2 points to the left of them on the ideological scale. The new women also average a difference of 0.2, also on the left.

Equally unconvincing are those attempts to explain cohesion as resulting from marginality. For one thing, the marginality of MPs has very little impact on propensity to rebel, once we control for the intake cohort.[43] Moreover, the scale of Labour's victory brought in many MPs who were not expected to win their seats, named the 'unlikely lads' by one of their number.[44] Importantly, these people were disproportionately likely to be unlikely lads rather than lasses (just 15 per cent of these MPs elected in the unexpected gains were women), because AWS applied only to key (winnable) and inheritor seats (where the incumbent MP was standing down). Therefore, the new women MPs did *not* sit in the most marginal seats. The average marginality of a new Labour woman MP in 1997 was 19 per cent; that of a new Labour man was 17 per cent. So while the new Labour women MPs did sit for more marginal seats than the rest of the PLP that was because they were newly elected, rather than because they were women, and compared to the male MPs of the new intake – who were twice as likely to rebel – they actually sat for slightly safer seats. It seems difficult therefore to attribute much significance to the marginality of their constituencies as a cause of their cohesion.

That said, the very scale of Labour's victory may produce a partial explanation for the differential cohesion. Many of these unexpected victors were largely unknown to the central party before their election, bringing fears within the party hierarchy that they might cause trouble once at Westminster. The day after the election, Peter Mandelson ordered every one of Labour's regional press officers to provide the party headquarters at Millbank with a list of 'little-known and potentially troublesome new MPs'.[45] They identified at least 20 'suspect' MPs.[46] And indeed, these unlikely victors were slightly more likely to have rebelled, although the differences were neither huge nor statistically significant.[47] Although not an effect of marginality *per se*, this might be a plausible explanation for a slightly lower level of rebellion among the new women.

OTHER CHARACTERISTICS

Of course, different MPs may respond to these various pressures in different ways, because of their different personal characteristics. Here we examine three variables previously found to relate to rebellion: education, group membership and previous political history.

There is little evidence that the answer lies in the MPs' educational backgrounds. Some 71 per cent of the new women had been educated at university, compared to 72 per cent of the new men. We can also swiftly reject membership of the Campaign Group. Three women from the 1997 intake joined the Campaign Group (5 per cent of the women elected in 1997), compared to six men (also 5 per cent).

A rare piece of evidence demonstrating some difference comes with the final variable, when we examine the previous political history of the MPs. The new women MPs were disproportionately likely *not* to have been local councillors. Almost three-quarters of the new Labour men (74 per cent) had been councillors, compared to exactly two-thirds of the new women (although this difference is not statistically significant). And since experience in local government appears to make MPs more rebellious, this is at least a plausible explanation for the different rates of cohesion.

MULTIVARIATE ANALYSIS

There appears, therefore, to be little evidence to support most of the attempts to explain away the difference between the new women and the new men. Only two of the variables examined point in a consistent direction. The unexpected victors (who were more likely to rebel) were disproportionately men. And MPs with a background in local government (who are more likely to rebel) were also disproportionately men. Other evidence is more mixed – such as with political roles – or appears to show no effect at all.

Of course, many of these variables are not independent of one another. Some may be exaggerating the effect of individual variables upon an MP's propensity to rebel. Others may be masking interrelationships. In order to find out which variables are exerting an independent influence on an MP's propensity to rebel, we therefore need some multivariate analysis.

The dependent variable utilized here is simply rebelled (coded as 1)/not rebelled (0). The independent variables are analysed in two stages. First, data on the backgrounds or characteristics of MPs, where we have data on all MPs, are used. Second, data from the BRS, where we have data for a minority of MPs, are added. Our second model is thus more fully developed, but suffers from a lower number of cases.

The first set of independent variables includes age (at time of 1997 election), percentage constituency marginality, unexpected victor (coded 1 for yes, 0 for no), university educated (coded 1 for yes, 0 for no), Campaign Group membership (coded 1 for yes, 0 for no), sex (coded 1 for women, 0 for men), and council experience (coded 1 for yes, 0 for no). The second model then adds in data from the BRS: ideology (using the tax/spend scale, since of all the ideological variables that best measured propensity to rebel), delegate role (coded 1 for yes, 0 for no), ambition for government office (coded 1 for yes, 0 for no), and, lastly, a variable measuring the difference between the MP's ideological position and their constituency party (where positive scores indicate that the party was to the right of the MP).

The results are shown in Table 8.7. The first model – using data on all MPs – finds three variables exerting a statistically significant impact on the propensity to rebel: age, university education and sex. Of these, the third is the most important for our purposes here, because it means that even once we control for everything else, and when examining just the new MPs, sex remains a significant variable. By contrast, a similar logistic regression (not reported here in full for reasons of space), concentrating on just the longer-serving MPs, does not find sex to be significant. The presence of sex as a significant independent variable among the new MPs, and its absence from the older MPs, confirms that what we have with the new women is not a sex effect, but something specific to that group of women MPs.

When we introduce the attitudinal data (Model 2), however, only two

TABLE 8.7 LOGISTIC REGRESSION, LABOUR REBELLIONS, NEW MPs, 1997–2001

	Model 1 *B*	*Model 2* *B*
Ideology		
Tax/spend	–	–0.90*
Roles		
Delegate	–	–10.84
Self-interest		
Ambition	–	–0.54
Age	0.12***	0.21**
Constituency party	–	0.31
% majority	–0.01	–0.10
Unexpected victor	–0.16	–0.10
Other characteristics		
University educated	–0.96*	–1.37
Campaign Group	10.26	16.85
Sex	-1.29**	–2.33
Council background	0.83	3.99
Constant	–5.96***	–7.73
% correctly predicted	78.0	86.4
Nagelkerke R^2	0.40	0.66
N	182	81

Note: * indicates $p<0.05$; ** $p<0.01$; *** $p<0.001$.

variables appear to remain statistically significant: ideology and age. Sex continues to exert an influence on the propensity to rebel, with women MPs being less likely to have rebelled, but the difference is no longer large enough (or consistent enough) to be statistically significant. Yet this model, because it is examining only the new MPs, and of the new MPs only those where there are attitudinal data from the BRS, is based on just 81 cases in total. The smaller the number of cases, *ceteris paribus*, the larger any differences need to be before they are significant. And even here, sex only just fails to be statistically significant.[48] What appears to be happening is that, once we control for everything else that might be explaining the differences, sex still appears to exert an influence on the propensity to rebel; even controlling for everything else, the women from the 1997 intake were less likely to rebel than their male peers. The difference is not large enough (or consistent enough) to be statistically significant (that is, large enough or consistent enough for there not to be the possibility that it was created by chance), but it still exists.

This finding does, though, help to put some of the claims about the behaviour of the new Labour women MPs into perspective. The initial large difference in behaviour between the new Labour women and the rest of the PLP becomes smaller (but still statistically significant) once we compare the new women with the new men. It becomes smaller still (and no longer statistically significant) once we control for the women's other characteristics. There *is* still a difference between the new Labour women and the new Labour men, but it is a difference of degree, not direction. But attempts to explain that difference away completely remain unconvincing.

A FEMINIZED STYLE OF POLITICS

However, the majority of the women MPs themselves do not seek to explain this difference away. Rather, they claim it is part of a different, feminized, style of political behaviour. The explanation for the new women's differential rate of cohesion, which receives the greatest support from the new Labour women MPs – being mentioned by more than half – is that women MPs employ a different style of politics.[49]

Importantly, this style of politics was perceived by many of the women to be both distinct from, and more effective than, a style of politics involving overt rebellion, the latter being perceived as reflecting a masculine mode of politics more concerned with gesture politics than effecting change. (Several of the women also thought that loyalty itself was a female attribute.)[50] Many of the new Labour women MPs were also forthright in their questioning of the assumption that voting with the government was a negative activity. As one said: 'I don't actually think that loyal women or loyal MP actually equals bad.'[51]

Rather than rebelling, the women MPs claim to operate 'behind the scenes': 'We've probably tend[ed] to use the tools that are available to us behind the scenes as a first course of action ... I have always found it possible to use the avenues that are open behind the scenes.'[52] They consider that criticism can be communicated to government in many different ways, through lobbying, private conversations and holding meetings with ministers and through the PLP's backbench groups:

> [A] lot of working behind the scenes goes on and I think [that] is not appreciated, anyone who thinks that … all the Labour women are too loyal, if I can put it that way, has not been at meetings with say the Home Secretary over hunting, with the Trade and Industry Secretary over employment rights.[53]

However, it is not just that many considered that they have a different style of politics, some believed that working behind the scenes was a more effective strategy than rebelling.

> If you are a sort of macho 'oh I'm going to vote against the government' … I don't [think] that your influence is even as much as the people that are saying 'look Jack, this is … not working' … you don't really get anywhere [by] being a rebel … people [who] vote against the Government [are] … not really doing anything other than making a gesture.[54]

Supporting the government in the lobby therefore ensures that they are listened to by ministers when they raise criticism: 'If those of us who genuinely vote with the government come along and say "this has got to stop", you know, people listen.'[55] This woman MP then added, discussing specifically the cut in lone parent benefit:

> I don't think that any government would have reversed it [the lone parent cut] if there had been a mass rebellion … if they'd won it by a handful of votes, I don't think then a few months later they would have turned it around.

Another MP agreed:

> I think particularly on that [lone parent] bill and on others there were women who have abstained or voted with the government … [they felt] we have been loyal, so what are you going to do about it? … we didn't vote against you we voted for you [pause] … we should have something in return, what are you going to do?[56]

In themselves, the new Labour women MPs' claims about their loyalty are revealing, for they show that many of the women MPs have thought through, and can defend, their decision to remain loyal to their party. Their loyalty appears to result not from them being spineless but, at least for more than half of them, from a belief in a different style of politics. Yet we have already demonstrated that a simple sex difference as an explanation of the women's loyalty does not stand up to empirical analysis. However, many of the new Labour women believed that their feminized style of politics is not shared by all women MPs (including their more established Labour colleagues): it is a gender and not a sex difference.[57]

Plausible as this is, though, we are faced with a problem: for this to explain the behavioural difference between the new Labour women MPs and the rest of the PLP, we need to show that they were *more likely* to practise this style of politics than other MPs. Male Labour MPs and longer-serving women MPs often reveal almost identical explanations for their loyalty.[58] They too work behind the scenes. They too take problems to ministers. They too often have a calculating and instrumental approach to cohesion and rebellion. The idea that the new Labour women MPs are more likely to use, or are more effective at using, such behind-the-scenes avenues is also a disputed one. One of the more established women MPs – once she had stopped laughing – described the idea that women were better at behind-the-scenes pressure as 'absolute nonsense' and 'an excuse'.[59] Even one of the new Labour women MPs argued that such behind-the-scenes contacts were less useful than they might appear:

> I do feel sometimes [that] people … who have not been in what I call the hard edge of politics before think that because they say something and they appeared to be listened to [that] that's a very big deal and actually I think it makes them think they've been listened to but really [they] have minimal impact … I'm probably over cynical.[60]

CONCLUSION

The lack of rebellions by the new Labour women MPs was one of the most striking features of the 1997 Parliament and one that attracted much criticism. As this chapter has shown there was a difference between the voting of the new Labour women and the rest of the PLP.

Many of the explanations that seek to explain away this difference do not stand up to empirical verification. Once we control for all of the variables, we find that the difference between the new men and the new women MPs fails to remain statistically significant, but only just (at the conventional measurement of $p<0.05$), even with a very small sample size. Some difference still remains.

We are left with three possible explanations. The first is that put forward by most of the new Labour women MPs' critics: that there was, for some reason, something second-rate about this particular batch of women MPs that was responsible for their differential rate of rebellion. It is not an argument that either of the authors of this chapter feels is convincing but there is almost no way of definitively disproving these sorts of claim.

The second explanation is that it is possible to explain the difference away, but that this analysis has failed to do so, either (i) because it has failed to include variables that are responsible for the difference; or because (ii) the data employed are not sufficiently fine to spot the differences between the different groups. Both are possibilities. For example, it could conceivably be that despite being similarly ambitious, the new Labour women MPs perceive the costs of rebelling to be greater than do the men. This could be (part of) the explanation for their behaviour. Unfortunately we have no way of knowing if this is the case or if other variables not examined here could explain the difference. Given what data are available, some difference still remains.

The dominant explanation put forward by the new women themselves is that they 'do' politics differently; their lack of rebellion is a sign of their reluctance to engage in what they considered to be macho politics. The problem is that it is extremely hard – if not impossible – ever to test this empirically. It is at best a plausible argument, one that awaits further research and one that is far more positive to the newly elected women than the standard media line that they are just too feeble to stand up to the nasty whips. Given that many of the other explanations appear to have little validity, it will continue to be used by many of the new Labour women MPs and their supporters, while their detractors will dismiss it as wishful thinking.

NOTES

1. P. Cowley (2002), *Revolts and Rebellions* (London: Politicos), pp. 24–9.
2. Anne Perkins, *Guardian* 29 April 1999.
3. Interview, 12 July 2000.
4. Interviews, 13 June 2000, 22 May 2000.

5. For a full discussion of this see Appendix 1.
6. P. Norton (1980), *Dissension in the House of Commons, 1974–1979* (Oxford: Clarendon Press), p. x.
7. Here we take 'in government' to include those who were Parliamentary Private Secretaries (PPSs), since a PPS is bound by collective responsibility not to vote against the government.
8. This figure may seem large, but it results from the extent to which (largely unnoticed) the composition of the lower echelons of the Blair government was substantially reshuffled during the four years between 1997 and 2001.
9. Cowley, *Revolts and Rebellions*, Chapters 2–5.
10. The difference becomes even sharper when we consider that once we remove the MPs who were in government (disproportionately male) the new women constituted 19 per cent of MPs on the backbenches at any point in the Parliament, and 17 per cent of the permanent backbenchers.
11. Remember, this is the figure once we remove all MPs in government for the entire Parliament. The raw figures – for the entire PLP – are 3 per cent and 21 per cent; the figures for those on the backbenches throughout the Parliament are 5 per cent and 35 per cent. These are a mere seven-fold difference, rather than a nine-fold difference.
12. US literature suggests that differences in behaviour are more likely at the early stages in the legislative cycle – in agenda-setting and policy formation – rather than at the stage of roll call voting (see D. Dodson [2001], 'The Impact of Women in Congress', paper presented to the Annual Meeting of APSA Women and Politics Special Session, San Francisco; B. Reingold [2000], *Representing Women* [Chapel Hill, NC and London: Universiy of North Carolina Press]; and Karin L. Tamerius [1995], 'Sex, Gender, and Leadership in the Representation of Women', in Georgia Duerst-Lahti and Rita Mae Kelly [eds], *Gender, Power, Leadership, and Governance* [Ann Arbor, MI: University of Michigan Press], pp. 93–112).
13. This summarizes Cowley, *Revolts and Rebellions*, Chapter 6.
14. See P. Cowley (1999), 'The Absence of War? New Labour in Parliament', *British Elections and Parties Review*, 9: 154–70.
15. The rebellious longer-serving women MPs include Dr Lynne Jones (who rebelled on 38 occasions), Gwyneth Dunwoody (27), Diane Abbott (26), Alice Mahon (25), Audrey Wise (25) and Ann Clwyd (24).
16. When we excluded all MPs who were in government at any time, it became significant.
17. If we examine just the permanent backbenchers, we find that the difference reduces slightly – to 45 per cent of the new men and 26 per cent of the new women – but it remains both sizeable and statistically significant.
18. Indeed, one of the authors (Cowley) was (mis)quoted saying something similar when early findings from this research were first published (*Observer* 20 September 1998). One male Labour MP also saw AWS as a cause of the high levels of cohesion, if for slightly different reasons. AWS was, he argued, 'without question, a device to get ultra-loyalists in place … an easier route in for ultra-loyalists' (Interview, 6 February 2001).
19. *Times* 7 February 1998; *Sunday Times* 4 October 1998.
20. Interview, 13 June 2000.
21. Interview, 21 March 2000.
22. Previous studies tended to debunk this belief. See, for example, J. Richard Piper (1991), 'British Backbench Rebellion and Government Appointments, 1945–87', *Legislative Studies Quarterly*, 16: 219–38; Norton, *Dissension in the House of Common*, p. 465; or A. King (1992), 'The Chief Whip's Clothes', in D. Leonard and V. Herman (eds), *The Backbencher and Parliament* (London: Macmillan), pp. 80–6. The Blair government did tend to exclude those who had voted against it in the division lobbies. See Cowley, *Revolts and Rebellions*, p. 108.
23. Interview, 22 June 2000.
24. Two other women MPs were explicit in recognizing the costs associated with rebelling. Reflecting on her rebelliousness, one woman MP admitted that it 'does disadvantage you … [it] does stand against you, probably' (interview, 21 June 2000; also, interview, 20 June 2000).
25. Interview, 21 June 2000.
26. Interviews, 13 June 2000 and 10 May 2000.
27. Interview, 21 June 2000.
28. Interview, 15 May 2000.
29. Cowley, *Revolts and Rebellions*, Chapter 6.

30. Ibid., pp. 113–14, 118.
31. See, for example, K. Krehbiel (1993), 'Where's the Party?', *British Journal of Political Science*, 23: 235–66; or K. Krehbiel (1999), 'Paradoxes of Parties in Congress', *Legislative Studies Quarterly*, 14: 31–64.
32. A low score indicates a left-wing, or pro-European, response.
33. Every new Labour woman who responded to the survey scored 1 on the question about the role of women in society, the most 'pro-women' response possible.
34. P=0.076.
35. A. Heath, G. Evans and J. Martin (1994), 'The Measurement of Core Beliefs and Values: the Development of Balanced Socialist/Laissez-faire and Libertarian/Authoritarian scales', *British Journal of Political Science*, 24: 115–31.
36. The new men averaged 12.7 on the socialism scale, compared to 12.6 for the new women. The scores on the libertarian/authoritarian scale were 13.2 and 14.2 respectively.
37. More precisely, in both cases, the new women were overwhelmingly tolerant, but they were *less* tolerant than were the men.
38. D. D. Searing (1994), *Westminster's World* (Cambridge, MA: Harvard University Press). See also the special issue of the *Journal of Legislative Studies* (1997) on 'Members of Parliament in Western Europe: Roles and Behaviour'.
39. Cowley, *Revolts and Rebellions*, pp. 106–7.
40. Ibid., pp. 109–10.
41. The median age of both new men and new women was 43. The new men and the new women also contain almost identical proportions of MPs aged over 50 (21.5 per cent and 21 per cent respectively).
42. For the folklore, see A. Ranney (1965), *Pathways to Parliament* (New York: Macmillan), p. 281; for the desires of the Labour leadership, see 'Labour Moves to Rein in Rebels', *Times* 27 May 1998; and for the almost complete lack of any effect, see Cowley, *Revolts and Rebellions*, pp. 111–13.
43. Cowley, *Revolts and Rebellions*, pp. 113–14.
44. Ibid., pp. 10–11.
45. D. Draper (1997), *Blair's Hundred Days* (London: Faber and Faber), p. 8.
46. *Sunday Times* 23 November 1997. One party insider described some of those elected as 'flotsam and jetsam left-wing candidates' (*Sunday Telegraph* 4 May 1997).
47. A total of 34 per cent of the 'unlikely lads' rebelled, compared to 25 per cent of the new MPs who expected (or realistically hoped) to win their seats, although this difference is not statistically significant (Cowley, *Revolts and Rebellions*, p. 114).
48. Sex: p=0.086; council experience: p=0.054.
49. For a full discussion of women's feminized style of politics see Chapter 10.
50. Interviews, 19 June 2000, 10 May 2000, 16 May 2000.
51. Interview, 22 May 2000.
52. Interview, 23 May 2000.
53. Interview, 15 May 2000.
54. Ibid.
55. Interview, 12 July 2000.
56. Interview, 20 June 2000.
57. See Chapter 10.
58. Cowley, *Revolts and Rebellions*, Chapters 8–9.
59. Interview, 4 July 2000.
60. Interview, 15 June 2000.

9

The Women's Minister and the Substantive Representation of Women

'A BIRD ON THE SHOULDER OF GOVERNMENT'[1]

A Women's Minister can act for women in the absence of women's descriptive representation.[2] With much government business conducted away from the Chamber of the Commons the Women's Minister can also compensate for backbench women MPs' limited influence. Yet, when combined with a large number of women representatives who are supportive, the Women's Minister is more likely to be in a position to act for women and to effect feminized change.[3]

Labour's Women's Minister, however, had an inauspicious start. Although the Labour Party had been committed to a Ministry for Women from the mid-1980s, by the time of the 1997 general election, the party was offering only a Women's Minister in the Cabinet.[4] And their appointment of the minister was fudged.[5] It was only after Harriet Harman was appointed Secretary of State for Social Security that she was recalled to have the Women's Minister brief added to her portfolio. Then Joan Ruddock was also appointed Women's Minister (Parliamentary Under Secretary of State). These appointments and the lack of ministerial pay accorded to Ruddock drew adverse criticism. But the post at least seemed to be in two pairs of 'feminist' hands. Moreover, Harman was in the Cabinet and it was Joan Ruddock's only brief.[6]

However, both Harman and Ruddock were sacked in Blair's first reshuffle just over a year later following, and some would argue as a result of the lone parent allowance débâcle.[7] They were replaced by Margaret Jay and Tessa Jowell in July 1998. This time both posts were part-time: Jay was Leader of the House of Lords and Jowell was Minister for Education and Employment. Furthermore, Jay was, at this time, concerned with Labour's reform of the House of Lords while Jowell admitted that only 20 per cent of her time was spent on her women's brief.[8] The fact that Jay was a member of the House of Lords also drew criticism: here was proof that New Labour wanted to minimize its commitment to the post and the substantive representation of women.[9] In addition, neither was regarded as a feminist. In a *Vogue* interview in March 1999 Jay stated: 'I'm not sure what feminism is in 1999. I don't feel part of a sisterhood. Who are they the sisters of, anyway?'[10]

Notwithstanding these developments – the changes in personnel, the part-time nature of the posts and the subsequent appointment of a Member of the House of Lords – Labour's Women's Ministers still had the potential to make a difference for women. And part of that potential was dependent upon relationships with Labour's women MPs. That many of the new Labour women MPs sought the substantive representation of women suggested that they would be supportive of the Women's Minister in principle. But were they happy with the establishment of the post in its actual form? And were they supportive of the women who filled the posts? Did they consider that the Women's Minister acted for women?

Perhaps unsurprisingly, support for the Women's Minster was widespread among the new Labour women MPs in 1997: 21 voiced general support for the position and there was only one response which could be interpreted as ambivalent or negative.[11] This MP talked of not having 'any problem' with a Women's Minister although she stated when probed further: 'Do [I] like it? Do [I] support it? Yes.'[12]

The most widely cited justification in support for the Women's Minister was that the minister would ensure the articulation and taking into account of women's concerns in the absence of women at the heart of government. This was based on the belief that in the absence of a Women's Minister women's concerns would not be included and/or prioritized.[13] Indeed, only one MP rejected the notion that the Women's Minister would ensure that women's concerns were fully represented.[14] For most, the Women's Minister would give extra emphasis to women's concerns[15] – '[it is] about saying these things are important' and giving 'extra emphasis'.[16] Two MPs also considered the position to have symbolic meaning, that is, it indicates that the government is 'serious' about looking at women's lives[17] and another noted that other European countries have similar posts.[18]

The Women's Minister was also seen as a strategic overseer or auditor of policy decisions, a post that is concerned with 'all the different departments'.[19] MPs talked variously of the minister being an 'extra resource', bringing in an 'extra focus', having 'extra time', and with the 'emphasis to make sure things are happening'; the role was about 'raising the profile of issues of particular concern [to] women' 'at [the] very highest level of government'. Another MP talked of the continual need for somebody to remind and prod government ministers and MPs towards change;[20] another, rather defensively, argued that although not ignored, women's concerns would be less noticeable and that the Women's Minister signifies an intrinsic value to women's concerns.[21] A colleague talked of the loss of a systematic standpoint and the corresponding dependence on the vagaries of individual departments and personnel and, in particular, their 'general outlook on this area of political life'.[22] One MP went as far as to say, accompanied with much laughter, that the Women's Minister, along with her Cabinet subcommittee of 'elder stateswomen' 'frightened ministers'.[23]

Three of the MPs provided illustrative examples of the way in which they considered that the absence of women in particular ministries corresponds with the absence and/or marginality of women's concerns. The first reiterated the view that women's concerns 'won't get addressed anywhere else' or will be 'too far down the agenda'.[24] In this MP's opinion, the question of the widening of women's opportunities in the defence forces was a defence issue, but it was not on the agenda of the Ministry of Defence because of the minister's maleness, the departmental culture and the male-dominated civil service.[25] In such circumstances the Women's Minister would ensure that the Ministry of Defence 'acts for women'.

A second MP argued that due to the pressures of governance, particularly of time, all 'thought of what it means for women flies out of the window'.[26] This occurs, in her opinion, because the men in government either lack the experiences that engender women's perspectives and/or because they 'disapprove a little bit of feminism'. Again, in such circumstances, the Women's Minister will 'say "oi" we are not going to do this welfare to work without it benefiting women'.[27]

The third MP felt that the Women's Minster would ensure that departments '*look more sensibly* at something that mostly affects women' (emphasis added).[28] When this MP was asked about what it is about the Women's Minister that would ensure 'sense' is brought to government decision-making she admitted that it means 'being probably more rounded' and that other ministries will have to 'say how will that affect everybody else'. Despite the de-gendered language employed by this MP – 'sensible' and 'more rounded' – the MP is talking about the inclusion of women and women's perspectives.

The indeterminacy of whether particular ministers and departments 'act for' women is further illustrated by two more of the new Labour women MPs. The first noted that 'some ministers and ministries, some areas and policies lent themselves very well [to] having [an] overview [of] all disadvantaged groups'.[29] She went on to suggest that areas such as crime and transport are not necessarily thought of as being gendered, but in reality, both have a 'huge impact on women's lives'. Furthermore, she claimed that it was possible to identify ministers who 'naturally' consider disadvantaged people when they are considering policy. However, her responses revealed that these ministers' 'natural' predisposition is dependent upon individual personality traits.

The second MP also talked about the Department of Transport as an example of a department whose decision-making needed to be supplemented by an input from a Women's Minister.[30] Although the (then) Secretary of State, John Prescott, and Minister of Transport, Gavin Strang, knew 'all about high speed links through the Channel tunnel', the MP claimed that they were unconscious of the gendered nature of transport policies 'because [it is] so long since they actually got their buggy and tried to get on a bus'.

The Women's Minister acts, then, as a 'big sister', policing the policies of those who are experientially different from women and indifferent, if not hostile, to gendered perspectives. Support for the interpretation that the Women's Minister acts to ensure that other ministers and departments are sensitive to gendered analysis is also forthcoming in those responses which indicated that there would be a time in the future when such a post would not be necessary; when women's concerns had become 'mainstreamed', the post, whose role it is to remind departments not to take decisions that are 'anti-woman or against women or make life worse for women', will be redundant.[31]

If the principle of a Women's Minister was largely supported by the new Labour women MPs, their concerns must also be recognized. There was little concern about the Labour Party's changed commitment from a Ministry of Women to a minister, although there was greater concern that the Women's Minister might have insufficient authority and be ghettoized, and many MPs were unhappy about the lack of pay accorded to Joan Ruddock.

Although a number of the women MPs discussed the current post by comparing it to the previous plans for a Ministry for Women in the 1980s, only one saw the change as wholly negative.[32] Perhaps this should not be surprising. Few of the new Labour women MPs would have been associated with the earlier plans. Others regarded the changes as appropriate. For example, one MP considered that while an institutional approach had been relevant to the 1980s when the Ministry for Women was 'going out ahead [and] establishing a base camp', she felt that this approach had been eclipsed by the greater presence of women in politics.[33] As a consequence, 'we have leapfrogged' the need for a ministry because women's presence in Parliament and across government would fulfil the roles envisaged under the more institutional approach. The current political culture, in her opinion, engendered the scrutiny of legislation to be undertaken by the Women's Minister, select committees and other 'short-term approaches'. However, it should be noted that she added the qualification that if the Women's Minister approach failed to deliver, 'we may have to go back to the more institutional way'. Another MP argued that though she had previously believed that the Women's Minister should have Cabinet rank, she had changed her mind.[34] Following consultation with women in her constituency she argued that women preferred to see women's voices 'heard' on all issues and she believed that this would be best achieved by the presence of greater numbers of women MPs, ministers and Cabinet ministers rather than with a separate Women's Ministry. The third MP who provided pragmatic acceptance of the change from ministry to minister did so on the basis that she preferred 'strategic units', which 'cut across ministries', rather than a single ministry, which might suffer from marginalization,[35] while the fourth admitted that she had always been in favour of the post but had 'never got terribly hung up on where it should be'.[36]

Of the seven MPs who voiced concerns about the lack of authority wielded by the Women's Minister four were among the 21 who articulated support for the minister in general.[37] Two MPs talked about the fact that the Women's Minister needed the support of the Prime Minister to be effective.[38] Although acting with the support of the Prime Minister could prove a valuable bargaining position *vis-à-vis* other ministers/ministries, in the absence of their support other ministers/ministries might feel empowered to deflect the Women's Minister's input. Either way – and Blair's support for the post has been called into question – these interpretations leave the impact of the Women's Minister dependent upon, and determined by, political actors over whom she may have little or no authority.

Indeed, nearly one-third of the women MPs were concerned that the Women's Minister might become marginal, 'isolated and pushed to one side', and only allowed to enter the debate after the decisions have been made,[39] although most of these MPs also voiced general support for the post. Concerns were raised that the establishment of a Women's Minister might suggest to other ministers and ministries that they did not need to include women's concerns within their frame of reference, that women's presence and a Women's Minister means that 'all the chaps don't have to worry about it'.[40]

Of the two women MPs who raised concerns about the possibility of the Women's Minister becoming ghettoized, and who had not indicated their support for the position in general, the first preferred integration rather than separatism – in effect the presence of women in all departments.[41] The second, drawing on her experience of local government, was concerned that the Women's Minister was a way of 'shutting women up'.[42]

The fudged appointment of Harriet Harman and Joan Ruddock as Women's Ministers was also raised by a number of the MPs. One MP made explicit criticism of the conjoining of the positions of Secretary of State for Social Security and the Minister for Women. She argued that not only is the remit of Social Security a full-time job in itself, but she also considered that conflict between the two posts was a distinct possibility.[43] The two roles were 'not necessarily compatible'. Another MP was more resigned to the situation and, while 'sorry' that Joan 'isn't a full minister' was prepared, because of her own pragmatism, to 'consolidate what we've got'.[44]

Nevertheless, a number of MPs highlighted the lack of payment made to Joan Ruddock on her appointment.[45] Their criticisms are based upon, first, the negative message this sends to colleagues,[46] in particular, the way in which it undermines the authority of the post and the post holder; and, second, their view that no male MP would have been asked to accept an unpaid ministerial post. In contrast, only one of the new Labour women MPs defended the non-payment on the basis that 'simple things happen like you run out of it [money]'.

While the 1997 interview data indicate the attitudes of the new Labour women MPs towards the post of the Women's Minister and their thoughts on the appointment of Harriet Harman and Joan Ruddock, it does not enable a systematic assessment of the impact of the Women's Minister. As one MP put it: '[the] proof of the pudding is in the eating', and remains to be researched.[47] However, three of the women MPs proffered evaluations. One was not 'overwhelmed' by what it had achieved in its first few months, the second considered that Harriet Harman was 'stunningly effective' and the third that the Women's Minister will have, and is having an effect.[48] Another of the MPs felt that the success of any Minister for Women was dependent upon a good relationship between the minister and the other women Labour MPs. She felt that the women members were the Women Minister's 'secret weapon'.[49] At the time of the 1997 interviews, however, this MP was concerned about the lack of meetings between the Women's Minister and the Labour women MPs and, consequently, about the success of the minister and her initiatives. The personality of the Women's Minister was also identified by one MP as critical to its success.[50]

THE MINISTER FOR WOMEN: ACTING FOR WOMEN, 1997–2000

The women MPs' thoughts on the post of the Women's Minister in 2000 continued to reflect many of the concerns they identified in 1997. This is not to say that they did not continue to support the existence of a Women's Minister, rather it was that they were disappointed by the way in which the Women's Minister had worked in practice.

Nevertheless, there were some MPs who were ambivalent about the post. One MP, who had earlier been critical of the lack of status accorded to the Women's Minister, admitted that she was unsure about the post because she was not convinced that there were issues that were women's issues.[51] Another acknowledged her dilemma between arguing for a Women's Minister who is 'proactive' for women and her concern that this suggests that women are a minority in society.[52] Yet, it was a lone MP who explicitly stated that she was not 'terribly supportive of the Minister for Women':[53]

> For some people …it is tremendously symbolically important, the fact …[that] someone's got an overview of what's happening…who hopefully, if there is a problem, would identify that…I think for some people [it] is absolutely crucial and [that] not to have it I think would send messages to some people, *it wouldn't to me*. (emphasis added)

Two MPs believed that when women's concerns and gendered analysis were on 'everyone's agenda' in the Cabinet the post of Women's Minister would be redundant, although only one felt that this stage had been achieved.[54] A third said that she felt 'a bit exasperated' that women's concerns were left to women and that she wanted all ministers to act for women, although she recognized that it would be for the Women's Minister to be the 'guiding light' 'leading the charge'.[55]

In contrast to these views, there were plentiful statements by other MPs that demonstrate that most of the new Labour women MPs wanted to see a more secure, authoritative and effective Women's Minister.[56]A few considered that the Women's Minister had had a 'bad start',[57] and been only a 'half-hearted' attempt.[58] Others were even more explicit: 'I would like to see it stronger really but I think they've made a start';[59] '[it] has become, you know, a very low part of the process … [it] hasn't had the profile it should have had';[60] 'it wasn't a poper post, it wasn't funded, there wasn't a salary with it, it doesn't have a particularly high profile or high status';[61] 'they haven't been allowed to have the impact they could have had';[62] '[it's] been completely marginalized and although each individual woman has tried to do her best, it hasn't work[ed]';[63] 'I get the impression that the women's agenda, such as it is, is a bit on the back burner'.[64] Another MP claimed that 'it doesn't do the job that we thought [it] … would be doing … as first mooted before the 1992 general election' so she could not say that she was 'enthralled by it', though she also felt that it was not going to get much 'more support than it's getting now and we have to be realistic about that'.[65]

Moreover, many of the MPs remained preoccupied and unhappy about the way in which Joan Ruddock had been unpaid and 'disgracefully' treated.[66] This was felt to be indicative of the government's, and according to one MP specifically Tony Blair's, view that the post of Women's Minister was relatively unimportant.[67]

There was also extensive criticism, by more than half of the MPs, that neither of the Women's Ministers following Ruddock's dismissal was full-time.[68] Two MPs' responses were heavy with sarcasm. One asked: 'Do we have *one*?' The other stated, when she was asked to reflect on the Minister for Women, 'both of them'.[69] Another MP forcefully stated her preference for a single minister: 'I think we … still should have, you know, a Women's Minister, maybe not a department, but certainly a minister whose job it is to speak up for women's issues.'[70] Others considered it insulting to 'add on' the women's brief to another brief: 'I think that's a role [Women's Minister] in itself and to tag it on to it … is an insult to women and an insult to her [the woman minister] in a way that she can do these two…that she can do it, tag it on.'[71]

The lack of a single Women's Minister was also felt to symbolize the continued lack of support for the post:

> Joan Ruddock did a good job and I was very sad when she went as a minister whose sole job was women and I think frankly we should have that back ... [when] women just get tacked on the end I mean it sends out all the wrong signals, you know, you have to send out signals about if you are serious.[72]

Yet another MP, once she had been reassured that her response would be anonymous, was prepared to be even more explicit in her criticism:

> Harriet and Joan were ... [I] suppose you would say they were both sort of feminists really and who would stick out for women's issues and it was ghastly what happened really, losing them both like that ... I think they were sacrificial lambs and I think it was quite damaging to the post of Women's Minister that they went ... I feel the post's been downgraded a bit since it's been given, you know to two people with other major responsibilities ... we haven't anybody who has just got the women's brief ... we have lost something.[73]

Other MPs were critical of the appointment of Margaret Jay because she was a Member of the House of Lords and therefore unelected and distanced from the women MPs,[74] although three MPs were explicit in their support for Jay.[75] One MP was also critical because she did not consider Jay to be sufficiently feminist,[76] while another argued that Jay's appointment was one of the reasons why she wanted to see the post empowered to 'actually kind of be able to get the other departments by the scruff of the neck ... and look how it [policy] affects women's lives'.[77] A colleague shared her concern:

> I am disappointed at the women [Jay and Jowell] who are in these positions, I am disappointed, probably not with the women themselves, but the profile they've been given or that they've sought for themselves, they haven't been as robust about these matters as we could have been.[78]

In terms of whether the MPs considered that the Women's Minister had effected feminized change there was a division between those who were clear that they had, even if sometimes this was hidden behind the scenes,[79] those who were less sure,[80] and others who felt little had been achieved. In the former group were those who made statements praising the Women's Ministers: '[the] work the Women's Ministers have done is, you know, very impressive'; 'some of their reports have been excellent, because they've come more or less a year before you've seen the policy'.[81] Other MPs praised them for their work on domestic violence and equal pay[82] and for their consultation with women in Britain.[83] Some also talked about how the Women's Minster acted as a resource.[84] Although one of these MPs recognized that they were themselves under-resourced, which meant that some of the information was not 'tremendously useful',[85] a couple of her colleagues disagreed.[86] Another MP stated simply that she had had lots of links with the Women's Minister.[87]

A few of the MPs also questioned the extent to which the substantive representation of women was occurring via the Women's Minister. One felt that other women ministers acted for women while another identified the lobbying of feminist organizations and the support of both male and female MPs as the dynamic for women's substantive representation.[88] Yet another argued that rather than 'going to the Women's Minister … I think about how can I organize my colleagues and sort it out … through the PLP's Women's Group'.[89]

There was also a single criticism that the minister and Women's Unit had lost sight of what it should be doing – 'women's rights in the workplace', the 'Sex Discrimination Act' and the media representation of the new Labour women MPs as 'Blair's Babes' – and had focused its attention on less important issues – 'lecturing girls on body image and on what they eat and how they look … talking in schools'. In this MP's opinion the Minister had turned into a 'big Mary Poppins nanny figure'.[90] However, her interpretation was contested by another MP, who argued that even if some of the issues and publicity had appeared 'gimmicky', they were, nevertheless, important issues. For this MP, issues such as anorexia and the representations of women by the modelling industry were important issues.[91] Moreover, she considered that such publicity had the additional benefit of raising the profile of the Women's Minister among the general public in a way that the minister's work on domestic violence may not. She also felt that although women's organizations and women survivors of domestic violence were aware of the government's actions, the wider community of women probably were not.

CONCLUSION

In both the 1997 and the 2000 data it is clear that the majority of the new Labour women MPs were supportive of the post of Women's Minister. Their responses demonstrate that they perceive the Minister as constituting an additional mechanism for the substantive representation of women. It is the Women's Minister's ability to articulate women's concerns at the heart of government and across departments that underpins their support for the post. A government in which there is no Women's Minister is regarded as deficient *vis-à-vis* the substantive representation of women. Thus, while the 1997 general election brought in greater numbers of women MPs, there was still widespread support for a Women's Minister to act for women and to hold the government to account for the substantive representation of women.

Notwithstanding their support, the women MPs demonstrated in 1997 and again in 2000, when it might be thought that the passage of time would have dampened down their anger, that they were unhappy about the way in which Harriet Harman and Joan Ruddock were appointed as Women's Ministers in the immediate aftermath of the 1997 general election. The MPs were also highly critical of their replacements being part-time and concerned about the lack of authority that the post wielded.

To be sure, many of the new Labour women MPs' criticisms of both the post and the women who have been Women's Ministers were often extensive but these reflect, rather than undermine, their support for the post. The women MPs do not want to see the Women's Minister marginalized *because* this would reduce the ability for the minister to ensure that other departments 'act for women'; they do not want to see the Women's Minister reliant upon the Prime Minister *because* this will limit the ability of the Women's Minister to transform government policy; and criticisms of how the post was set up are strongly put *because* they wanted the Women's Minister to be a Cabinet minister with a single responsibility to 'act for women'.

NOTES

1. This heading is drawn directly from one of the interviews, though it is not clear whether the pun was intended.
2. J. Squires and M. Wickham-Jones (2002), 'Mainstreaming in Westminster and Whitehall', *Parliamentary Affairs*, 55, 1: 59; C. Short (1996), 'Women and the Labour Party', in J. Lovenduski and

P. Norris (eds), *Women in Politics* (Oxford: Oxford University Press), pp. 24–5. In addition, Squires and Wickham-Jones argue that a Women's Minister who engages with women's groups, increases women's knowledge and participation in formal politics and projects a more women-friendly image of government, should increase women's numerical representation as more women are encouraged to seek selection as parliamentary candidates (Squires and Wickham-Jones, 'Mainstreaming in Westminster and Whitehall', pp. 58–9). See also J. Squires and M. Wickham-Jones (forthcoming), 'New Labour, Gender Mainstreaming and the Women and Equality Unit', *British Journal of Politics and International Relations*.

3. M. Sawer (2002), 'The Representation of Women in Australia', *Parliamentary Affairs*, 55, 1: 17.
4. There would also be a Women's Unit, housed in the Department of Social Security. Squires and Wickham-Jones, 'Mainstreaming in Westminster and Whitehall', p. 61; S. Bashevkin (2000), 'From Tough Times to Better Times', *International Political Science Review*, 4; Short, 'Women in the Labour Party'.
5. Bashevkin, 'From Tough Times to Better Times', p. 417.
6. Ibid., p. 418.
7. Harriet Harman was replaced as Secretary of State for Social Security by Alistair Darling on 27 July 1998, Joan Ruddock was Parliamentary Under Secretary of State until 28 July 1998 when Baroness Jay of Paddington became Leader of the House of Lords and Minister for Women.
8. Squires and Wickham-Jones, 'Mainstreaming in Westminster and Whitehall', p. 67.
9. Bashevkin, 'From Tough Times to Better Times', p. 418.
10. *Vogue*, March 1999.
11. Interviews 3 (18–12–97), 4 (30–07–97), 10 (08–07–97), 11 (23–07–97), 12 (11–06–97), 14 (03–07–97), 15 (14–10–97), 17 (05–11–97), 18 (12–06–97), 19 (10–12–97), 22 (08–09–97), 23 (29–07–97), 24 (07–04–97), 25 (01–07–97), 26 (30–07–97), 27 (08–07–97), 28 (09–07–97), 29 (06–08–97), 30 (10–06–97), 31 (08–07–97) and 32 (19–11–97).
12. Interview 20 (09–07–97).
13. Interviews 3 (18–12–97), 4 (30–07–97), 10 (08–07–97), 11 (23–07–97), 14 (03–07–97), 17 (05–11–97), 19 (10–12–97), 22 (08–08–97), 24 (07–04–97) and 25 (01–07–97). Many of the new Labour women MPs provided multiple arguments in support of the post.
14. Interview 23 (29–07–97).
15. Interviews 3 (18–12–97), 10 (08–07–97), 19 (10–12–97), 23 (29–07–97) and 30 (10–06–97).
16. Interviews 3 (18–12–97), 4 (30–07–97), 14 (03–07–97), 17 (05–11–97), 19 (10–12–97), 24 (07–04–97), 26 (30–07–97), 27 (08–07–97) and 30 (10–06–97).
17. Interviews 18 (12–06–97) and 28 (09–07–97).
18. Interview 17 (05–11–97).
19. Interviews 3 (18–12–97), 19 (10–12–97), 22 (08–09–97), 23 (29–07–97), 24 (07–04–97) and 25 (01–07–97).
20. Interview 3 (18–12–97).
21. Interview 4 (30–07–97).
22. Interview 19 (10–12–97).
23. Interview 4 (30–07–97).
24. Interview 17 (05–11–97).
25. The issue of the impact of a male-dominated civil service is identified by four MPs (interviews 14 [03–07–97], 16 [24–11–97], 17 [05–11–97] and 20 [01–08–97]).
26. Interview 11 (23–07–97).
27. The way in which this woman MP frames her response indicates that she is eliding the terms 'women's' and 'feminist'.
28. Interview 24 (07–04–97).
29. Interview 26 (30–07–97).
30. Interview 30 (10–06–97).
31. Interviews 3 (18–12–97), 27 (08–07–97) and 14 (03–07–97). The latter suggested that equality was needed throughout the system before this should occur, and she made explicit reference to women's presence in the civil service. This suggests that the arguments for women's substantive representation are not limited to elected positions.
32. Short, 'Women and the Labour Party'.
33. Interview 6 (12–11–97).

34. Interview 31 (08–07–97).
35. Interview 20 (01–08–97).
36. Interview 15 (14–10–97).
37. Interviews 11 (23–07–97), 12 (11–06–97), 18 (12–06–97) and 28 (09–07–97) in respect of the former, and interviews 1 (14–12–97), 16 (24–11–97) and 20 (01–08–97) regarding the latter.
38. Interviews 11 (23–07–97) and 18 (12–06–97).
39. See notes 40–43 below.
40. Interview 12 (11–06–97). Interviews 11 (23–07–97), 12 (11–06–97), 17 (05–11–97), 24 (07–04–97), 26 (30–07–97), 28 (09–07–97), 29 (06–08–97) and 30 (10–06–97).
41. Interview 33 (19–06–97).
42. Interview 28 (09–07–97).
43. Interview 1 (04–12–97).
44. Interview 9 (03–11–97).
45. Interviews 9 (29–10–97), 15 (14–10–97), 29 (06–08–97), 32 (19–11–97) and 33 (19–06–97).
46. Interview 15 (14–10–97).
47. Interview 11 (23–07–97) also argues that it is too soon to evaluate the impact of the Women's Minister.
48. Interviews 16 (24–11–97), 5 (23–06–97) and 32 (19–11–97) respectively.
49. Interview 20 (01–08–97).
50. Interview 15 (14–10–97).
51. Interview 27 (17–05–00).
52. Interview 29 (15–05–00).
53. Interview 31 (10–07–00).
54. Interviews 9 (22–06–00) and 14 (08–06–00).
55. Interview 18 (12–07–00).
56. Interviews 1 (12–07–00), 4 (21–06–00) and 5 (22–05–00).
57. Interview 3 (14–06–00).
58. Interviews 14 (08–06–00) and 27 (17–05–00).
59. Interview 16 (26–07–00).
60. Interview 2 (13–06–00).
61. Interview 27 (17–05–00).
62. Interview 28 (12–07–00).
63. Interview 9 (22–06–00).
64. Interview 29 (15–05–00).
65. Interview 24 (10–05–00).
66. Interviews 2 (13–06–00), 3 (14–06–00), 8 (20–06–00), 9 (22–06–00), 18 (12–07–00), 22 (16–05–00), 27 (17–05–00) and 29 (15–05–00).
67. Interview 18 (12–07–00). See also interview 22 (16–05–00), who considered that Blair viewed the post as a 'single issue' and therefore it causes him 'alarm'.
68. Interviews 1 (12–07–00), 3 (14–06–00), 4 (21–06–00), 5 (22–05–00), 8 (20–06–00), 9 (22–06–00), 14 (08–06–00), 15 (23–05–00), 18 (12–07–00), 22 (16–05–00), 23 (19–06–00), 25 (21–06–00) and 29 (15–05–00).
69. Interviews 5 (22–05–00) and 14 (08–06–00).
70. Interview 4 (21–06–00).
71. Interview 9 (22–06–00).
72. Interview 18 (12–07–00).
73. Interview 25 (21–06–00). Although the interviews did not directly address the issue of the sacking of Harriet Harman, support for her was forthcoming. One MP felt that she had been consciously marginalized (Interview 5 [22–05–00]) while another considered that she was 'pushed off her perch' (Interview 6 [13–06–00]). Harman was, according to this MP, respected by her colleagues and she was credited with continuing to advocate women's concerns, concerns which Harman was seen to feel 'passionately about'.
74. Interviews 5 (22–05–00), 9 (22–06–00), 23 (19–06–00), 25 (21–06–00), 28 (12–07–00), 29 (15–05–00) and 31 (10–07–00).
75. Interviews 9 (22–06–00), 28 (12–07–00) and 31 (10–07–00).
76. Interview 8 (20–06–00).
77. Interview 16 (26–07–00).

78. Interview 6 (13–06–00).
79. Interviews 2 (13–06–00), 12 (15–06–00), 3 (14–06–00), 15 (23–05–00) and 24 (10–05–00).
80. Interview 3 (14–06–00).
81. Interviews 4 (21–06–00) and 6 (13–06–00).
82. Interview 13 (13–06–00).
83. Interviews 13 (13–06–00) and 24 (10–05–00).
84. Interviews 6 (13–06–00), 14 (08–06–00), 29 (15–05–00) and 24 (10–05–00).
85. Interview 14 (08–06–00).
86. Interviews 5 (22–05–00) and 27 (17–05–00).
87. Interview 25 (21–06–00).
88. Interviews 1 (12–07–00) and 24 (10–05–00).
89. Interview 24 (10–05–00).
90. Interview 5 (22–05–00). See also interview 22 (16–05–00) who was critical of the 'headline' that stated that she was critical of women becoming hairdressers.
91. Interview 13 (13–06–00).

10

A Feminized Style of Politics?

INTRODUCTION

The contention that women practise politics in a different way from men is widely held. Women are expected to reject confrontation and adversarial politics in favour of a co-operative and consensual style.[1] Women politicians are considered to be 'more caring, practical, approachable, honest, principled, and hardworking'.[2] At the time of the 1997 general election, such presumptions were widely reported in the press. Headlines included: 'Winning women to overturn male culture of the Commons'; 'Sisterhood signals end to macho politics'.[3] Clare Short, the senior Labour MP, similarly expected that the presence of greater numbers of women MPs following the general election would 'bring a change' in the 'ya-boo culture of the House of Commons'.[4] But on what basis is it claimed that women have a different style of politics from men? Was the expectation that the new Labour women MPs would do politics differently shared by those MPs who were expected to act in this feminized way? And were they able to act like women in a Parliament renowned for its aggressive style?

PERCEPTIONS OF A FEMINIZED STYLE OF POLITICS

Many of the new Labour women MPs in 1997 believed that the increased presence of women MPs would make a difference to the style of politics practised in the House of Commons. Women, it was claimed, do not 'stand up and waffle on for about thirty-five minutes in the Chamber'.[5] Women's approach is 'more direct' and there is less 'going around in circles'. There is 'dialogue or trialogue' (*sic*), rather than an opposition between a correct government position and an incorrect opposition stance.[6] There is also less aggression and more co-operation, teamwork, inclusiveness, consultation and a willingness to listen.[7] Women MPs talk in more concrete ways and apply arguments to 'real people'.[8] One MP argued that women MPs derive their arguments and perspectives from personal experiences rather than relying upon 'scientific research',[9] while another MP stated '[I don't] know of anything I find more uplifting' than the respect that women accord each other during debates at the Labour Women's Conference.[10]

The difference in style between women and men MPs is, according to the new Labour women MPs, due to women and men's differently gendered socialization and experiences. As one MP acknowledged, the 'directness' of women's approach derives from their experiences of 'dealing with millions of things at once', their desire to 'move on to something else' and their more 'holistic' approach.[11] Two MPs also contended that part of the reason for the women MPs' co-operation in the 1997 Parliament was the sense of cohesion and collective identity that was engendered by the greater numbers of women elected.[12]

Interestingly, one MP saw women's use of a different language as a dynamic for feminized change: 'language', she argued, 'can change things' because it can 'challenge' the terms in which issues are discussed and can 'encourage people to be gender-balanced'.[13]

Many of the women MPs were keen to criticize the dominant, masculinized style of the House of Commons. There was extensive criticism of the 'convoluted', 'old-fashioned speaking styles' of the House and of MPs' tendency to refer to 'people in the third person'.[14] One MP, drawing on a pensions debate early in the 1997 Parliament, recalled how 'all the men without exception talked about pension actuaries, [the] size [of] pension funds, [and] lots of statistics'.[15]

There was also criticism of male MPs' aggressive and confrontational style – of men 'behaving badly'.[16] One MP termed this masculinized style of politics 'babies in the play pen' politics.[17] Another stated that in mixed-sex meetings within Parliament the women MPs found 'just getting [a] word in edgeways [is] very difficult'.[18] While a number of MPs talked about the importance of alcohol to the House, it was, one claimed a 'boys' club' in which some 'hit the bars'[19] and 'drunks go … through the lobby at 10 p.m.'.[20]

Singled out as particularly bad was Conservative male MPs' behaviour. One MP recalled how, in agricultural questions, a Labour member had asked about what action the government was taking to protect birds. At this, the 'Tories fell about' and the 'Speaker had to intervene'.[21] Another contended that Conservative men 'do not know how to handle us' because they lack the 'culture' of engaging with women.[22] Interestingly, one MP talked about how a Conservative woman MP acknowledged, through a physical sign across the floor of the House, her criticism of the 'abominable' behaviour of her Conservative male colleagues.[23]

A couple of MPs contended that such male behaviour would 'never happen' on the Labour benches. Indeed, they considered that the newly elected Labour men were similarly critical of the behaviour and rituals – the 'schoolboyish theatricality' – of the House.[24] Moreover, one of the new Labour woman MPs considered that their presence had, even in the short time between their election in 1997 and the first round of interviews, ensured that the House of Commons had become 'a bit more civilized', although she admitted that 'you do hear remarks'.[25]

The responses from new Labour women MPs which appear to reject the notion that women and men have different approaches to politics varied. One woman felt that such analysis relies upon a crude division between women and men, and is underpinned by an implicit association of goodness with women's behaviour.[26] Another rejected outright that her behaviour is, or will fit, some kind of women's mode of political operation and that women are, by their very natures 'nice and caring and sharing'.[27] Furthermore, she added that women who have previously been successful in British politics – Barbara Castle, Shirley Williams, Margaret Thatcher, Ann Taylor, Margaret Beckett and Clare Short – have been 'hard and tough [and] played the game like one of the boys', though her conclusion that these successful women 'played like the boys' raises the question of whether women are able to function in a feminized way and be successful.

Indeed, some of the women clearly felt that their style was less valued by their parliamentary colleagues:

> [A] premium is put upon what is predominantly a male style of political practice, which is quite aggressive and quite confrontational … [a] debating society style of presentation which men are often much better at, have more confidence in doing, taught more to do and doesn't necessarily make for any greater government.[28]

Others agreed. One MP recounted how she had been admonished by a professional speechwriter who maintained that one must 'back up everything with figures' because this is 'what [male (read proper)] politicians do'.[29] A second MP reflected upon the criticisms that were levelled at Harriet Harman MP in the 1992 Parliament in a debate with the senior Conservative MP Michael Portillo.[30] She argued that it was inevitable that Harman was regarded to have lost the debate. Portillo's aggressive style, the way in which he 'shout[ed] her down' and denied her the opportunity 'to say what she want[ed] to say' is the accepted norm of engagement across the floor of the House. Therefore, fellow MPs and political commentators would rate Portillo's performance positively and regard Harman's negatively. At the same time, however, this MP believed that Harman could not have adopted, even if she had wanted to, the current 'rules of the game'. Had she taken a similarly aggressive approach towards Portillo her behaviour, according to this MP, would have transgressed gender norms and she would have been criticized for being a 'strident cow'. In any case, as another MP forcefully stated, women should not become like men and 'behave badly' because this accepts rather than transforms the dominant style of the House.[31]

Yet, whether women MPs can resist the process of assimilation was disputed. On the one hand, one MP maintained her belief that some space is available for women representatives to act in 'a womanly fashion'.[32] On the other hand, another MP admitted that she participated in debates more frequently than she wished to because she sought to counter the charge that women MPs are 'too afraid' to speak in debates even though this ran the risk of speaking in debates on which she had little expertise.[33]

ACTING LIKE WOMEN: THREE YEARS ON

The interviews in 2000 enabled the women MPs to reconsider their initial perceptions and reflect upon women's and men's styles after having experienced life in the House of Commons for three years. They also enabled a discussion of whether all women share the feminized style, in particular, whether party differences make a difference, and the extent to which women MPs are able to act like women in an institution that many regarded as masculinized, questions that were not explored fully in the earlier interviews.

Just under two-thirds of the new Labour women MPs argued in 2000 that women had a different political style.[34] Of those who disagreed, one felt that she had not seen any 'hard evidence' of a feminized style,[35] and a second that she did not consider that you could identify the sex of an MP on the basis of their 'pattern' of behaviour.[36] But the majority subscribed to the view that women do have a different style of politics. Women prefer a 'less combative and aggressive style'.[37] They 'don't do as much standing up, shouting on the floor of the House'.[38] Women are more 'measured'.[39] Another MP, while admitting that some women are 'shouty', said she preferred to adopt an approach in which one recognizes that there will have been 'some merit in what was done before'.[40] There was also a belief that the women operated not as individuals, but as part of teams. As one MP said: 'It's important for politicians to recognize they don't achieve things on their own.'[41] A colleague felt that women were more likely to recognize this: 'Women will step back and not say "look what I've done for you" they will say … "look what we have done".'[42]

Women MPs also claimed they spoke in a different language.[43] This is the 'language everybody understands'; women are 'not prone to political babble [and] jargon'.[44] They look at issues 'from a personal perspective rather than just looking at the sort of pounds, shilling and pence type of approach to things';[45] 'women don't want to know global sums … [they want to know that] every primary school will get between three and nine thousand pounds'.[46]

Women's political style is also characterized by working behind the scenes (as discussed in Chapter 8): women MPs prefer 'private meetings', informal or semi-formal contacts with ministers in contrast to macho, gesture politics.[47] As one MP stated: 'Hansard' is merely the 'tip of the iceberg' of what women MPs are doing in the House.[48]

Three years on many of the new Labour women MPs remained critical of the House of Commons' masculinized style. A shared sense in which, to use some well-worn clichés, the House still constitutes 'an old boys' club' or a 'boys' prep school'[49] – even if the reality was not quite so bad as one MP had envisaged[50] – was evident. Other criticisms included the theatricality of the Chamber,[51] its childishness,[52] its inefficiency,[53] and that it is negatively perceived by the electorate.[54] Another MP bluntly stated that it was populated by a 'bunch of wankers'.[55] However, one MP, while initially rejecting such descriptions, acknowledged that it adequately describes some of the spaces within the House, although she maintained that you could choose where to 'hang out'.[56]

In terms of a different political language, male MPs were again identified as having a different style. They had a tendency towards repetition: 'men always do want to say it again';[57] 'there is so much duplication going on from one male speaker to another'.[58] This MP continued, laughing, that she recognized 'that's an old truism about men and women, but it's true'. Women are 'less likely to shout out a cutting remark', said another,[59] although this particular MP recognized that she was generalizing. A third MP agreed: 'A lot of men, you know, like the sound of their own voice.'[60]

Male MPs were also identified as scrutinizing women's presence, appearance and performance, with male Conservative MPs regarded, once again, as the worst offenders.[61] One woman felt that they just did not know 'quite how to handle' women MPs other than by ridiculing them.[62] Another felt, however, that her contributions to debates were often ignored by male colleagues from all parties:

> I gave quite a long speech which mentioned several things ... other speakers later mentioned and ... nearly all of them made no reference to ... [the] fact that I had already said certain things, but [they] mentioned other men, including men from other parties so it's like this invisible women thing, you are sort of patted on the head but you are not taken notice of.[63]

Yet, many of the MPs (who discussed this) believed that things have improved, although some admitted that it was difficult to judge the change because they had no direct comparison. There was a sense in which it was felt that women MPs and women's concerns were less likely to be received amidst laughter and 'sniggering';[64] that there was less 'ya-boo' politics;[65] that the Chamber was a slightly softer place;[66] that women MPs were less 'defensive and embattled';[67] that sexual harassment would not be tolerated;[68] and that women have 'humanized'[69] and had a civilizing influence.[70] However, three MPs argued that while the 1997 numbers were an improvement upon previous Parliaments, there was still an insufficient number of women MPs to effect considerable change.[71] One colleague believed the opposite, however – that the Labour women MPs formed 'some sort of mass that can have an impact rather than being ... picked off'.[72]

A FEMINIZED STYLE OF POLITICS: GENDER AND PARTY DIFFERENCES

Some of the women MPs' responses indicated that not all women MPs shared the feminized style of politics. The difference in style between women and men is not determined by sex so much as gender. Older, 'successful' women MPs were regarded as employing the traditional masculinized style and were perceived as 'male'.[73] In contrast, 'new men' were considered more likely to share women's political style.[74] As one woman put it, 'maybe it's a generational thing'. Some of the 'new men', by which she meant those 'younger than 60' and not simply those who were first elected in 1997,[75] were 'equally shocked' by the norms of behaviour in the House.[76]

Party identity was also felt to be an important determinant. The new Labour women MPs were asked about their attitudes towards, and experiences of, having acted with women MPs from the other parties – behaviour that might indicate a more co-operative, consensual and less adversarial style of politics. However, acting with other women was limited in the 1997 Parliament because of the small numbers of women MPs from the other parties.[77] Indeed, five MPs stated that they had not experienced cross-party co-operation with other women MPs,[78] and another noted that it 'doesn't happen much',[79] although one of these thought it 'could be a good idea'.[80]

The question remains, though, whether there would be more extensive cross-party co-operation if the other parties had more women MPs. There was a clear indication among the new Labour women MPs that they had had productive relationships with women Liberal Democrat MPs. The Liberal Democrat women MPs were felt to have a 'genuine interest in women'[81] and have 'similar views on certain things'.[82] Two of the three Liberal Democrat women MPs were particularly singled out for praise.[83] And one MP talked about how, if she was sponsoring an Early Day Motion (EDM) a particular Liberal Democrat woman MP 'would be an automatic one I would go to'.[84] Indeed, one MP noted that the Liberal Democrat women MPs supported the campaign against Mike Tyson,[85] while another talked about how there was a shared concern between Labour and Liberal Democrat women regarding a commitment to women's equal numerical representation in the Scottish Parliament.[86] In contrast, only one MP stated that she did not really know any of the Liberal Democrat women.[87]

With regard to Conservative women MPs, the new Labour women MPs' responses suggested that greater co-operation with Conservative women was not likely even if there were greater numbers of them. Not only are Conservative women MPs in a minority in their party, the Conservative Party itself is regarded as ideologically hostile to feminist perspectives.[88] As one MP put it, 'the [Tory] women are just so different'.[89] Another MP concluded, on the basis of conversations with Conservative women MPs, that there was 'phenomenal sexism' in the party and it was 'very nasty'.[90] One MP, however, felt a sense of regret for Conservative women MPs:

> I feel quite sad for the Tory women ... because in order to survive they've really had to capitulate most of their ... femininity; they've had to join the male agenda, live it, breathe it and now they are it, which is really sad.[91]

Moreover, one of the MPs recounted how two Conservative women MPs had agreed with Early Day Motions regarding Mike Tyson – an indication of attitudinal convergence between (admittedly a minority) of Conservative and Labour women MPs – but had neither signed the EDM nor spoken out in public. This Labour MP was clearly disappointed in the behaviour of the Conservative women, particularly because she considered that many EDMs are not partisan. At the same time, she was not surprised that they had not been prepared to endorse publicly the EDM because she considered that 'women in the Conservative Party have a very rough time' because it 'is deeply sexist'.[92]

Notwithstanding this interpretation, one of the MPs indicated that in the future the possibility for cross-party co-operation between Labour and Conservative women might be improved as the 'young ones tend to be more feminist'. Two separate MPs identified a particular Conservative woman MP as an example of a younger, 'more feminist' Conservative woman MP.[93] The Labour women MPs' interpretation suggests, at least in their opinion, that it is the particular configuration of their gender and party identities that prevents cross-party co-operation between Conservative and Labour women MPs at this time. In the future, as the party and gender identities of Conservative women MPs change, some Conservative women MPs might, therefore, adopt a more feminized style of politics and act for women.

THE HOUSE OF COMMONS: CAN WOMEN ACT LIKE WOMEN?

Although many of the women MPs clearly supported the contention that they have a different style of politics, a number of them suggested that the dominant masculinized style of the House was not conducive to women acting in a feminized way.[94] For example, one woman MP spoke with regret that she and other women MPs had been unable to act differently 'to the extent I would like to see',[95] while a colleague stated that 'the culture here is very strong ... you really have to learn to operate within it or you are lost'. Another MP concurred: '[The Chamber is an] institutional framework that demands performance, that demands adversarial conduct.'[96] In such a context, trying to 'impose a different kind of culture is a very long-term process'.[97]

The notion that women MPs may not feel comfortable in the Chamber was evident in a few of the interview discussions.[98] Four MPs directly stated this.[99] Another simply stated that she preferred to use other means,[100] while two MPs used the term 'alien' to describe how they felt.[101] In contrast, only one woman MP explicitly stated that she felt comfortable in the Chamber.[102]

One of the new Labour woman MPs talked extensively about how she experienced the House. She had 'no problems with the robustness of politics' and considered that she was capable of fighting back 'if any man is sexist to me', although she considered that her background in local government had given her the experience to 'fight back'.[103] Another of her colleagues' responses also indicated that she was more than capable of coping with Parliament. This MP asserted: 'I wouldn't allow a man to make me feel uncomfortable.'[104] But, as she continued discussing this she started to say how she needed 'lots of reassurance at home' that she was 'up to the job'. When she was probed about whether she had felt such insecurity in her previous career she admitted: 'You're right I didn't … and of course … women dominated the profession.'

Some of the new Labour women MPs also recalled how colleagues had criticized their style of politics. For example, one MP felt that they were regarded as naïve for talking in everyday language.[105] Another recalled that one of the whips had said to her that she was 'too quiet' and that she didn't do 'enough barracking and shouting'.[106] And a third took issue with the ways in which women's style was judged negatively against the male norm.[107]

One of the women's responses to this negative judgement was that she would not be 'put off by men' and that women had to 'carry on doing it their way'.[108] When probed further as to whether this would reduce the impact of women MPs' interventions she was adamant that women had to 'stick to' their approach, although the laughter which accompanied her responses, and her qualification 'I know what you are saying', suggested that she was not unaware of the tension in her comments. Namely, that in the short term, at least, there may be a cost associated with women employing a style of politics that is regarded as less legitimate, less effective and is, hence, able to be ignored.

That women MPs perceive that their effectiveness may be limited by their style is supported further by two additional MPs. Both were discussing the Labour Party's plans for the modernization of Parliament (referring here to ending debates in the early evening and some timetabling of legislation). In both cases, Margaret Beckett MP (then Leader of the House) was directly criticized for seeking consensus in the face of deliberate obstruction.[109] As one of the MPs put it: 'She ain't going to get it [consensus].'[110] When this woman was asked about the apparent contradiction between her own preference for a feminized style of politics and her criticism of Beckett, she admitted that her two comments were contradictory. However, she then added that she was more concerned about the outcome rather than the means: 'I'm a collaborative person and if you can achieve it that [way] … [but] the outcome is ultimately what I am here for.'

In institutions where women's feminized style of politics is less valued, such as the House of Commons (at least according to many of the new Labour women MPs), women politicians seem to face a choice between assimilation or resistance, between adopting the male 'game playing' or 'standing out against it'.[111] Many of the new Labour women MPs who were critical of the House's dominant masculinized style were, unsurprisingly, reluctant to adopt it. One MP, who considered that she probably could behave differently, stated that she simply did not 'like those sorts of arguments'.[112] Another colleague was even more explicit about the choice she faced:

> I am still struggling not to involve myself in the cheering and the booing, in the 'ya-booing', in the confrontational style of this place and I still don't want to exploit the system … I want to be here, be respected for what I do, for how I do it … there are issues here which are taken as confrontational simply because that is the style of the place and it's a good way to have a knock about and harm politically one or other party; that is stupid, I do not want ever to find myself involved in that style.[113]

When it was suggested to this MP that it might be personally advantageous and/or be beneficial in terms of the arguments/concerns she was advocating to reject the feminized style she added: 'I don't think at the parliamentary level I've had many opportunities or that I would have had the kind of character to take them, that's not my style and I would find it quite difficult.' Other MPs, too, were explicit in recognizing the dangers, in their view, of assimilation. One asked, 'how do you not get sucked into that?'[114] This was particularly difficult for this MP because she acknowledged that she needed to participate in supporting her front bench against the Opposition. A second MP also admitted that she could get 'more stuck into the debates' if she wanted to but that she 'just [didn't] see the point of it'.[115] Again, she recognized that she could 'enjoy' this practice, that it was attractive to her at one level, and that she 'could get drawn into it'. However, at the same time she regarded it as 'playing games' and sought to resist the temptation. Another colleague considered that it was 'almost impossible to resist and to behave different[ly]':

> The pressures to produce ... the outcomes demanded by the system are almost irresistible ... the pressure to make a joke, to make a smart remark ... the very fact that you know what you are trying to do is either promote an argument or to find holes in somebody else's argument ... is a very adversarial process.[116]

Another of the MPs admitted that she had had to 'compromise' and learn to 'put [herself] about as an individual' in order to be regarded as a successful MP.[117]

Taking, perhaps, a 'realist' position, one of the women MPs considered that there came a point when 'you have to stick the knife' or 'the stiletto' in because that was what was demanded by the 'system'. However, her ambivalence was also revealed when she added that this should be achieved in a 'way ... which isn't unpleasant and adversarial'.[118] As another of the MPs acknowledged, 'I think you have to be strong, vigorous and decisive'.[119] She had come to reject the notion that 'if one stood up and spoke in a very quiet voice when one was putting over one's point that was somehow more effective'.

There were some women MPs who accepted the norms, or at least some of the norms, of male parliamentary behaviour. For example, one MP felt that she had over time begun to understand the meaning of 'ya-boo' politics.[120] While she had initially regarded Prime Minister's Questions (PMQs) as 'outrageous', she had subsequently revised her opinion and now regarded it as fulfilling the function of 'rallying the troops'. When she was asked about the claim that women's numerical representation is negatively affected because of how Prime Minister's Questions is perceived by women, she replied that there was a responsibility for women MPs to say to women who might seek selection that 'you don't have to be afraid'. Another MP agreed that women MPs could perform well on the floor of the House because they 'could learn a real turn of phrase'.[121]

CONCLUSION

There is a widely shared appreciation among many of the new Labour women MPs that (some) women have a different, feminized, style of politics. If anything, their perception has been strengthened over time. Yet it is not because women are biologically different from men which causes them to act in a feminized way. The difference is a gender and not a sex difference. It is also determined by party identity and the gendered environment in which they act.

In the House of Commons, the women MPs consider that the alternative feminized style is regarded as less legitimate and less effective. They also experience pressure to conform to the masculinized style, a style of which many are critical. Yet, even if women politicians choose to adopt the masculinized norms, their ability to 'master' them is open to question. As one woman MP phrased it: 'Imagine if we all did start shouting and yelling ... then we would be strident ... you actually can't win.'[122] However, if women MPs choose to act like women there may be costs.

Furthermore, the responses from a number of the women MPs suggest that some of them are choosing not to engage fully in the Chamber because they do not wish to have to adopt its masculinized style. As one MP admitted, because she could not 'relate at all' to the 'ya-boo' style, she was 'finding other ways of ... getting questions [addressed]'. But if women MPs are 'turning away' from the Chamber, this raises the question of whether women MPs can still make a difference and act for women. It also raises the possibility that the particular women MPs who choose not to participate fully in the Commons' Chamber will not be regarded as fulfilling their roles as MPs.[123] If this happened, it might have repercussions in terms of women's individual career prospects, collectively for women's numerical representation in Parliament and in government as well as for the substantive representation of women.[124]

Nevertheless, if one wanted to argue for women's political presence on the basis that women representatives have a different style of politics, then new Labour women MPs in the 1997 Parliament provide supportive evidence: a majority consider that they have a different style of politics from their male parliamentary colleagues.

NOTES

1. P. Norris (1996), 'Women Politicians: Transforming Westminster?', in J. Lovenduski and P. Norris (eds), *Women in Politics* (Oxford: Oxford University Press), p. 93. C. Bochel and J. Briggs (2000), 'Do Women Make a Difference?', *Politics*, 20, 2: 66–7; F. Mackay (2001), *Love and Politics* (London: Continuum), p. 108. See also Mo Mowlam talking about the Women's Coalition in Northern Ireland (M. Mowlam [2002], *Momentum* [London: Hodder and Stoughton], p. 146).
2. Norris, 'Women Politicians', p. 100.
3. *Guardian* 3 May 1997; *Observer* 4 May 1997.
4. J. Lovenduski (1997), 'Gender Politics: a Breakthrough for Women?', *Parliamentary Affairs*, 50, 4: 717.
5. Interview 16 (24–11–97).
6. Interview 9 (29–10–97).
7. Interviews 9 (29–10–97), 15 (14–10–97), 18 (12–06–97), 2 (10–07–97) and 19 (10–12–97).
8. Interview 14 (03–07–97).
9. Interviews 23 (29–07–97) and 26 (30–07–97).
10. Interview 24 (07–04–97).
11. Interview 16 (24–11–97).
12. Interviews 18 (12–06–97) and 1 (04–12–97). Interview 29 (06–08–97) also talked of her experience of other new Labour women MPs as being supportive.
13. Interview 7 (09–97).
14. Interview 5 (23–06–97).
15. Interview 26 (30–07–97). This woman considered that during the debate women MPs were conscious of the different language adopted by men and women participants. See also interviews 14 (03–07–97) and 34 (19–06–97).
16. Interviews 9 (29–10–97), 15 (14–10–97) and 24 (07–04–97).
17. Interview 18 (12–06–97). Interview 11 (23–07–97) recalled a conversation with a woman who had been elected in the 1970s and who noted the 'oppressive attitudes' of men in the House.
18. Interview 15 (14–10–97). Prior to the 1997 general election this MP was a top-level public sector employee.
19. Interview 19 (10–12–97).
20. Interview 20 (01–08–97).
21. Interview 1 (04–12–97).
22. Interview 33 (19–06–97).
23. Interview 14 (03–07–97).
24. Interviews 17 (05–11–97) and 18 (12–06–97).
25. Interview 16 (24–11–97).
26. Interview 6 (12–11–97).
27. Interview 5 (23–06–97).
28. Interview 17 (05–11–97).
29. Interview 26 (30–07–97).
30. Interview 24 (07–04–97).
31. Interview 3 (18–12–97).
32. Interview 26 (30–07–97).
33. Interview 17 (05–11–97).
34. Interviews 1 (12–07–00), 2 (13–06–00), 3 (14–06–00), 4 (21–06–00), 5 (22–05–00), 7 (13–06–00), 8 (20–06–00), 9 (22–06–00), 14 (8–06–00), 15 (23–05–00), 16 (26–07–00), 18 (12–07–00), 23 (19–06–00), 24 (10–05–00) and 33 (13–06–00).
35. Interview 12 (14–05–00).
36. Interview 31 (10–07–00).
37. Interview 5 (22–05–00).
38. Interview 23 (19–06–00).
39. Interview 8 (20–06–00).
40. Interview 7 (13–06–00).
41. Interviews 31 (10–07–00), 2 (13–06–00) and 9 (22–06–00).
42. Interview 3 (14–06–00).

43. L. Karvonen, G. Djupsund and T. Carlson (1995), 'Political Language', in L. Karvonen and P. Selle (eds), *Women in Nordic Politics* (Aldershot: Dartmouth), pp. 343–79.
44. Interview 23 (19–06–00).
45. Interview 2 (13–06–00).
46. Interview 9 (22–06–00).
47. Interviews 2 (13–06–00), 3 (14–06–00), 14 (08–06–00), 15 (23–05–00), 18 (12–07–00), 22 (16–05–00), 23 (19–06–00), 24 (10–05–00) and 31 (10–07–00).
48. Interview 15 (23–05–00).
49. Interviews 2 (13–06–00), 9 (22–06–00) and 18 (12–07–00).
50. Interview 3 (14–06–00).
51. Interviews 15 (23–05–00) and 24 (21–06–00).
52. Interview 18 (12–07–00).
53. Interview 25 (21–06–00).
54. Interview 15 (23–05–00).
55. Interview 14 (08–06–00).
56. Interview 31 (10–07–00).
57. Interview 29 (15–05–00).
58. Interview 13 (13–06–00).
59. Interview 8 (20–06–00). See also interview 7 (13–06–00).
60. Interview 16 (26–07–00).
61. Interviews 14 (08–06–00), 29 (15–05–00) and 22 (16–05–00).
62. Interview 1 (12–07–00).
63. Interview 29 (15–05–00).
64. Interviews 1 (12–07–00), 2 (13–06–00), 7 (13–06–00), 22 (16–05–00) and 23 (19–06–00).
65. Interview 1 (12–07–00).
66. Interview 27 (17–05–00).
67. Interview 18 (12–07–00).
68. Interview 1 (12–07–00).
69. Interview 24 (10–05–00).
70. Interview 33 (13–06–00).
71. Interview 14 (8–06–00), 16 (26–07–00) and 29 (15–05–00).
72. Interview 13 (13–06–00).
73. Interview 3 (14–06–00) and 14 (8–06–00).
74. Interviews 1 (12–07–00), 3 (14–06–00), 9 (22–06–00), 14 (08–06–00) and 18 (12–07–00).
75. Interview 14 (08–06–00).
76. Interview 18 (12–07–00). The 'new men' are regarded as those whose life experiences are less structured by conventional gender roles. See Chapter 5.
77. Interviews 7 (13–06–00), 3 (14–06–00), 24 (10–05–00), 29 (15–05–00) and 31 (10–07–00).
78. Interviews 4 (21–06–00), 9 (22–06–00), 12 (15–06–00), 16 (26–07–00) and 24 (10–05–00).
79. Interview 25 (21–06–00).
80. Interview 9 (22–06–00).
81. Interview 24 (10–05–00).
82. Interview 8 (20–06–00).
83. Interviews 8 (20–06–00), 24 (10–05–00), 25 (21–06–00) and 29 (15–05–00).
84. Interview 25 (21–06–00).
85. Interview 18 (12–07–00).
86. Interview 3 (14–06–00).
87. Interview 7 (13–06–00).
88. Interviews 13 (13–06–00), 24 (10–05–00), 27 (17–05–00), 29 (15–05–00), 31 (10–07–00).
89. Interview 22 (16–05–00).
90. Interview 23 (19–06–00).
91. Interview 7 (13–06–00).
92. Interview 18 (12–07–00). A second MP considered that on another issue there was some Conservative support in private but that the Conservative women MPs were 'still stuck in using [a report] as a partisan point-scoring issue'. This, she considered, was 'very unhelpful' (interview 13 [13–06–00]).
93. Interview 22 (16–05–00).

94. In an interview with Jackie Ashley in the *Guardian* (27 January 2003), Helen Liddell, the Secretary of State for Scotland, 'hinted that some of her perceived toughness is a result of the system, not her personality'.
95. Interview 28 (12–07–00). See also interview 5 (22–05–00).
96. Interview 4 (21–06–00). See also interview 24 (10–05–00).
97. Interview 28 (12–07–00). See also interview 14 (8–06–00).
98. Interviews 4 (21–06–00), 14 (08–06–00), 16 (26–07–00) and 31 (10–07–00).
99. Interviews 14 (08–06–00), 15 (23–05–00), 16 (26–07–00) and 25 (21–06–00).
100. Interview 23 (19–06–00).
101. Interviews 25 (21–06–00) and 2 (13–06–00). One MP talked about how she did not know how she would have felt in the previous Parliament where the numbers of women were much less, implying that, for her, numbers matter (interview 29 [15–05–00]).
102. Interview 5 (22–05–00).
103. Interview 18 (12–07–00).
104. Interview 24 (10–05–00).
105. Interview 23 (19–06–00).
106. Interview 1 (12–07–00). She also suggested that some new men were also less likely to adopt the traditional masculinized norms of behaviour.
107. Interview 18 (12–07–00).
108. Interview 5 (22–05–00).
109. Interviews 2 (13–06–00) and 9 (22–06–00).
110. Interview 9 (22–06–00).
111. C. S. King (1995), 'Sex-role Identity and Decision-styles: How Gender Helps Explain the Paucity of Women at the Top', in G. Duerst-Lahti and R. M. Kelly (eds), *Gender, Power, Leadership and Governance* (Ann Arbor, MI: University of Michigan Press), p. 67.
112. Interview 7 (13–06–00).
113. Interview 9 (22–06–00).
114. Interview 13 (13–06–00).
115. Interview 15 (23–05–00).
116. Interview 4 (21–06–00).
117. Interview 9 (22–06–00).
118. Interview 33 (13–06–00).
119. Interview 5 (22–05–00).
120. Interview 24 (10–05–00).
121. Interview 31 (10–07–00).
122. Interview 22 (16–05–00).
123. Interview 25 (21–06–00).
124. For reports of the resignation of the Secretary of State for Education Estelle Morris in 2002, in which the male style of politics is widely discussed, see the *Guardian* 24 and 25 October 2002.

11

Conclusion: Theorizing Women Making a Difference

While the 101 Labour women MPs in the 1997 Parliament have been acknowledged for effecting some changes – adding colour to the House, changing the food served in Parliament's restaurants to include ciabatta and mozzarella with 'menus boast[ing] tiny hearts printed next to low-fat offerings and tiny ticks to denote vegetarian'[1] – the dominant representation of them has been one of loyalty, timidity and tears. Most importantly, they are said to have failed women. The shadow of the reduction in lone parent allowance loomed large over their heads.

It was not supposed to have been like this. Although feminist conceptions of representation do not premise the case for women's political presence solely on the substantive representation of women – the case is also made in terms of justice, symbolic representation, and on the basis that women politicians have a different style of politics – it was this stronger claim of a link between women's descriptive and substantive representation that had intuitive appeal. What was one to make of the apparent disjuncture between feminist theories and the *actualité* of the substantive representation of women by women representatives? Were those who had rejected the argument for descriptive representation right all along?

This book started from the premise that a more nuanced conceptualization of women's political representation is more likely to emerge through theoretically informed empirical research. The study of real women – of explicating how, and on what basis, women representatives perceive and practise the representation of women – would provide 'situated knowledge' that would help us reconsider traditional and feminist conceptions of representation.[2] In other words, to know more about the relationship between women's descriptive, symbolic and substantive representation and whether women representatives have a different political style (between the presence of women representatives and the difference they make) it is useful, if not necessary, to study the attitudes and behaviour of women representatives in real political environments.

RECLAIMING DESCRIPTIVE REPRESENTATION: WOMEN'S POLITICAL PRESENCE

Many feminists have reclaimed descriptive representation, arguing that who our representatives are matters after all.[3] But it matters not just to feminists; for many of the newly elected Labour women MPs it matters too. Many agreed that the House of Commons should be descriptively representative in terms of sex. Moreover, they argued for women's political presence *because* they accept the link between the identity of the representative and the representative's attitudes and behaviour. According to the women MPs, the presence of women in Parliament is not simply about justice, symbolism or a feminized style of politics, it is about acting for women (although it is about all of these too). Indeed, from the 1997 interview data, it looked as if many of the newly present Labour women MPs would seek to act for women: the substantive representation of women by the new Labour women MPs looked promising.

CRITICAL MASS: NUMBERS ARE NOT EVERYTHING

Why should the presence of women representatives make a difference? When theorizing the relationship between women's descriptive and substantive representation simply determining the numbers of women present in particular political institutions is inadequate. This is not to say that numbers do not matter, but the concept of critical mass hides more than it reveals.[4] It tells us nothing about the party identity of the women present, nor does it tell us anything about whether they accept gendered analysis. It also ignores the particular context within which the women representatives act. The relationship between women's presence and women making a difference for women is therefore better conceptualized in terms of recognizing different women representatives operating in different gendered environments.[5] This approach suggests that empirical research should identify and account for the places and conditions under which women representatives 'act for' women.

THE COMPLICATED RELATIONSHIP BETWEEN WOMEN'S DESCRIPTIVE AND SUBSTANTIVE REPRESENTATION: GENDER AND PARTY

Mindful of essentialism, Mansbridge's more sophisticated understanding of descriptive representation where 'shared experiences' rather than 'visible characteristics' are crucial in determining the relationship between characteristics and actions, is of great theoretical importance.[6] Women substantively represent women not on the basis of shared sex but on the basis of shared gendered experiences. The new Labour women MPs were similarly aware of this distinction. The basis upon which they claimed to act for women was their shared gendered experiences rather than any simple notion of shared sex.

Yet, as was stated in Chapter 3, too often there is an unconscious elision between the substantive representation of women by women representatives and the feminist substantive representation of women by feminist women representatives. But feminist minds must not be confused with women's bodies. Some women representatives may reject 'feminism', but they may still act for women, albeit in a different way (and one which feminists might find unappealing).[7] Recognizing this demands that gender is theorized in a more complex way than a simple feminist/non-feminist dichotomy. Thus, rather than 'attitudinal feminism' being a predictor of acting for women, establishing that so many of the new Labour women MPs identified themselves as feminists tell us about the likely direction of their 'acting for' women – in a feminist rather than non-feminist direction.[8]

Any comprehensive account of the relationship between women's presence and the substantive representation of women in Westminster must also recognize that women MPs are party representatives. Although in principle women representatives may share a feminized agenda, one cannot presume that all women will agree on, or that there is, a 'women's' response to that agenda. In practice, the nature of the substantive representation is influenced by the representatives' party (at least in political systems where parties are dominant) as well as their gender identity. This is not to argue, in a reductionist way, that women representatives of particular parties think *x* or *y* about a particular women's concern; there is room for intra-party differences. To illustrate: a woman MP's analysis of the childcare issue will be informed by the way in which she conceptualizes both the role of the state in providing childcare (party identity) as well as the way in which she considers women's roles as the carers of children (gender identity). Thus, if a particular woman believes in a minimal state and that women's primary role is to bear and care for children, she is unlikely to support the state provision of childcare.

The importance of rejecting a simple deterministic relationship between women's presence and acting for women and of recognizing the intersection of gender and party identities is supported by the empirical data presented in this book. As one MP acknowledged, not all women MPs seek to act for women – a statement that reflects Phillips's warning that the substantive representation of women by women representatives is not guaranteed.[9] Furthermore, although many of the women MPs believed that their presence meant that women's concerns would be articulated, they recognized at the same time the impact of party identity: 'It's when you come to the next stage about proposed policy and solutions then [you] get the divergence.'

In the discussions concerning cross-party co-operation with other women MPs, women Liberal Democrat MPs were depicted as having a 'genuine interest in women' and 'similar views on certain things' to the Labour women MPs. In contrast, Conservative women were 'different' and greater co-operation with Conservative women MPs was not considered likely. However, gender and party identities are not fixed. There may well be a greater likelihood of cross-party co-operation between Labour and Conservative women MPs over time, as the younger Conservative women 'tend to be more feminist', as one MP put it.

GENDERED ENVIRONMENTS

Whether women representatives seek to act for women is one question; determining whether they can, in practice, act for women is another.[10] This is because establishing women representatives' gender and party identity tells us something of the complicated relationship between women's descriptive and substantive representation, but it does not tell us anything about the environments in which women representatives seek to act for women.

By looking at Parliament, government and the constituency (Chapters 6–10) a more complex picture is painted of when and how women MPs act for women. The interview data in 1997 and 2000 are strongly suggestive of a link between women's descriptive and substantive representation (Chapters 5–9). In 2000 nearly two-thirds argued that they had articulated women's concerns in the House, more than one-half considered that women's constituents had accessed them in greater numbers and more than three-quarters that their presence had engendered contact between themselves and women's organizations in the constituency.

While many of the women MPs claimed (as discussed in Chapter 7) that they had articulated women's concerns in Parliament since their election – 'if we hadn't had all these women here ... I don't think this childcare strategy ... would have had all the money it's had' – there was also recognition that it was not always possible to act for women. In part this is because of party discipline. But it is also about the acceptance of women's concerns and feminist analysis. There was a widely held belief that if a woman MP is ambitious she cannot afford to be regarded as acting for women too often or too forcefully. Indeed, one MP felt that she had 'better not be seen to be just identified with' women's concerns because of her association with women's concerns in her pre-parliamentary career, while a second considered that feminized change would only come about when women MPs were no longer 'threatened' or 'endangered'.

However, the House of Commons should not be regarded as a single space in which women MPs act. Although the Chamber of the House was not considered particularly conducive to acting for and like women, the women MPs identified other spaces within the House where they could act for women. MPs considered that they had been able to re-gender the agenda of their select committees and they felt comfortable discussing women's concerns in the PLP's Women's Group.

Similarly, women MPs were confident that their presence in the constituency had made a real difference. They claimed that women constituents and women's groups were accessing them and raising women's concerns (Chapter 6). In the constituency women MPs seem to find it easier to act for women as they represent the interests of individuals (particularly those whose identity or interests they share) and because party identity and inter-party conflict are often less important. This finding, rather than undermining the main argument, suggests that the relative importance of gender and party identities may differ in respect of the different sites of representation.

How women do politics is also a determinant of the substantive representation of women. Many of the women MPs considered that there was such a thing as a feminized style of politics (Chapter 10). However, many also considered that their style was less well regarded. Although many of those who were critical of the dominant, masculinized style resisted the pressure to adopt it, there was some recognition that women MPs' ability to transform the parliamentary political agenda is likely to be reduced if they act like women; acting for women might be dependent upon acting like men.

WOMEN'S DIFFERENCES

As feminist research and practice has demonstrated, any simple understanding of 'women' is misplaced. If women are not the same, and experience the world in different ways, the basis upon which women can act for women – shared gender experiences – is questioned. As a consequence, the political presence of different kinds of women seems necessary, as well as desirable.

Yet, Mansbridge's claim that women representatives need not have personally shared the same particular experiences because of women's wider shared experiences and their more diffuse consciousness of 'being a woman' in a gendered society is an important theoretical development.[11] If she is correct, then, arguably, the class and ethnic identity of the women representatives present in our political fora is irrelevant, at least in terms of the substantive representation of women. Thus, the fact that the 1997 intake of Labour women MPs was overwhelmingly white and middle-class is rendered unproblematic in relation to the substantive representation of women, even if it remains problematic in terms of justice and symbolic representation.

While many of the women MPs understood the basis upon which they could act for women as premised upon shared gender identity, this is not to say that they were not, at the same time, cognizant of the complexity of women's identities. And while there was a sense that acting for black women was different from representing white women – as one MP stated, she would have to 'do some work' and 'listen more' – there was also an appreciation among the responses that women's gender is shared by women who also have other different identities. The new Labour women MPs' discussion of women's differences suggests that they do not perceive that this prevents the substantive representation of women. Their interpretations support Mansbridge's analysis that women need not have personally shared the same experiences in order for them to be in a position to act for other women. Women representatives' appreciation of 'being a woman' in a gendered society combines with specific actions, for example, listening to and establishing relationships with different women. The discussion in Chapter 6 emphasized the MPs' belief that black and Asian women were contacting them and raising their concerns with them in the constituency.

Now, it might be that some will claim that this is the same argument that underpins the assertion that men can act for women. If men representatives listen to women, establish contact and lines of accountability with them, then women representatives do not need to be present. However, the difference is the presumption that shared gender identity is perceived to function still between women representatives and the women they are acting for in a way that it cannot with men or, at least, cannot with most men.

WOMEN'S LEGISLATIVE RECRUITMENT

If women should be present in our political forum as a guarantee (albeit unguaranteed) for the substantive representation of women, achieving women's numerical representation takes on even greater importance. And it is by no means an easy task. It took most of the twentieth century to get the percentage of the House of Commons that was female above 10 per cent.

Although explanations for women's numerical representation are multidimensional, Chapter 3 demonstrated that in 1997 the key to understanding the increased numbers of women MPs elected to the House of Commons was the Labour Party's policy of AWS. However, the policy did not transform the Labour Party into a party at one with selecting women as parliamentary candidates.[12] There was a great deal of intra-party hostility, little support from the party leadership, and at times the policy was subverted on the ground. The new Labour women MPs were, though, overwhelmingly supportive of AWS: they recognized how important it was. They also recognized that many of the women who were able to overcome the barriers of legislative recruitment are atypical women – a significant insight that explicitly links women's numerical representation with other concepts of representation.

In the absence of mechanisms of positive discrimination in the Labour Party, or any other party for that matter – AWS having been declared illegal in 1996 – the numbers of women elected to the House of Commons in 2001 unsurprisingly declined. Policies of exhortation and the provision of training for women seeking candidature failed to deliver. It seemed that the parties had little demand for women candidates. Achieving women's greater numerical representation appears, therefore, dependent upon 'long-term policies of positive discrimination'.[13] Moreover, the discussion in Chapter 3 underlines the importance of recognizing that analysis of women's legislative recruitment must be a continual process, and one which is cognizant of changes in the recruitment procedures of political parties (as well as changes in any of the other levels of analysis contained within the explanatory frameworks).

The most important change that has occurred since the 2001 general election is the passage of the Sex Discrimination (Election Candidates) Act. The passage of this Act constitutes an important example of women representatives making a difference in politics by 'acting for' women. In this instance, the reality supports the theoretical link suggested in feminist theory between women's descriptive and substantive representation: male members of both Houses (especially backbenchers) were conspicuous by their absence. As Ann Widdecombe asked: 'Are all the men in this place sound asleep?' Yet although most male members chose not to attend the debates, those who did supported the Bill. In fact, the only MPs who opposed the Bill at Second Reading in the Commons were all women, a fact that highlights the importance of recognizing that the relationship between women's descriptive and substantive representation is complicated.

NOTES

1. *Guardian* 17 September 1999.
2. J. Squires (1999), *Gender in Political Theory* (Cambridge: Polity Press), p. 227; F. Mackay (2001), *Love and Politics* (London: Continuum).
3. A. Phillips (1998), 'Democracy and Representation', in A. Phillips (ed.), *Feminism and Politics* (Oxford: Oxford University Press), pp. 224–40.
4. D. Dodson (2001), 'The Impact of Women in Congress', paper presented to the Annual Meeting of APSA Women and Politics Special Session, San Francisco; D. Dahlerup (1988), 'From a Small to a Large Minority', *Scandinavia Political Studies*, 11, 4; J. Lovenduski (2001), 'Women and Politics', in P. Norris (ed.), *Britain Votes 2001* (Oxford: Oxford University Press); B. Reingold (2000), *Representing Women* (Chapel Hill, NC: University of North Carolina Press).
5. Lovenduski, 'Women and Politics'; G. Duerst-Lahti (2001), 'Institutions, Ideologies, and the Possibility of Equal Political Participation', paper presented to the Annual Meeting of APSA Women and Politics Special Session, San Francisco; Dodson, 'The Impact of Women in Congress'.
6. J. Mansbridge (1999), 'Should Blacks Represent Blacks and Women Represent Women?', *Journal of Politics*, 6, 3: 635–6.
7. Dodson, 'The Impact of Women in Congress', pp. 19–20.

8. See Chapter 5. J. Lovenduski (1990), 'Feminism and West European Politics: an Overview', in D. W. Urwin and W. E. Paterson (eds), *Politics in Western Europe Today* (London: Longman), p. 158.
9. A. Phillips (1995), *A Politics of Presence* (Oxford: Oxford University Press), p. 83.
10. J. Lovenduski (1997), 'Gender Politics', *Parliamentary Affairs*, 50, 4: 708–19.
11. Mansbridge, 'Should Blacks Represent Blacks and Women Represent Women?'.
12. B. Criddle (1997), 'MPs and Candidates', in D. Butler and D. Kavanagh (eds), *The British General Election of 1997* (Basingstoke: Macmillan), pp. 186–209.
13. J. Squires and M. Wickham-Jones (2001), *Women in Parliament* (Manchester: EOC), p. xii; L. Shepherd-Robinson and J. Lovenduski (2002), *Women and Candidate Selection* (London: Fawcett Society), p. 2; M. Russell (2000), *Women's Representation in UK Politics* (London: The Constitution Unit); M. Russell (2001), *The Women's Representation Bill* (London: The Constitution Unit).

EPILOGUE

The Sex Discrimination (Election Candidates) Act

The Labour Party's 2001 election manifesto committed a returning Labour government to introduce legislation that would permit positive discrimination in the selection of parliamentary candidates. Belatedly, Tony Blair had realized that the numbers of women in the House of Commons would decline at the 2001 general election.[1] As a consequence both of internal (from women MPs and party activists) and external pressure (from women's lobby groups such as the Fawcett Society and the EOC) to act, and emboldened by academic research that demonstrated that legal change was possible,[2] the Queen's speech of June 2001 promised 'legislation to allow political parties to make positive moves to increase the representation of women in public life'. Although the Bill had to be introduced in the first session to be effective, as selections for the devolved bodies and the next general election would take place in 2002/3, it only just made it into the Queen's speech: Patricia Hewitt (not yet Women's Minister) and Stephen Byers (then Secretary for Transport, Local Government and the Regions) had to fight for its inclusion during Cabinet and Blair's support was vital 'to guarantee its inclusion'.[3]

The Sex Discrimination (Election Candidates) Bill was introduced in the Commons on 17 October 2001. The Bill sought to exclude from the operation of the Sex Discrimination Act 1975 and the Sex Discrimination (Northern Ireland) Order 1976 certain matters relating to the selection of candidates by political parties. It introduces a new section 42A to the Sex Discrimination Act. This dis-applies the anti-discrimination rules in Parts 2 to 4 of the Act (including section 13) from arrangements which 'regulate the selection by a political party registered under the Political Parties, Elections and Referendums Act 2000 of candidates in an election for Parliament' and 'are adopted for the purpose of reducing the inequality in the numbers of men and women elected, as candidates of *that* party, to be members of the body concerned'. The Bill's remit includes elections for Westminster, the European Parliament, the Scottish Parliament and National Assembly for Wales and local government elections, although it excludes election for the Mayor of London and other directly elected Mayors.

The Bill was permissive rather than prescriptive. As Stephen Byers, the Secretary of State for Transport, Local Government and the Regions made clear, it allows political parties choice and flexibility … [it] does not force political parties to take any steps'. Although the government prefers to use the term 'positive action', the Bill would allow procedures and practices that are usually considered 'positive discrimination'.[4] Clause 3, a 'sunset' clause, causes the provisions of the Bill to expire at the end of 2015, unless a Statutory Instrument is passed to ensure its continuation.

The Bill received its Second Reading in the House of Commons on 24 October, had its Committee Stage on 6 and 8 November, with the Report Stage and Third Reading on 14 November. Its First Reading in the Lords was on 15 November, its Second on 20 December and, with no amendments tabled, the motion for Committee stage was discharged. The Bill received its Third Reading (without debate) on 28 January 2002. It received Royal Assent on 26 February 2002.

In the Commons there was front bench cross-party support for the Bill. At Second Reading in the Commons all but three of the MPs who spoke (Ann Widdecombe, Virginia Bottomley and Lady Hermon, Conservatives and Ulster Unionist respectively) supported the Bill, and it passed without a division either at Second or Third Reading in the Commons. The Commons Committee stage of the Bill was also relatively consensual. In the Lords there was similarly no division and the Bill was debated only at Second Reading even though there had been expectations within the government that the Bill would meet with stiff opposition.[5]

This consensus in favour of the legislation, in both Houses and across parties, might have reflected a conversion on behalf of those who had previously been hostile to positive discrimination and/or AWS. Indeed, Theresa May (then Shadow Secretary of State for Transport) admitted at Second Reading in the Commons that 'parties move on in their attitudes'. It might also have reflected a changed political environment in which it was no longer acceptable to oppose the principle of the Bill, at least among parliamentarians in Parliament: not one MP or peer argued that women should not be present in greater numbers in the House of Commons. But parliamentary support for the Bill also reflected the Bill's permissive rather than prescriptive nature. There almost certainly would have been greater inter-party argument and greater opposition in general had the Bill forced political parties to introduce positive action and/or discrimination.

There was disagreement among parliamentarians regarding whether the Sex Discrimination (Election Candidates) Bill was compatible with the European Union Law on equal treatment (the Equal Treatment Directive [76/207/EEC] which provides for equal treatment in relation to access to employment and promotion, vocational training and working conditions), the European Convention on Human Rights and other international human rights law. The government confidently put forward its belief that the Bill was compatible with both EU legislation and the UK's international human rights obligations.[6] The UN Human Rights Committee (General Comment No. 18 on the International Covenant for Civil and Political Rights [ICCPR]), Article 7 of the Convention on the Elimination of All Forms of Discrimination Against Women (ICEDAW, 1979) and Article 4 of the 1986 UN Convention on the Elimination of All Forms of Discrimination Against Women (CEDAW) all allow for positive action.[7]

Notwithstanding the government's confidence, opposition MPs continued to contest the government's interpretations in the Commons and Lords debates and in the Commons Standing Committee and Report Stage. Indeed, Lord Lester of Herne Hill QC, a specialist in human rights and discrimination law, argued that the Bill was only compatible with EU law because 'it does not *require* any action which could conceivably breach the principle of equality, properly understood, which includes proportionate and necessary measures to tackle inequality'.

THE PASSAGE OF THE SEX DISCRIMINATION (ELECTION CANDIDATES) BILL

In arguing for the Bill, many MPs and peers, from all parties, stated that women should be present in the House of Commons in greater, if not proportionate, numbers. Even the three women MPs who spoke against the Bill at Second Reading in the Commons supported this principle. While many of the speakers, either explicitly or implicitly, argued that women were currently 'under-represented' in Parliament, they did so in ways that suggested that the meaning of women's political representation was simple or uncontested and which left untheorized why women's presence matters.

Arguments that premise women's political presence on a feminized style of politics found only little support in both Houses. This is not to say that members did not believe that women practise a different style of politics or were not critical of the masculinized norms of the House, merely that they did not employ this argument in support of the Bill.

MPs and peers were more supportive of symbolic arguments. They were therefore more in tune with feminists who argue that women's presence is symbolically important than with Lord Norton, who argued that symbolic representation was 'not central to the debate' on the Bill.

The parliamentary debates also saw discussion of women's substantive representation. Yet, for the most part, MPs and peers chose not to employ this argument, at least not in its strongest interpretation, and some MPs rejected this argument outright. However, there was a tendency for MPs and peers to articulate a weaker interpretation, namely, the argument that women's political presence brings 'women's experiences' into Parliament. At the same time they appeared reluctant to accept the assumption that women MPs act for women, even though their statements imply that women's presence will make a difference. This reticence is also evident where individual members make conflicting statements, rejecting the substantive representation of women argument, arguing that women do bring 'women's experiences' into politics and that Labour women MPs had acted for women since their election in greater numbers in 1997. Again, this suggests concern that members prefer to leave the argument that women representatives will act for women implicit.

The apparent reluctance of many MPs and peers to articulate explicitly a strong interpretation of women's substantive representation might have reflected the contested nature of the link between women's descriptive and substantive representation. That women MPs have different experiences from men might appear to MPs and peers (and others) as self-evident, whereas arguing that women should be present in the House of Commons to ensure women's substantive representation might be perceived as more likely to be challenged. Nevertheless, it is important to recognize that a number of Labour MPs and peers, including current and ex-Cabinet ministers, were prepared to argue for women's presence on the basis that women MPs act for women. This was an important party difference.

The most widely articulated argument in support of the Bill was, however, the justice argument. Members of all parties in both Houses considered that it was the difficulties faced by women seeking (s)election that justified the Bill, in particular that women prospective parliamentary candidates suffer negative discrimination in the parties' selection processes. MP after MP and peer after peer came forward to admit to the existence of selectorate discrimination.

That members premised their arguments in support of the Bill on the justice argument – the least contentious concept of representation – might, of course, have been strategic. The justice argument does not carry with it other conceptions of representation, in particular the attendant assumption that women representatives will make a difference or 'act for' women. Thus, mainstream conceptions of representation, such as party or constituency representation, are not disturbed. As a consequence, MPs and peers might have felt that it was a 'safe' argument to articulate in support of women's political presence.

CONCLUSION

The enactment of the Sex Discrimination (Election Candidates) Bill is a cause for celebration for those who advocate women's greater political presence. It is, as Lovenduski states, a watershed in British politics: British political parties are now permitted to introduce positive discrimination in the selection of candidates.[8] The Act's easy passage through Parliament – where its principle that there should be greater numbers of women elected to the House of Commons was uncontested – also suggests that the political climate has finally changed. Although an important part of the explanation for the Act's successful passage in Parliament was its permissive rather than prescriptive nature, the passage of the Sex Discrimination (Election Candidates) Bill constitutes, nevertheless, an important example of women representatives making a difference in politics by 'acting for' women.

Yet, because the Sex Discrimination (Election Candidates) Act permits, but does not prescribe, what political parties should do, women's political presence is still not assured in the UK. Each political party must decide if and how to respond to the legislation. Arguments for measures that have been proven to increase the number of women MPs, such as AWS, still need to be won. During the debates in Parliament party differences were apparent. The Conservatives made their hostility to AWS clear; the Liberal Democrats were left lamenting their Party Conference's rejection of AWS in 2002 and calling for proportional representation. In contrast, there was strong support for AWS from the Labour benches in both the

Commons and Lords, suggesting that Labour women MPs and peers would argue for their reintroduction.

Labour did, indeed, agree to introduce AWS in 'at least 50 per cent of the seats in every region where the sitting Labour MP is retiring' with a target of 35 per cent women MPs in each English and Welsh region. Sitting MPs intending to stand down had to indicate their intention by 23 December 2002. These seats could then volunteer to be an AWS. But if there were not enough voluntary AWS, then the National Executive Committee (NEC) would impose them. Any MP declaring their intention to stand down after the deadline would automatically be classed as a late retirement and declared an AWS, although the NEC retained the power to authorize exceptions in special circumstances.

With this deadline now passed the picture is far from rosy.[9] Only a dozen or so Labour MPs announced their intention to retire. This figure throws doubt on whether there will be sufficient turnover to achieve the Labour Party's target. Women's increased representation in the PLP has become dependent upon late retirements and the NEC not parachuting 'favoured sons' into these seats. There are also concerns that if all the vacant seats became AWS, hostility against women and positive discrimination will, once again, become vocal. An apparent conflict between the selection of women and the selection of ethnic minority candidates has already been articulated and differential treatment of 'favoured white sons' hinted at.[10]

The Conservatives, who have historically had problems of supply as well as demand, have acknowledged their difficulties in (s)electing women for Parliament. Theresa May, the Party Chairman, has repeatedly exhorted local associations to select a greater diversity of candidates. Furthermore, the party has engaged in greater 'outreach' efforts and reformed their selection procedures. Acceptance on the party's Approved List, the first stage in being selected as a parliamentary candidate, is determined by successful attendance at a Parliamentary Assessment Board (PAB). In reviewing its procedures the party drew on the services of Professor Jo Silvester, an occupational psychologist. An MP's job description was drawn up which reflected the reality of MPs' varied roles – it would 'show local associations that the skills of being an MP are not just about standing up and speaking'[11] – and aspirant candidates now undertake a range of practical exercises and tests that reflect this. Assessors were also fully trained.

Notwithstanding these positive developments, developments which it was felt would demonstrate women's competencies in terms of the new definition of what makes a good MP (communication and intellectual skills, relating to people, leading and motivating, having resilience and drive, and political communication),[12] May's exhortation appears to be falling on deaf ears. Although greater numbers of women are now on the Approved List and are therefore more likely to be seen by the party's selectorates, the expectation that women will be, as a consequence, selected has not been fulfilled. It seems that candidates are, *contra* May, still selected on the basis of who the local association 'are going to enjoy having a drink with on a Sunday morning':[13] only nine women have been selected to stand in 60 of the party's winnable seats. Moreover, one prospective women candidate overheard the chairwoman of the Conservative Women's Club (*sic*) state: 'Up from London, and single – but you know, we did feel we ought to have at least one woman on the list.'[14]

That there is a 'tension' between the objectives of those who wish to see an increase in the numbers of women MPs and local selectorates' independence in selecting their candidate is clear and is recognized by Central Office. Yet, in February 2003 May remained optimistic that subsequent selections would see greater numbers of women selected.[15] Only time will tell if her optimism that 'good women' will be selected is well placed. And it will be interesting to see what other options might then be considered. Although opposed to AWS, May has, in the past, advocated 50:50 sex shortlists[16] (even though the efficacy of such mechanisms were called into question in 2001).[17] Whether she chooses to go down this road and/or whether she is in a position to do so, in a party suspicious of, if not hostile to, positive action and positive discrimination, remains to be seen.[18]

The Liberal Democrats' procedures for selecting candidates for Parliament are guided by rules that repeatedly emphasize the importance of fairness, objectivity and equal opportunities. Prospective candidates must be approved, members of the Selection Committee should be trained (and should be composed of 'a balanced number of men and women') and clear selection criteria used. The party also has a sex quota at the shortlisting stage:

> Subject to there being a sufficient number of applicants of each sex, shortlists of three or four must include at least one member of each sex and shortlists of five or six must include at least two members of each sex (the One-third Rule); there must also be due regard for the representation of ethnic minorities.

The Liberal Democrats also have the Gender Balance Task Force (GBTF), an organization set up to increase women's participation through mentoring, training and support. Yet while there is clear support for positive discrimination among some of the women in the party, especially the older women, and the party leadership, this is countered, particularly by young women. It looks, therefore, as though the Liberal Democrats will fail to respond to the opportunities provided by the Sex Discrimination (Election Candidates) Act. Until greater numbers of the party are supportive of positive discrimination it is unlikely that the GBTF will seek even to put the issue back on the agenda. In the meantime, they are left trying to ensure that its selection procedures are fair and that 'confident' and 'trained' women are present when local selectorates select their candidates.

NOTES

1. J. Lovenduski (2001), 'Women and Politics', in P. Norris (ed.), *Britain Votes 2001* (Oxford: Oxford University Press).
2. M. Russell (2000), *Women's Representation in UK Politics* (London: The Constitution Unit); M. Russell (2001), *The Women's Representation Bill* (London: The Constitution Unit).
3. Lovenduski, 'Women and Politics', p. 192.
4. J. Lovenduski (1993), 'Introduction: the Dynamics of Gender and Party', in J. Lovenduski and P. Norris (eds), *Gender and Party Politics* (London: Sage), pp. 8–11.
5. Private information.
6. Russell, *Women's Representation in UK Politics*; Russell, *The Women's Representation Bill.*
7. Russell, *The Women's Representation Bill.*
8. Lovenduski, 'Women and Politics', p. 193.
9. *Guardian* 27 December 2002, 24 December 2002, 31 December 2002.
10. 'Blocking of Asian candidates stirs row over Labour shortlists' (*Guardian* 29 January 2003) and 'Labour can trade gender for race' (*Guardian* 10 January 2003).
11. *Guardian* 22 January 2003 and 3 February 2003.
12. *Guardian* 3 February 2003.
13. *Guardian* 3 February 2003.
14. *Observer* 26 January 2003.
15. *Guardian* 3 February 2003.
16. 'Tories Appoint First Chairwoman', *Guardian* 24 July 2002.
17. J. Squires and M. Wickham-Jones (2001), *Women in Parliament* (Manchester: EOC), p. xii; L. Shepherd-Robinson and J. Lovenduski (2002), *Women and Candidate Selection* (London: Fawcett Society), p. 2; Lovenduski, 'Women and Politics', p. 187.
18. *Independent* 8 January 2003. One candidate, Sue Catling (an advocate of positive discrimination), has been subject to, in her opinion, a 'witch hunt' by her local association, which, she feels, is seeking to push her 'out by a campaign of sexism'. It should, however, be noted that she has received support from Central Office and senior politicians such as Gillian Shephard (*Telegraph* 31 January 2003, 8 February 2003, 11 March 2002, 8 March 2002).

APPENDIX 1

Research Design and Research Methods

This book is based on interviews with more than half of the Labour women MPs first elected in 1997. They were interviewed at two points during the 1997 Parliament, first in 1997 and then in the summer of 2000. In 1997 34 of the 65 newly elected Labour women MPs were interviewed. Three years on, 23 of these MPs agreed to be reinterviewed. The decision to interview only women MPs reflected the research aims but also follows a tradition of feminist research.[1]

The participating new Labour women MPs in both 1997 and 2000 broadly reflected the whole population of newly elected Labour women MPs with regard to a range of characteristics, including age, size of majority and socio-economic breakdown of constituencies. However, being selected on an all-women shortlist (AWS) was a statistically significant difference between the participating and non-participating women MPs in 1997. Of the 34 new Labour women MPs interviewed in 1997, 23 were selected on endorsed all-women shortlists compared with 12 out of the 31 new Labour women MPs who did not participate. The interviewed women were also more likely to represent constituencies with higher percentages of professional/managerial constituents.

Most of the interviews on both occasions were conducted at Westminster, either in the MPs' offices, in the tearooms or on the terrace. One interview in 1997 took place in the MP's home. A couple of interviews were conducted over the phone. Most of the interviews lasted approximately one hour and were tape-recorded. Anonymity was guaranteed. The MPs' responses were transcribed. Where the presentation of part of a transcript was thought likely to reveal the identity of the woman, thereby undermining the anonymity guarantee, permission to reproduce the statement was sought or the number of the interview removed from the text.[2]

The interviews were based upon interview guides (presented in Appendix 2). Interview guides engendered 'guided conversations'[3] in which the women MPs were able to talk both at length and in depth about how they conceived and experienced representation.[4] I hoped that the women MPs' situated knowledge would throw new light on feminist conceptions of representation.[5]

During the interviews the women were able to talk about what they considered 'important and relevant' 'in their own words'.[6] They could demonstrate why they held particular attitudes and opinions. Moreover, the coherency of their arguments could be examined and, if necessary (for example, if their responses appeared 'less than frank', something elite interviews are prone to), probes could be introduced so that their responses could be clarified and elaborated upon.[7]

My observations of the women MPs during the interview conversations also constitute data and helped in the interpretation of the interview transcripts.[8] The intonation of the women MPs' statements, the 'knowing smile' or accompanying laughter helped me to analyse a particular woman MP's perspective or argument. Having a woman interview other women is sometimes said to enhance the quality of the interview conversation.[9] In this instance, arguably, it increased the numbers of new Labour women MPs who were prepared to participate, especially in 2000.

I acknowledge that the interview data are the new Labour women MPs' perceptions and experiences of representation rather than observations of their behaviour. Moreover, I accept, as Lovenduski and Norris point out, that 'without independent verification it is difficult to evaluate the validity of self-reported claims'.[10] Thus, I recognize that few strong claims about the behaviour of the women MPs can be made on the basis of these data. Nevertheless, by drawing on two data sets it is possible to explore the attitudes of the women MPs at two points in the 1997 Parliament, that is, before and after they had acquired experience as MPs.

In addition to my interview data, Chapter 8 draws on research by Philip Cowley. The data were gathered by Philip Cowley and Mark Stuart as part of a project into MPs' voting in the 1997 Parliament, funded by the Leverhulme Trust and the University of Hull. The data are the complete voting records of the 1997 Parliament, along with some data from previous Parliaments, two surveys of British MPs (the 1997 British Representation Survey [BRS] and the Study of Parliament Group Survey [SPG]), and approximately 90 interviews with male and female MPs conducted by Philip Cowley between 1997 and 2001.

The published records of divisions (that is, votes) yields a mass of what David Truman termed 'hard data' about the voting of MPs.[11] Yet the data are not perfect. Printing errors (such as the names of MPs being mixed up) are not frequent but neither are they rare. Some errors are obvious (such as when a minister votes against their own government, for example), but others have to be (and were) resolved by checking with the MPs concerned. A further drawback of divisions in the House of Commons is that, unlike in some legislative chambers (including the Scottish Parliament, for example), abstentions cannot be formally recorded.[12] The party managers (the whips) may formally sanction an absence from a vote – it may be accidental or it may be deliberate. There is no information on the record that allows us to establish, at least not systematically, the causes of absences. For the purposes of systematic analysis over time, therefore, we have to rely on the votes cast.

The 1997 BRS, directed by Pippa Norris in collaboration with Joni Lovenduski, Anthony Heath, Roger Jowell and John Curtice, was a national survey of prospective parliamentary candidates and MPs from all major parties standing in the 1997 British general election. The survey was conducted in mid-1996 and garnered a total of 999 positive responses (a response rate of 61 per cent). Of these, the data set records 277 respondents as having been elected in May 1997, of whom 179 were Labour.

The SPG survey, directed by Michael Rush and Philip Giddings, looked at the socialization of British MPs. Questionnaires were sent in 1999 to all newly elected MPs and to a sample of longer-serving MPs, producing an overall positive response rate of 44 per cent, of which 129 respondents were Labour MPs.

NOTES

1. S. Reinharz (1992), *Feminist Methods in Social Research* (Oxford: Oxford University Press), p. 19; Chapman cited in V. Randall (1991), 'Feminism and Political Analysis', *Political Studies*, 39: 520.
2. The Political Studies Association (2000), 'Guidelines for Good Professional Conduct', www.psa.ac.uk/about/Publications/Professional_Conduct; S. Sarantakos (1998), *Social Research* (Basingstoke: Macmillan), p. 24.
3. Lofland cited in N. Fielding (1993), 'Qualitative Interviewing', in N. Gilbert (ed.), *Researching Social Life* (London: Sage), p. 136.
4. F. Devine (1995), 'Qualitative Methods', in D. Marsh and G. Stoker (eds), *Theory and Methods in Social Science* (Basingstoke: Macmillan), p. 138; Fielding, 'Qualitative Interviewing', p. 138.
5. F. Mackay (2001), *Love and Politics* (London: Continuum), p. 13.
6. J. B. Manheim and R. C. Rich (1995), *Empirical Political Analysis* (London: Longman), p. 162; Reinharz, *Feminist Methods in Social Research*, p. 19.
7. Devine, 'Qualitative Interviewing'; D. Richards (1996), 'Elite Interviewing: Approaches and Pitfalls', *Politics*, 16, 3: 200–1.

8. Devine, 'Qualitative Interviewing', p. 138.
9. Chapman cited in Randall, 'Feminism and Political Analysis'; K. F. Punch (1998), *Introduction to Social Research* (London: Sage), pp. 178–80; Sarantakos, *Social Research*; Rheinharz, *Feminist Methods in Social Research.*
10. J. Lovenduski and P. Norris, 'Westminster Women: the Politics of Presence', *Political Studies*, 51: 84–102.
11. D. Truman (1959), *The Congressional Party: A Case Study* (New York: Wiley).
12. Proposals in 1998 to allow the recording of abstentions met with a positive reaction from parliamentarians, although nothing has happened as yet. See The Sixth Report from the Select Committee on Modernisation of the House of Commons, 'Voting Methods', HC 799 (London: HMSO, 1998).

APPENDIX 2

Interview Guides

INTERVIEW GUIDE, 1997

Participation
- Interest in politics
- Political experience
- Reasons stood for Parliament
- Qualities/skills of MPs
- Ambitions

Recruitment
- Experience of the (s)election process
- Selectorates' criteria
- Explanations of women's numerical under-representation
- All-women shortlists
- Numbers of Conservative and Liberal Democrat women MPs

Representation
- Understanding of representation

Symbolic representation
- Symbolic representation
- Role model effect

Microcosmic representation
- Women's microcosmic representation in the House of Commons
- Identity, attitudes and behaviour
- Participation and representation
- Gender and representation

Substantive representation
- Effect of women's participation in politics
- Effect of 101 Labour women MPs

- Effect of Labour women in/on government
- Views on Women's Minister/ministries

Party representation
- Gender and party representation

Women
- Women's similarities and differences

Feminism
- Identify as a feminist?
- Definition feminism

INTERVIEW GUIDE, 2000

Personal
- Achievements
- Seeking reselection? Why? Ambitions for a second term
- Responsibilities within Parliament/interests

Women's legislative recruitment
- Labour Party selection for next election/AWS
- Acted as role model?
- Tensions between home and the House of Commons

Constituency representation
- Experiences of being a constituency MP
- Increased access? Outreach?
- Feminized agenda?
- Women's differences

Parliament
- Your impact
- Articulating women's concerns?
- Acted for women? Examples
- With other Labour women MPs
- Cross-party?
- Committees

Loyalty

- Why new Labour women are loyal
- Lone parent cut
- PLP
- Modernization of the House
- Critical mass

Feminized style of politics

- Agree?
- Impact of party
- Experiences in the House

Government

- Minister for Women
- Acting for women

Party

- Other political parties 'act for' women?

Representation

- Consciously represent women?
- Shared perspectives on women's issues?
- Represent different women?

Bibliography

Abdela, L. *Women With X Appeal* (London: Optima, 1989).

Acker, J., Barry, K. and Esselveld, J. 'Objectivity and Truth: Problems in Doing Feminist Research', *Women's Studies International Forum*, 5, 4 (1983): 423–35.

Allan, G. 'Qualitative Research', in G. Allan and C. Skinner (eds), *Handbook for Research Students in the Social Sciences* (London: The Falmer Press, 1991), pp. 177–89.

Allan, G. and C. Skinner (eds), *Handbook for Research Students in the Social Sciences* (London: The Falmer Press, 1991).

Appleton, A. and Mazur, A. G. 'Transformation or Modernization: the Rhetoric and Reality of Gender and Party Politics in France', in J. Lovenduski and P. Norris (eds), *Gender and Party Politics* (London: Sage, 1993), pp. 86–112.

Arat, Y. 'A Woman Prime Minister in Turkey: Did it Matter?', *Women and Politics*, 19, 4 (1998): 1–22.

Arber, S. 'The Research Process', in N. Gilbert (ed.), *Researching Social Life* (London: Sage, 1993), pp. 2–51.

Arber, S. 'Designing Samples', in N. Gilbert (ed.), *Researching Social Life* (London: Sage, 1993), pp. 68–93.

Arblaster, A. *The Rise and Decline of Western Liberalism* (Oxford: Basil Blackwell, 1984).

Atkinson, V. and Spear, J. 'The Labour Party and Women: Policies and Practices', in M. J. Smith and J. Spear (eds), *The Changing Labour Party* (London: Routledge, 1992), pp. 151–67.

Baer, D. L. 'Political Parties: the Missing Variable in Women and Politics Research', *Political Research Quarterly*, 46 (1993): 547–76.

Ball, A. *Modern Politics and Government* (London: Macmillan, 1983).

Barkman, K. 'Politics and Gender: the Need for Electoral Reform', *Politics*, 15, 3 (1995): 141–6.

Barry, J. with Honour, T. and Palnitkar, S. 'Gender and Local Governance in Mumbai and London', paper presented to Colloque du CESCIB Université Paris VIII, November 1998.

Bartle, J. 'Why Labour Won – Again?', in A. King (ed.), *Britain at the Polls* (London: Chatham House, 2002), pp. 164–206.

Bashevkin, S. (ed.), *Women and Politics in Western Europe* (London: Frank Cass, 1985).

Bashevkin, S. 'From Tough Times to Better Times', *International Political Science Review*, 4 (2000): 407–24.

Beckman, P. R. and D'Amico, F. 'Conclusion: an End and a Beginning', in F. D'Amico and P. R. Beckman (eds), *Women in World Politics: An Introduction* (Westport, CT: Bergin and Garvey, 1995), pp. 199–213.

Beetham, D. 'The Plant Report and the Theory of Political Representation', *Political Quarterly*, 63, 4 (1992): 460–7.

Bell, C. and Roberts, H. *Social Researching* (London: Routledge, 1984).

Bernstein, R. A. 'Why are there so Few Women in the House?', *Western Political Quarterly*, 39, 1 (1986): 155–64.

Bickford, S. 'Reconfiguring Pluralism: Identity and Institutions in the Inegalitarian Polity', *American Journal of Political Science*, 43, 1 (1999): 86–108.

Birch, A. H. *Representation* (Basingstoke: Macmillan, 1971).

Birch, A. H. *The Concepts and Theories of Modern Democracy* (London: Routledge, 1993).

Blair, T. *New Britain: My Vision of a Young Country* (London: Fourth Estate, 1996).

Bledsoe, T. and Herring, M. 'Victims of Circumstances: Women in Pursuit of Political Office', *American Political Science Review*, 84, 1 (1990): 213–23.

Boals, K. 'Political Science', *Signs*, 1, 1 (1975): 161–74.

Bochel, C. and Briggs, J. 'Do Women Make a Difference?', *Politics*, 20, 2 (2000): 63–8.

Bochel, J. and Denver, D. 'Candidate Selection in the Labour Party: What the Selectors Seek', *British Journal of Political Science*, 13, January (1983): 45–69.

Bogdanor, V. *What is Proportional Representation?* (Oxford: Martin Robertson, 1984).

Bourque, S. and Grossholtz, J. 'Politics, an Unnatural Practice: Political Science Looks at Female Participation', in A. Phillips (ed.), *Feminism and Politics* (Oxford: Oxford University Press, 1998): 23–43.

Bowles, G. and Klein, R. D. *Theories of Women's Studies* (London: Routledge, 1989).

Bratton, K. A. and Haynie, K. L. 'Agenda Setting and Legislative Success in State Legislatures: The Effects of Gender and Race', *Journal of Politics*, 61, 3 (1999): 658–79.

Breitenbach, E. 'Out of Sight, Out of Mind? The History of Women in Scottish Politics', *Scottish Affairs*, 2 (1993): 58–70.

Brennan, G. and Hamlin, A. 'On Political Representation', *British Journal of Political Science*, 29 (1999): 109–27.

Bristow, S. L. 'Women Councillors – an explanation of the Under-representation of Women in Local Government', *Local Government Studies*, May/June (1980): 73–90.

Brivati, B. and Bale, T. *New Labour in Power* (London: Routledge, 1997).

Brookes, P. *Women at Westminster: An Account of Women in the British Parliament 1918–1966* (London: Peter Davies, 1967).

Brooks, R., Eagle, A. and Short, C. *Quotas Now: Women in the Labour Party* (London: Fabian Society, 1990).

Brown, A. *Women in Scottish Politics* (Edinburgh: Unit for the Study of Government in Scotland at Edinburgh University, 1991).

Brown, A. 'Women and Politics in Scotland', in J. Lovenduski and P. Norris (eds), *Women in Politics* (Oxford: Oxford University Press, 1996), pp. 28–42.

Brown, A. and Galligan, Y. 'Views from the Periphery: Changing the Political Agenda for Women in the Republic of Ireland and in Scotland', *West European Politics*, 2 (1993): 165–89.

Brown, A., McCrone, D. and Lindsay, P. *Politics and Society in Scotland* (Basingstoke: Macmillan, 1996).

Bryman, A. *Quantity and Quality in Social Research* (London: Routledge, 1996).

Burrell, B. C. 'Women Candidates in Open Seat Primaries for the US House: 1968–1990', *Legislative Studies Quarterly*, XVII, 4 (1992): 493–509.

Burrell, B. C. 'Party Decline, Party Transformation and Gender Politics: the USA', in J. Lovenduski and P. Norris (eds), *Gender and Party Politics* (London: Sage, 1993), pp. 291–308.

Cabinet Office. *Delivering for Women: Progress So Far* (London: COI, 1998).

Campbell, B. *The Iron Ladies: Why Do Women Vote Tory?* (London: Virago, 1987).

Carroll, S. J. 'Woman Candidates and Support for Feminist Concerns: the Closet Feminist Syndrome', *Western Political Quarterly*, 37 (1984): 307–23.

Carroll, S. J. 'Women's Autonomy and the Gender Gap', in C. M. Mueller (ed.), *The Politics of the Gender Gap* (London: Sage, 1988), pp. 237–56.

Carroll, S. J. *Women as Candidates in American Politics* (Bloomington and Indianapolis: Indiana University Press, 1994).

Castles, F. G. 'Female Legislative Representation and the Electoral System', *Politics*, 1 (1981): 21–6.

Caul, M. 'Women's Representation in Parliament: the Role of Political Parties', *Party Politics*, 5, 1 (1999): 79–99.

Chamberlayne, P. 'Women and the State: Changes in the Roles and Rights in France, West Germany, Italy and Britain, 1970–1990', in J. Lewis (ed.), *Women and Social Policies in Europe* (Aldershot: Edward Elgar, 1993), pp. 170–93.

Chapman, J. 'The Feminist Perspective', in D. Marsh and G. Stoker (eds), *Theory and Methods in Political Science* (Basingstoke: Macmillan, 1995), pp. 94–114.

Childs, S. 'The New Labour Women MPs in the 1997 British Parliament', *Women's History Review*, 9, 1 (2000): 55–73.

Childs, S. 'Conceptions of Representation and the Passage of the Sex Discrimination (Election Candidates) Bill', *Journal of Legislative Studies*, 8, 3 (2002): 90–108.

Childs, S. 'The Sex Discrimination (Election Candidates) Act, *Representation*, 39, 2 (2003): 83–92.

Childs, S. and Withey, J. 'Signing for Women: Women MPs and the Signing of Early Day Motions in the 1997 Parliament', paper presented at PSA Annual Conference, University of Leicester, April 2003.

Christy, C. A. 'Economic Development and Sex Differences in Political Participation', *Women and Politics*, 4, 1 (1984): 7–34.

Christy, C. A. *Sex Differences in Political Participation: Processes of Change in Fourteen Nations* (New York: Praeger, 1987).

Christy, C. A. 'Trends in Sex Differences in Political Participation: a Comparative Perspective', in M. Githens, P. Norris and J. Lovenduski (eds), *Different Roles, Different Voices* (New York: HarperCollins, 1994), pp. 27–37.

Clark, J. 'Getting There: Women in Political Office', in M. Githens, P. Norris and J. Lovenduski (eds), *Different Roles, Different Voices* (New York: HarperCollins, 1994), pp. 99–110.

Clarke, S. E., Staeheli, L. A. and Brunell, L. 'Women Redefining Local Politics', in D. Judge, G. Stoker and H. Wolman (eds), *Theories of Urban Politics* (London: Sage, 1995), pp. 205–27.

Clegg, S. 'Feminist Methodology – Fact or Fiction?', *Quality and Quantity*, 19 (1985): 83–97.

Cockburn, C. 'Strategies for Gender Democracy', *European Journal of Women's Studies*, 3, 7 (1996): 7–26.

Cohen, S. 'Body, Space and Presence: Women's Social Exclusion in the Policies of the European Union', *European Journal of Women's Studies*, 5 (1998): 367–80.

Cook, C. and Taylor, I. *The Labour Party* (London: Longman, 1980).

Cook, J. and Fonow, M. M. 'Knowledge and Women's Interests', in J. McCarl Nielson (ed.), *Feminist Research Methods* (Boulder, CO and San Francisco: Westview Press, 1990), pp. 69–93.

Coole, D. *Women in Political Theory* (Hemel Hempstead: Harvester Wheatsheaf, 1993).

Coole, D. 'Is Class a Difference that Makes a Difference?', *Radical Philosophy*, 77 (1996): 17–25.

Corrin, C. *Feminist Perspectives on Politics* (London: Longman, 1999).

Costain, A. N. 'Representing Women: the Transition from Social Movement to Interest Group', in E. Bonepath and E. Stoper (eds), *Women, Power and Policy* (Oxford: Pergamon, 1988), pp. 26–47.

Cowley, P. 'The Absence of War? New Labour in Parliament', *British Elections and Parties Review*, 9 (1999): 154–70.

Cowley, P. *Revolts and Rebellions* (London: Politicos, 2002).

Cowley, P. and Childs, S. (2002) 'An Uncritical Critical Mass', in P. Cowley, *Revolts and Rebellions* (London: Politicos, 2002).

Criddle, B. 'MPs and Candidates', in D. Butler and D. Kavanagh (eds), *The British General Election of 1992* (Basingstoke: Macmillan, 1992), pp. 211–30.

Criddle, B. 'MPs and Candidates', in D. Butler and D. Kavanagh (eds), *The British General Election of 1997* (Basingstoke: Macmillan, 1997), pp. 186–209.

Criddle, B. 'MPs and Candidates', in D. Butler and D. Kavanagh (eds), *The British General Election of 2001* (Basingstoke: Palgrave, 2002), pp. 182–207.

Currell, M. *Political Woman* (London: Croom Helm, 1974).

Dahlerup, D. 'Overcoming the Barriers: an Approach to How Women's Issues are Kept from the Political Agenda', in J. H. Stiehm (ed.), *Women's Views of the Political World of Men* (New York: Transnational Publishers, 1984), pp. 33–66.

Dahlerup, D. 'From a Small to a Large Minority: Women in Scandinavian

Politics', *Scandinavian Political Studies*, 11, 4 (1988): 275–98.
Dalley, J. *Diana Mosley: A Life* (London: Faber and Faber, 1999).
D'Amico, F. and Beckman, P. R. (eds), *Women in World Politics* (Westport, CT: Bergin and Garvey, 1995).
Darcy, R. and Hadley, D. 'Black Women in Politics', *Social Science Quarterly*, 69, 3 (1988): 629–45.
Darcy, R., Welch, S. and Clark, J. *Women, Elections and Representation* (Lincoln, NB and London: University of Nebraska Press, 1994).
Darcy, R., Welch, S. and Clark, J. 'Women, Elections and Representation', in M. Githens, P. Norris and J. Lovenduski (eds), *Different Roles, Different Voices* (New York: Harper Collins, 1994), pp. 89–93.
Dargie, C. 'Observation in Political Research', *Politics*, 18, 1 (1998): 65–71.
Denby, M. 'Women in Parliament and Government', in L. Middleton (ed.), *Women in the Labour Movement* (London: Croom Helm, 1977), pp. 175–90.
Denver, D. 'Britain: Centralized Parties with Decentralized Selection', in M. Gallagher and M. Marsh (eds), *Candidate Selection in Comparative Perspective: The Secret Garden of Politics* (London: Sage, 1988), pp. 47–71.
Devine, F. *Affluent Workers Revisited* (Edinburgh: Edinburgh University Press, 1992).
Devine, F. 'Studying Voting Behaviour', in *Issues in Sociology and Social Policy* (Liverpool: University of Liverpool, 1994).
Devine, F. 'Qualitative Methods', in D. Marsh and G. Stoker (eds), *Theory and Methods in Political Science* (Basingstoke: Macmillan, 1995), pp. 137–53.
Devine, F. and Heath, S. *Sociological Research Methods in Context* (Basingstoke: Macmillan, 1999).
Dexter, L. A. *Elite and Specialized Interviewing* (Evanston, IL: Northwestern University Press, 1970).
Diamond, I. and Hartsock, N. 'Beyond Interests in Politics', in A. Phillips (ed.), *Feminism and Politics* (Oxford: Oxford University Press, 1998), pp. 193–223.
Diggs, B. J. 'Practical Representation', in J. R. Pennock and J. W. Chapman (eds), *Representation* (New York: Atherton Press, 1968), pp. 28–37.
Dodson, D. 'The Impact of Women in Congress', paper presented to the Annual Meeting of APSA Women and Politics Special Session, San Francisco, 2001.
Draper, D. *Blair's Hundred Days* (London: Faber and Faber, 1997).

Driver, S. and Martell, L. *New Labour: Politics after Thatcherism* (Cambridge: Polity Press, 1998).

Drucker, H. M. *Doctrine and Ethos in the Labour Party* (London: George Allen and Unwin, 1979).

Duerst-Lahti, G. 'Institutions, Ideologies, and the Possibility of Equal Political Participation', paper presented to the Annual Meeting of APSA Women and Politics Special Session, San Francisco, 2001.

Duerst-Lahti, G. and Mae Kelly, R. *Gender, Power, Leadership and Governance* (Ann Arbor, MI: University of Michigan Press, 1995).

Duerst-Lahti, G. and Mae Kelly, R. 'On Governance, Leadership and Gender', in G. Duerst-Lahti and R. Mae Kelly (eds), *Gender, Power, Leadership and Governance* (Ann Arbor, MI: University of Michigan Press, 1995), pp. 11–37.

Duerst-Lahti, G. and Verstegen, D. 'Making Something of Absence: the 'Year of the Woman' and Women's Representation', in G. Duerst-Lahti and R. Mae Kelly (eds), *Gender Power Leadership and Governance* (Ann Arbor, MI: University of Michigan Press, 1995), pp. 213–38.

Duverger, M. *The Political Role of Women* (Paris: UNESCO, 1955).

Eagle, M. and Lovenduski, J. *High Time or High Tide for Labour Women* (London: Fabian Society, 1998).

Edwards, J. 'Women's Committees: a Model for Good Local Government?', *Policy and Politics*, 17, 3 (1989): 221–5.

Egan, M. 'Gendered Integration: Social Policies and the European Market', *Women and Politics*, 19, 4 (1998): 23–52.

Electoral Commission. 'Candidates at a General Election Factsheet', www.electoralcommission.org.uk (2002).

Elgood, J., Vinter, L. and Williams, R. *Man Enough for the Job? A Study of Parliamentary Candidates* (Manchester: EOC, 2002).

Eulau, H. 'Changing Views of Representation', in I. de Sola Pool (ed.) *Contemporary Political Science* (New York: McGraw-Hill, 1967), pp. 53–85.

Evans, G. 'Is Gender on the "New Agenda"?', *European Journal of Political Research*, 24 (1993): 135–58.

Evans, J. 'Women and Politics: a Re-appraisal', *Political Studies*, 28, 2 (1980): 210–21.

Evans, J. 'The Good Society? Implications of a Greater Participation by Women in Public Life', *Political Studies*, 32 (1984): 618–26.

Fainsod Katzenstein, M. 'Feminism and the Meaning of the Vote', *Signs*, 10, 1 (1984): 4–26.

Fielding, N. 'Qualitative Interviewing', in N. Gilbert (ed.), *Researching Social Life* (London: Sage, 1993), pp. 135–53.

Fielding, N. 'Ethnography', in N. Gilbert (ed.), *Researching Social Life* (London: Sage, 1993), pp. 154–71.

Finch, J. 'It's Great to Have Someone to Talk to': the Ethics and Politics of Interviewing women', in C. Bell and H. Roberts (eds), *Social Researching* (London: Routledge, 1984), pp. 71–86.

Fisher, J. *British Political Parties* (Hemel Hempstead: Prentice Hall, 1996).

Francis, J. G. and Peele, G. 'Reflections on Generational Analysis: Is There a Shared Political Perspective between Men and Women?', *Political Studies*, 26, 3 (1978): 363–74.

Frazer, E. and Lacey, N. *The Politics of Community* (Hemel Hempstead: Harvester Wheatsheaf, 1993).

Fuchs Epstein, C. and Laub Coser, R. (eds), *Access to Power: Cross-national Studies of Women and Elites* (London: George Allen and Unwin, 1981).

Galligan, Y. 'Party Politics and Gender in the Republic of Ireland', in J. Lovenduski and P. Norris (eds), *Gender and Party Politics* (London: Sage, 1993), pp. 147–67.

Galligan, Y., Ward, E. and Wilford, R. *Contesting Politics: Women in Ireland, North and South* (Boulder, CO: PASI Press and Westview Press, 1999).

Geddes, A. 'The *Logic* of Positive Action', *Party Politics*, 1, 2 (1995): 275–85.

Geddes, A., Lovenduski, J. and Norris, P. 'Candidate Selection: Reform in Britain', *Contemporary Record*, April (1991): 19–22.

Genovese, M. A. (ed.), *Women as National Leaders* (London: Sage, 1993).

Gilbert, N. (ed.), *Researching Social Life* (London: Sage, 1993).

Gilbert, N. 'Research, Theory and Method', in N. Gilbert (ed.), *Researching Social Life* (London: Sage, 1993), pp. 18–31.

Gilbert, N. 'Writing about Social Research', in N. Gilbert (ed.), *Researching Social Life* (London: Sage, 1993), pp. 328–344.

Gill, B. *Winning Women: Lessons from Scotland and Wales* (London: Fawcett Society, n.d.).

Gill, B. *Where is Worcester Woman? Women's Voting Intentions and Political Priorities 2001* (London: Fawcett Society, n.d.).

Githens, M., Norris, P. and Lovenduski, J. (eds), *Different Roles, Different Voices* (New York: HarperCollins, 1994).

Gluck Mezey, S. 'Does Sex Make a Difference? A Case Study of Women in Politics', *Western Political Quarterly*, 31 (1978): 492–501.

Goot, M. and Reid, E. 'Women: If not Apolitical, then Conservative', in J. Siltanen and M. Stanworth (eds), *Women and the Public Sphere: A Critique of Sociology and Politics* (London: Hutchinson, 1984), pp. 122–36.

Grant, J. 'I Feel Therefore I am: a Critique of Female Experience as the Basis for a Feminist Epistemology', *Women and Politics*, 7, 2 (1987): 99–114.

Graves, P. M. *Labour Women, Women: in British Working-Class Politics 1918–1939* (Cambridge: Cambridge University Press, 1994).

Grey, S. 'Does Size Matter?', in K. Ross (ed.) *Women, Politics and Change* (Oxford: Oxford University Press, 2002).

Gugin, L. C. 'The Impact of Political Structure on the Political Power of Women: a Comparison of Britain and the United States', *Women and Politics*, 6, 4 (1986): 37–56.

Haavio-Mannila, E. et al. (eds), *Unfinished Democracy: Women in Nordic Politics* (Oxford: Pergamon Press, 1985).

Hacker, H. M. 'Women as a Minority Group', *Social Forces*, 30 (1951): 60–90.

Halberg, M. 'Feminist Epistemology: an Impossible Project?', *Radical Philosophy*, 53 (1989): 3–7.

Halford, S. 'Women's Initiatives in Local Government: Where Do They Come from and Where are They Going?', *Policy and Politics*, 16, 4 (1988): 251–9.

Hansard Society. *The Report of the Hansard Society Commission on Women at the Top* (London: Hansard Society for Parliamentary Government, 1990).

Harding, S. (ed.) *Feminism and Methodology* (Bloomington, IN and Milton Keynes: Indiana University Press and Open University Press, 1987).

Harman, H. *The Century Gap* (London: Vermillion, 1993).

Harmer, H. *The Labour Party 1900–1998* (London: Longman, 1999).

Hayes, B. C. and McAllister, I. 'Gender, Party Leaders and Election Outcomes in Australia, Britain and the United States', *Comparative Political Studies*, 30, 1 (1997): 3–26.

Heath, A., Evans, G. and Martin, J. 'The Measurement of Core Beliefs and Values: the Development of Balanced Socialist/Laissez-faire and Libertarian/Authoritarian scales', *British Journal of Political Science*, 24 (1994): 115–31.

Hedlund, G. 'Women's Interests in Local Politics', in K. B. Jones and A. G. Jonasdottir (eds), *The Political Interests of Gender: Developing Theory and Research with a Feminist Face* (London: Sage, 1990), pp. 79–105.

Hicks Stiehm, J. 'The Man Question', in J. Hicks Stiehm (ed.), *Women's View of the Political World of Men* (New York: Transnational Publishers, 1984), pp. 205–24.

High-Pippert, A. and Comer, J. 'Female Empowerment: the Influence of Women Representing Women', *Women and Politics*, 19, 4 (1998): 53–66.

Hills, J. 'Candidates: the Impact of Gender', *Parliamentary Affairs*, 34 (1981): 221–8.

Hills, J. 'Women Local Councillors – a Reply to Bristow', *Local Government Studies*, January/February (1982): 61–71.

Hills, J. 'Life-style Constraints on Formal Political Participation – Why So Few Women Local Councillors in Britain?', *Electoral Studies*, 2, 1 (1983): 39–52.

Hinton, J. 'Essay in Labour Statistics, Women and the Labour Vote, 1945–50', *Labour History Review*, 57, 3 (1992): 59–62.

Hoskyns, C. and Rai, S. M. 'Gender, Class and Representation: India and the European Union', *The European Journal of Women's Studies*, 5 (1998): 345–65.

House of Commons. *The Speaker, Factsheet M2* (London: House of Commons, 2002).

Inglehart, M. 'Political Interest in West European Women: an Historical and Empirical Comparative Analysis', *Comparative Political Studies*, 14, 3 (1981): 299–326.

Inter-Parliamentary Union. *Women and Political Power* (Geneva: IPU, 1992).

Inter-Parliamentary Union. *Plan of Action: To Correct Present Imbalances in the Participation of Men and Women in Political Life* (Geneva: IPU, 1994).

Inter-Parliamentary Union. *Women in Parliaments 1945–1995: A World Statistical Survey* (Geneva: IPU, 1995).

Janova, M. and Sineau, M. 'Women's Participation in Political Power in Europe', *Women's Studies International Forum*, 15, 1 (1992): 115–28.

Jennings, M. K. and Farah, B. G. 'Ideology, Gender and Political Action: a Cross-national Survey', *British Journal of Political Science*, 10, 2 (1980): 219–40.

Jonasdottir, A. G. 'On the Concept of Interest, Women's Interests, and the Limitations of Interest Theory', in K. B. Jones and A. G. Jonasdottir (eds), *The Political Interests of Gender: Developing Theory and Research with a Feminist Face* (London: Sage, 1990), pp. 33–65.

Jones, C. 'Qualitative Interviewing', in G. Allan and C. Skinner (eds), *Handbook for Research Students in the Social Sciences* (London: The Falmer Press, 1991), pp. 203–14.

Jones, K. B. 'Towards the Revision of Politics', in K. B. Jones and A. G. Jonasdottir (eds), *The Political Interests of Gender, Developing Theory and Research with a Feminist Face* (London: Sage, 1990), pp. 11–32.

Jones, K. B. and Jonasdottir, A. G. (eds) *The Political Interests of Gender: Developing Theory and Research with a Feminist Face* (London: Sage, 1990).

Jones, K. B. and Jonasdottir, A. G. 'Introduction: Gender as an Analytic Category in Political Theory', in K. B. Jones and A. G. Jonasdottir (eds), *The Political Interests of Gender: Developing Theory and Research with a Feminist Face* (London: Sage, 1990), pp. 1–10.

Journal of Legislation Studies. 'Members of Parliament in Western Europe: Roles and Behaviour', *Journal of Legislative Studies*, Special issue (1997).

Judge, D. *Representation* (London: Routledge, 1999).

Karvonen, L., Djupsund, G. and Carlson, T. 'Political Language', in L. Karvonen and P. Selle (eds), *Women in Nordic Politics* (Aldershot: Dartmouth, 1995), pp. 343–79.

Karvonen, L. and Selle, P. 'Introduction: Scandinavia – a Case Apart', in L. Karvonen and P. Selle (eds), *Women in Nordic Politics* (Aldershot: Dartmouth, 1995), pp. 3–23.

Kay, S. A. 'Feminist Ideology, Race and Political Participation: a Second Look', *Western Political Quarterly*, 38 (1985): 476–84.

Kelly, J. and McAllister, I. 'Ballot Paper Cues and the Vote in Australia and Britain: Alphabetic Voting, Sex, and Title', *British Public Opinion Quarterly*, 48 (1984): 452–66.

King, A. 'The Chief Whip's Clothes', in D. Leonard and V. Herman (eds), *The Backbencher and Parliament* (London: Macmillan, 1972), pp. 80–6.

King, C. S. 'Sex-role Identity and Decision-styles: How Gender Helps Explain the Paucity of Women at the Top', in G. Duerst-Lahti and R. M. Kelly (eds), *Gender, Power, Leadership Governance* (Ann Arbor, MI: University of Michigan Press, 1995), pp. 67–92.

Klein, E. 'The Gender Gap: Different Issues, Different Answers', *Brookings Review*, 3 (1985): 33–7.

Knoche Fulenwider, C. 'Feminist Ideology and the Political Attitudes and Participation of White and Minority Women', *Western Political Quarterly*, 34, 1 (1981): 17–28.

Kogan, D. and Kogan, M. *The Battle for the Labour Party* (London: Kogan Page, 1982).

Kolinsky, E. 'Political Participation and Parliamentary Careers: Women's Quotas in West Germany', *West European Politics*, 14, 1 (1991): 56–72.

Krehbiel, K. 'Where's the Party?', *British Journal of Political Science*, 23 (1993): 235–66.

Krehbiel, K. 'Paradoxes of Parties in Congress', *Legislative Studies Quarterly*, 14 (1999): 31–64.

Lather, P. 'Feminist Perspectives on Empowering Research Methodologies', *Women's Studies International Forum*, 11, 6 (1988): 569–81.

Levy, C. 'Counting Women in the Past, Present and Future of Women in Scottish Politics', in A. Brown (ed.), *Women in Scottish Politics* (Edinburgh: Unit for the Study of Government in Scotland at Edinburgh University, 1991), pp. 17–23.

Levy, C. 'A Woman's Place? The Future Scottish Parliament', in L. Paterson (ed.), *Scottish Government Yearbook 1992* (Edinburgh: Unit for the Study of Government in Scotland, 1992), pp. 59–73.

Lewis, K. E. and Bierly, M. 'Toward a Profile of the Female Voter: Sex Differences in Perceived Physical Attractiveness and Competence of Political Candidates', *Sex Roles*, 22, 1 & 2 (1990): 1–12.

Lovenduski, J. 'Toward the Emasculation of Political Science: the Impact of Feminism', in D. Spender (ed.), *Men's Studies Modified* (Oxford: Pergamon Press, 1981), pp. 83–97.

Lovenduski, J. *Women and European Politics* (Brighton: Wheatsheaf, 1986).

Lovenduski, J. 'Implementing Equal Opportunities in the 1980s: an Overview', *Public Administration*, 67 (1989): 7–18.

Lovenduski, J. 'Feminism and West European Politics: an Overview', in D. W. Urwin and W. E. Paterson (eds), *Politics in Western Europe Today* (London: Longman, 1990), pp. 137–61.

Lovenduski, J. 'Introduction: the Dynamics of Gender and Party', in J. Lovenduski and P. Norris (eds), *Gender and Party Politics* (London: Sage, 1993), pp. 1–15.

Lovenduski, J. 'Will Quotas Make Women More Women-Friendly?', *Renewal*, 2, 1 (1994): 9–18.

Lovenduski, J. 'Sex, Gender and British Politics', in J. Lovenduski and P. Norris (eds), *Women in Politics* (Oxford: Oxford University Press, 1996), pp. 3–18.

Lovenduski, J. 'Gender Politics: a Breakthrough for Women?', *Parliamentary Affairs*, 50, 4 (1997): 708–19.

Lovenduski, J. 'Women and Politics', in P. Norris (ed.), *Britain Votes 2001* (Oxford: Oxford University Press, 2001).

Lovenduski, J. and Hills, J. (eds), *The Politics of the Second Electorate: Women and Public Particiation* (London: Routledge and Kegan Paul, 1981).

Lovenduski, J. and Norris, P. 'Selecting Women Candidates: Obstacles to the Feminization of the House of Commons', *European Journal of Political Research*, 17 (1989): 533–62.

Lovenduski, J. and Norris, P. 'Party Rules and Women's Representation: Reforming the British Labour Party', in I. Crewe et al. (eds), *British Elections and Parties Yearbook* (Hemel Hempstead: Harvester Wheatsheaf, 1991), pp. 189–206.

Lovenduski, J. and Norris, P. *Gender and Party Politics* (London: Sage, 1993).

Lovenduski, J. and Norris, P. 'The Recruitment of Parliamentary Candidates', in L. Robins, H. Blackmore and R. Pyper (eds), *Britain's Changing Party System* (London: Leicester University Press, 1994), pp. 125–46.

Lovenduski, J. and Norris, P. 'Labour and the Unions: After the Brighton Conference', *Government and Opposition*, 29, 2 (1994): 201–17.

Lovenduski, J. and Norris, P. *Women in Politics* (Oxford: Oxford University Press, 1996).

Lovenduski, J. and Norris, P. (2003) 'Westminster Women: the Politics of Presence', *Political Studies*, 51, 84–102.

Lovenduski, J., Norris, P. and Burness, C. 'The Party and Women', in A. Seldon and S. Ball (eds), *Conservative Century: The Conservative Party since 1900* (Oxford: Oxford University Press, 1994), pp. 611–35.

Lovenduski, J. and Randall, V. *Contemporary Feminist Politics* (Oxford: Oxford University Press, 1993).

McCarl Nielson, J. (ed.) *Feminist Research Methods* (Boulder, CO and San Francisco, CA: Westview Press, 1990).

McDonald, O. 'Women in the Labour Party', in L. Middleton (ed.), *Women in the Labour Movement* (London: Croom Helm, 1977), pp. 22–37.

McDougall, L. *Westminister Women* (London: Vintage, 1998).
Mackay, F. *Love and Politics* (London: Continuum, 2001).
McKenzie, C. *Quotable Women* (Edinburgh: Mainstream Publishing, 1992).
McLean, I. 'Forms of Representation and Systems of Voting', in D. Held (ed.), *Political Theory Today* (Cambridge: Polity Press, 1991), pp. 172–96.
McRae, S. 'Women at the Top: the Case of British National Politics', *Parliamentary Affairs*, 90, 3 (1990): 341–7.
McRae, S. *Women at the Top, Progress after Five Years* (London: Hansard Society, 1996).
McRobbie, A. 'The Politics of Feminist Research: Between Talk, Text, and Action', *Feminist Review*, 12 (1982): 46–57.
Mactaggart, F. 'Women in Parliament: Their Contribution to Labour's First 1,000 Days', research paper prepared for the Fabian Society (London: Fabian Society, 2000).
Mandelson, P. and Liddle, R. *The Blair Revolution, Can New Labour Deliver?* (London: Faber and Faber, 1996).
Manheim, J. B. and Rich, R. C. *Empirical Political Analysis* (London: Longman, 1995).
Mansbridge, J. 'Feminism and Democracy', *American Prospect*, 1 (1990): 126–39.
Mansbridge, J. 'Should Blacks Represent Blacks and Women Represent Women? A Contingent "Yes" ', *Journal of Politics*, 61, 3 (1999): 628–57.
Maynard, M. 'Methods, Practice and Epistemology: the Debate about Feminism and Research', in M. Maynard and J. Purvis (eds), *Researching Women's Lives from a Feminist Perspective* (London: Taylor and Francis, 1994), pp. 10–26.
Maynard M. and Purvis, J. 'Introduction: Doing Feminist Research', in M. Maynard and J. Purvis (eds), *Researching Women's Lives from a Feminist Perspective* (London: Taylor and Francis, 1994), pp. 1–9.
Meehan, E. *Citizenship and the European Community* (London: Sage, 1993).
Millns, S. and Whitty, N. *Feminist Perspectives on Public Law* (London: Cavendish, 1999).
Mossuz-Lavau, J. and Sineau, M. *Women in the Political World in Europe* (Strasbourg: Council of Europe, 1984).
Mowlam, M. *Momentum* (London: Hodder and Stoughton, 2002).
Moyser, G. and Wagstaffe, M. *Research Methods for Elite Studies* (London: Allen and Unwin, 1987).

Mueller, C. M. *The Politics of the Gender Gap: The Social Construction of Political Influence* (London: Sage, 1988).

Nicholson, B. 'From Interest Group to (Almost) Equal Citizenship: Women's Representation in the Norweigan Parliament', *Parliamentary Affairs*, 46, 2 (1993): 255–64.

Nicholson, E. *Secret Society – Inside and Outside – the Conservative Party* (London: Indigo, 1996).

Norris, P. 'The Gender Gap in Britain and America', *Parliamentary Affairs*, 38, 2 (1985): 192–201.

Norris, P. 'Women's Legislative Participation in Western Europe', *West European Politics*, 8, 4 (1985): 90–101.

Norris, P. 'Conservative Attitudes in Recent British Elections: an Emerging Gender Gap?', *Political Studies*, 34 (1986): 120–8.

Norris, P. *Politics and Sexual Equality* (Brighton: Wheatsheaf, 1987).

Norris, P. 'Gender Differences in Political Participation in Britain: Traditional, Radical and Revisionist Models', *Government and Opposition*, Winter (1991): 56–74.

Norris, P. 'Conclusions: Comparing Legislative Recruitment', in J. Lovenduski and P. Norris (eds), *Gender and Party Politics* (London: Sage, 1993), pp. 309–30.

Norris, P. 'Labour Party Factionalism and Extremism', in A. Heath, R. Jowell and J. Curtice (eds), *Labour's Last Chance? The 1992 Election and Beyond* (Aldershot: Dartmouth, 1994), pp. 173–90.

Norris, P. 'The Impact of the Electoral System on the Election of Women to National Legislatures', in M. Githens, P. Norris and J. Lovenduski (eds), *Different Roles, Different Voices* (New York: HarperCollins, 1994), pp. 114–21.

Norris, P. 'Political Participation', in M. Githens, P. Norris and J. Lovenduski (eds), *Different Roles, Different Voices* (New York: HarperCollins, 1994), pp. 25–6.

Norris, P. 'Elections and Political Attitudes', in M. Githens, P. Norris and J. Lovenduski (eds), *Different Roles, Different Voices* (New York: HarperCollins, 1994), pp. 47–50.

Norris, P. 'Political Recruitment' in M. Githens, P. Norris and J. Lovenduski (eds), *Different Roles, Different Voices* (New York: HarperCollins, 1994), pp. 85–8.

Norris, P. 'Labour Party Quotas for Women', in D. Broughton, D. M. Farrell, D. Denver and C. Rallings (eds), *British Elections and Parties Yearbook 1994* (London: Frank Cass, 1995), pp. 167–80.

Norris, P. 'Women Politicians: Transforming Westminster?', in J. Lovenduski and P. Norris (eds), *Women in Politics* (Oxford: Oxford University Press, 1996), pp. 91–104

Norris, P. 'Mobilizing the Women's Vote', *Parliamentary Affairs*, 49, 1 (1996): 333–42

Norris, P. *Passages to Power* (Cambridge: Cambridge University Press, 1997).

Norris, P. *Women, Media, and Politics* (Oxford: Oxford University Press, 1997).

Norris, P. 'A Gender-Generation Gap', http://www.ksg.harvard.edu/people/pnorris/Gendergap.htm (1998).

Norris, P. 'New Politicians? Changes in Party Competition at Westminster', in P. Norris and G. Evans (eds), *Critical Elections* (London: Sage, 1999), pp. 22–43.

Norris, P. 'Gender: a Gender–Generation Gap?', in P. Norris and G. Evans (eds), *Critical Elections* (London: Sage, 1999), pp. 148–63.

Norris, P., Carty, R. K., Erickson, L., Lovenduski, J. and Simms, M. 'Party Selectorates in Australia, Britain and Canada: Prolegomena for Research in the 1990s', *The Journal of Commonwealth and Comparative Politics*, 28, 2 (1990): 219–45.

Norris, P. and Lovenduski, J. 'Pathways to Parliament', *Talking Politics*, 1, 3 (1989): 90–4.

Norris, P. and Lovenduski, J. 'Women Candidates for Parliament: Transforming the Agenda?', *British Journal of Political Science*, 19, 1 (1989): 106–15.

Norris, P. and Lovenduski, J. 'Gender and Party Politics in Britain', in J. Lovenduski and P. Norris (eds), *Gender and Party Politics* (London: Sage, 1993), pp. 35–59.

Norris, P. and Lovenduski, J. 'If Only More Candidates Came Forward: Supply-side Explanations of Candidate Selection in Britain', *British Journal of Political Science*, 23 (1993): 373–408.

Norris, P. and Lovenduski, J. *Political Recruitment* (Cambridge: Cambridge University Press, 1995).

Norris, P., Lovenduski, J. and Vallance, E. 'Do Candidates Make a Difference?, *Parliamentary Affairs*, 45, 4 (1992): 496–517.

Norton, N. H. 'Analysing Roll-Call Voting Tools for Content: Are Women's Issues Excluded from Legislative Research', *Women and Politics*, 17, 4 (1997): 47–69.

Norton, P. *Dissension in the House of Commons, 1974–1979* (Oxford: Clarendon Press, 1980).

Norton, P. 'Dear Minister ... The Importance of MP-to-Minister Correspondence', *Parliamentary Affairs*, 35 (1982): 59–72.

Norton, P. and Wood, D. *Back From Westminster* (Lexington, KY: University of Kentucky Press, 1993).

Nuss, S. 'Female Representation in Political Life: Global Progress and Prospects for the Future', *International Journal of Sociology of the Family*, 16, Spring (1986): 1–18.

Oakley, A. 'Interviewing Women: a Contradiction in Terms', in H. Roberts (ed.), *Doing Feminist Research* (London: Routledge, 1995), pp. 30–61.

Okin, S. M. *Women in Western Political Thought* (Princeton, NJ: Princeton University Press, 1979).

Parry, G., Moyser, G. and Day, N. *Political Participation and Democracy in Britain* (Cambridge: Cambridge University Press, 1992).

Pateman, C. *The Disorder of Women* (Cambridge: Polity Press, 1989).

Pateman, C. *Participation and Democratic Theory* (Cambridge: Cambridge University Press, 1991).

Peake, L. 'Women in the Campaign and in the Commons', in A. Geddes and J. Tonge (eds), *Labour's Landslide: The British General Election 1997* (Manchester: Manchester University Press, 1997), pp. 165–77.

Pennock R. J. 'Political Representation: an Overview', in J. R. Pennock and J. W. Chapman (eds), *Representation* (New York: Atherton Press, 1968), pp. 3–27.

Pennock, J. R. and Chapman, J. W. (eds) *Representation* (New York: Atherton Press, 1968).

Perrigo, S. 'Socialist-Feminism and the Labour Party: Some Experiences from Leeds', *Feminist Review*, 23 (1986): 101–8.

Perrigo, S. 'Gender Struggles in the British Labour Party from 1979 to 1995', *Party Politics*, 1, 3 (1995): 407–17.

Perrigo, S. 'Women and Change in the Labour Party 1979–1995', in J. Lovenduski and P. Norris (eds), *Women in Politics* (Oxford: Oxford University Press, 1996), pp. 118–31.

Phillips, A. *Engendering Democracy* (Cambridge: Polity Press, 1991).

Phillips, A. *Democracy and Difference* (Cambridge: Polity Press, 1993).

Phillips, A. *The Politics of Presence* (Oxford: Clarendon Press, 1995).

Phillips, A. 'Why Does Local Democracy Matter', in L. Pratchett and D. Wilson (eds), *Local Democracy and Local Government* (Basingstoke: Macmillan, 1996), pp. 20–37.

Phillips, A. (ed.) *Feminism and Politics* (Oxford: Oxford University Press, 1998).

Phillips, A. 'Democracy and Representation: Or, Why Should It Matter Who Our Representatives Are?', in A. Phillips (ed.), *Feminism and Politics* (Oxford: Oxford University Press, 1998).

Pilcher, J. 'The Gender Significance of Women in Power: British Women Talking about Margaret Thatcher', *European Journal of Women's Studies*, 2, 4 (1995): 493–508.

Pitkin, H. F. *The Concept of Representation* (Berkeley, CA: University of California Press, 1967).

Pitkin, H. F. 'Commentary: the Paradox of Representation', in J. R. Pennock and J. W. Chapman (eds), *Representation* (New York: Atherton Press, 1968), pp. 38–42.

Pitkin, H. F. *Representation* (New York: Atherton Press, 1969).

The Political Studies Association 'Guidelines for Good Professional Conduct', www.psa.ac.uk/about/Publications/Professional_Conduct.htm (2000).

Porter, E. 'Women and Politics in Northern Ireland', *Politics*, 18, 1 (1998): 25–32.

Procter, M. 'Analysing Survey Data', in N. Gilbert (ed.), *Researching Social Life* (London: Sage, 1993), pp. 239–54.

Pugh, M. 'Labour and Women's Suffrage' in K. D. Brown (ed.), *The First Labour Party 1906–1914* (London: Croom Helm, 1985), pp. 233–53.

Punch, K. F. *Introduction to Social Research* (London: Sage, 1998).

Quaile Hill, K. and Hurley, P. A. 'Dyadic Representation Reappraised', *American Journal of Political Science*, 43, 1 (1999): 109–37.

Raaum, N. C. 'The Political Representation of Women: a Bird's Eye View', in L. Karvonen and P. Selle (eds), *Women in Nordic Politics* (Aldershot: Dartmouth, 1995), pp. 25–55.

Randall, V. *Women and Politics: An International Perspective* (Basingstoke: Macmillan, 1987).

Randall, V. 'Feminism and Political Analysis', *Political Studies*, 39 (1991): 513–32.

Randall, V. 'Feminism and Political Analysis', in M. Githens, P. Norris and J. Lovenduski (eds), *Different Roles, Different Voices* (New York: HarperCollins, 1994), pp. 4–16.

Randall, V. and Waylen, G. *Gender, Politics and the State* (London: Routledge, 1998).

Randon Hershey, M. 'The Year of the Woman?', in M. Githens, P. Norris and J. Lovenduski (eds), *Different Roles, Different Voices* (New York: HarperCollins, 1994), pp. 111–14.

Ranney, A. *Pathways to Power* (London: Macmillan, 1965).

Rao, N. 'Representation in Local Politics: a Reconsideration and some New Evidence', *Political Studies*, 46, 1 (1998): 19–35.

Rasmussen, J. 'The Role of Women in British Parliamentary Elections', *Journal of Politics*, 39 (1977): 1044–54.

Rasmussen, J. 'Female Political Career Patterns and Leadership Disabilities in Britain: the Crucial Role of Gatekeepers in Regulating Entry to the Political Elite', *Polity*, 13, 4 (1981): 600–20.

Rasmussen, J. 'Women Candidates in British By-elections: a Rational Choice Interpretation of Electoral Behaviour', *Political Studies*, 29 (1981): 265–74.

Rasmussen, J. 'Women's Role in Contemporary British Politics: Impediments to Parliamentary Candidature', *Parliamentary Affairs*, 36, 3 (1983): 300–15.

Rasmussen, J. 'The Electoral Costs of Being a Woman in the 1979 British General Election', *Comparative Politics*, July (1983): 461–75.

Rasmussen, J. 'The Political Integration of British Women: the Response of a Traditional System to a Newly Emergent Group', *Social Science History*, 7, 1 (1983): 61–95.

Rasmussen, J. 'Women in Labour: the Flapper Vote and Party System Transformation in Britain', *Electoral Studies*, 3, 1 (1984): 47–63.

Rees, T. 'Ethical Issues', in G. Allan and C. Skinner (eds), *Handbook for Research Students in the Social Sciences* (London: The Falmer Press, 1991), pp. 140–51.

Reeve, A. and Ware, A. *Electoral Systems* (London: Routledge, 1992).

Reingold, B. 'Concepts of Representation among Female and Male State Legislators', *Legislative Studies Quarterly*, 17 (1992): 509–37.

Reingold, B. *Representing Women* (Chapel Hill, NC and London: University of North Carolina Press, 2000).

Reinharz, S. *Feminist Methods in Social Research* (Oxford: Oxford University Press, 1992).

Richard Piper, J. 'British Backbench Rebellion and Government Appointments, 1945–87', *Legislative Studies Quarterly*, 16 (1991): 219–38

Richards, D. 'Elite Interviewing: Approaches and Pitfalls', *Politics*, 16, 3 (1996): 199–204.

Roberts, H. 'Some of the Boys Won't Play', in D. Spender (ed.), *Men's Studies Modified* (Oxford: Pergamon Press, 1981), pp. 73–81.

Roberts, H. 'Putting the Show on the Road: the Dissemination of Research Findings', in C. Bell and H. Roberts (eds), *Social Researching* (London: Routledge, 1989), pp. 199–212.

Roberts, H. (ed.), *Women's Health Count* (London: Routledge, 1990).

Roberts, H. (ed.), *Doing Feminist Research* (London: Routledge, 1995).

Roberts, H. 'Ten Years On', in H. Roberts (ed.), *Doing Feminist Research* (London: Routledge, 1995), pp. xiii–xxi.

Roddick, J. 'The Struggle for Representation in Europe', in A. Brown (ed.), *Women in Scottish Politics* (Edinburgh: Unit for the Study of Government in Scotland at Edinburgh University, 1991), pp. 4–16.

Rogers, B. *52%: Getting Women's Power into Politics* (London: The Women's Press, 1983).

Ross, K. 'Gender and Party Politics: How the Press Reported the Labour Leadership Campaign, 1994', *Media, Culture and Society*, 17 (1995): 499–509.

Ross, K. 'Women's Place in "Male" Space', *Parliamentary Affairs*, 55, 1 (2002): 189–201.

Ross, K. and Sreberny-Mohammadi, A. 'Playing House – Gender, Politics and the News Media in Britain', *Media, Culture and Society*, 19 (1997): 101–9.

Rowbotham, S. 'Feminism and Democracy', in D. Held and C. Pollit (eds), *New Forms of Democracy* (London: Sage, 1986), pp. 78–109.

Rule, W. 'Why Women Don't Run: the Critical Contextual Factors in Women's Legislative Recruitment', *Western Political Quarterly*, 34, 1 (1981): 60–77.

Rule, W. 'Electoral Systems, Contextual Factors and Women's Opportunity for Election to Parliament in Twenty-three Democracies', *Western Political Quarterly*, 40, 3 (1987): 477–98.

Rush, M. *The Selection of Parliamentary Candidates* (London: Nelson, 1969).

Russell, M. *Women's Representation in UK Politics* (London: The Constitution Unit, 2000).

Russell, M. *The Women's Representation Bill* (London: The Constitution Unit, 2001).

Sapiro, V. 'Gender Politics, Gendered Politics: the State of the Field', in W. Crotty (ed.), *Political Science: Looking to the Future* (Evanston, IL: Northwestern University Press, 1991), pp. 165–87.

Sapiro, V. 'When are Interests Interesting', in A. Phillips (ed.), *Feminism and Politics* (Oxford: Oxford University Press, 1998), pp. 161–92.

Sarantakos, S. *Social Research* (Basingstoke: Macmillan, 1998).

Sawer, M. 'The Representation of Women in Australia', *Parliamentary Affairs*, 55, 1 (2002): 5–18.

Seale, C. *The Quality of Qualitative Research* (London: Sage, 1999).

Searing, D. D. 'The Role of the Good Constituency Member and the Practice of Representation in Great Britain', *Journal of Politics*, 47 (1985): 348–81.

Searing, D. D. *Westminster's World* (Cambridge, MA: Harvard University Press, 1994).

Seyd, P. and Whitely, P. *Labour's Grass Roots* (Oxford: Clarendon Press, 1992).

Shanley, M. L. and Pateman, C. *Feminist Interpretations and Political Theory* (Cambridge: Polity Press, 1991).

Shepherd-Robinson, L. and Lovenduski, J. *Women and Candidate Selection* (London: Fawcett Society, 2002).

Short, C. 'Women and the Labour Party', in J. Lovenduski and P. Norris (eds), *Women in Politics* (Oxford: Oxford University Press, 1996), pp. 19–27.

Siltanen, J. and Stanworth, M. *Women and the Public Sphere: A Critique of Sociology and Politics* (London: Hutchinson, 1984).

Silverman, D. *Qualitative Methodology and Sociology* (Vermont, CT: Gover, 1985).

Silverman, D. *Doing Qualitative Research* (London: Sage, 2000).

Simms, M. 'Two Steps Forward, One Step Back: Women and the Australian Party System', in J. Lovenduski and P. Norris (eds), *Gender and Party Politics* (London: Sage, 1993), pp. 16–34.

Skard, T. and Haavio-Mannila, E. 'Equality Between the Sexes – Myth or Reality in Norden?', *Daedalus*, 113 (1984): 141–67.

Skjeie, H. 'The Rhetoric of Difference: on Women's Inclusion into Political Elites', *Politics and Society*, 19, 2 (1991): 233–63.

Skjeie, H. 'Ending the Male Political Hegemony: the Norweigan Experience', in J. Lovenduski and P. Norris (eds), *Gender and Party Politics* (London: Sage, 1993), pp. 231–62.

Spelling, L. 'Quangos: Political Representation and Women Consumers of Public Services', *Policy and Politics*, 25, 2 (1997): 119–28.

Squires, J. 'Rethinking Representation', paper presented to the Political Studies Association Annual Conference, University of York, 1995.

Squires, J. 'Quotas for Women: Fair Representation?', in J. Lovenduski and P. Norris (eds), *Women in Politics* (Oxford: Oxford University Press, 1996), pp. 73–90.

Squires, J. *Gender in Political Theory* (Cambridge: Polity Press, 1999).

Squires, J. and Wickham-Jones, M. *Women in Parliament* (Manchester: EOC, 2001).

Squires, J. and Wickham-Jones, M. 'Mainstreaming in Westminster and Whitehall', *Parliamentary Affairs*, 55, 1 (2002): 57–70.

Squires, J. and Wickham-Jones, M. 'New Labour, Gender Mainstreaming and the Women and Equality Unit', *British Journal of Politics and International Relations* (forthcoming).

Sreberny-Mohammadi, A. and Ross, K. 'Women MPs and the Media: Representing the Body Politic', in J. Lovenduski and P. Norris (eds), *Women in Politics* (Oxford: Oxford University Press, 1996), pp. 105–17.

Stacey, J. 'Can there be a Feminist Ethnography?', *Women's Studies International Forum*, 11, 1 (1988): 21–7.

Stacey, M. and Price, M. *Women, Power and Politics* (London: Tavistock, 1981).

Stanley, L. *Feminist Praxis* (London: Routledge, 1990).

Stanley, L. and Wise, S. 'Feminist Research, Feminist Consciousness and Experiences of Sexism', *Women's Studies International Quarterly*, 2 (1979): 359–74.

Stanley, L. and Wise, S. *Breaking Out Again* (London: Routledge, 1993).

Starkey, D. *Elizabeth* (London: Vintage, 2001).

Stephenson, M. *The Best Man for the Job: The Selection of Women Parliamentary Candidates* (London: Fawcett Society, 1997).

Steurnagel, G. A. 'Reflections on Women and Political Participation', *Women and Politics*, 7, 4 (1987): 3–13.

Stokes, W. 'Women and Political Representation', paper presented to the Political Studies Association Annual Conference, University of York, 1995.

Studlar, D. T. and McAllister, I. 'Political Recruitment to the Australian Legislature: Toward an Explanation of Women's Electoral Disadvantages', *The Western Political Quarterly*, 42, 2 (1991): 467–85.

Studlar, D. T. and McAllister, I. 'Candidate Gender and Voting in the 1997 General Election: Did Labour Quotas Matter?' *Journal of Legislative Studies*, 4, 3 (1998): 72–91.

Studlar, D. T. and McAllister, I. 'Does a Critical Mass Exist?', *European Journal of Political Research*, 41, 2 (2002): 233–53.

Studlar, D. T., McAllister, I and Ascui, A. 'Electing Women to the British Commons: Breakout from the Beleaguered Beachhead?', *Legislative Studies Quarterly* 13, 4 (1988): 515–28.

Studlar, D. T., McAllister, I. and Hayes, B. C. 'Explaining the Gender Gap in Voting: a Cross-national Analysis', *Social Science Quarterly*, 79, 4 (1998): 779–98.

Studlar, D. T. and Welch, S. 'Understanding the Iron Law of Andrarchy: Effects of Candidate Gender on Voting in Scotland', *Comparative Political Studies*, 20, 2 (1987): 174–91.

Studlar, D. T. and Welch, S. 'Does District Magnitude Matter? Women Candidates in London Local Elections', *Western Political Quarterly*, 44 (1991): 457–66.

Studlar, D. T. and Welch, S. 'The Party System and the Representation of Women in English Metropolitan Boroughs', *Electoral Studies*, 111, 1 (1992): 62–6.

Studlar, D. T. and Welch, S. 'A Giant Step for Womankind? Women Candidates and the 1992 General Election', in D. Denver (ed.), *British Elections and Parties Yearbook 1993* (Hemel Hempstead: Harvester Wheatsheaf, 1993), pp. 216–28.

Tamerius, K. L. 'Sex, Gender, and Leadership in the Representation of Women', in G. Duerst-Lahti and R. Mae Kelly (eds), *Gender, Power, Leadership and Governance* (Ann Arbor, MI: University of Michigan Press, 1995), pp. 93–112.

Taylor, C. *Multiculturalism and the Politics of Recognition* (Princeton, NJ: Princeton University Press, 1992).

Thane, P. 'The Women of the British Labour Party and Feminism, 1906–1945', in H. L. Smith (ed.), *British Feminism in the Twentieth Century* (Aldershot: Edward Elgar, 1990), pp. 124–43.

Thomas, S. *How Women Legislate* (Oxford: Oxford University Press, 1994).

Thomas, S. and Welch, S. 'The Impact of Gender on Activities and Priorities of State Legislators', *Western Political Quarterly* (1991): 445–55.

Thomas, S. and Wilcox, C. *Women and Elective Office* (Oxford: Oxford University Press, 1998).

Thorpe, A. *A History of the British Labour Party* (Basingstoke: Macmillan, 1997).

Tobin, A. 'Lesbianism and the Labour Party: the GLC Experience', *Feminist Review*, 34 (1990): 56–66.

Travers, A. 'Radical Democracy's Feminist Potential', *Praxis International*, 12, 3 (1992): 269–83.

Truman, D. *The Congressional Party: A Case Study* (New York: Wiley, 1959).

Vacher Dod. *The Vacher Dod Guide to the New House of Commons 1997* (London: Vacher Dod Publishing, 1997).

Vallance, E. *Women in the House* (London: The Athlone Press, 1979).

Vallance, E. 'Women Candidates and Electoral Preference', *Politics*, 1 (1981): 27–31.

Vallance, E. 'Where Power is, Women are Not', *Parliamentary Affairs*, 35, 2 (1982): 218–9.

Vallance, E. 'Women Candidates in the 1983 General Election', *Parliamentary Affairs*, 37, 3 (1984): 301–9.

Vallance, E. 'Two Cheers for Equality: Women Candidates in the 1987 General Elections', *Parliamentary Affairs*, 41 (1988): 86–91.

Vallance, E. and Davies, E. *Women of Europe: Women MEPs and Equality Policy* (Cambridge: Cambridge University Press, 1986).

Vickers, J. 'Toward a Feminist Understanding of Representation', in J. Arscott and L. Trimble (eds), *In the Presence of Women* (Toronto: Harcourt Brace, 1997), pp. 20–46.

Voet, R. 'Political Representation and Quotas: Hannah Pitkin's Concept(s) of Representation in the Context of Feminist Politics', *Acta Politica*, 27, 4 (1992): 389–403.

Voet, R. 'Women as Citizens', *Australian Feminist Studies*, 19 (1994): 61–77.

Waller, R. and Criddle, B. *The Almanac of British Politics* (London: Routledge, 1996).

Watts Powell, L., Brown, C. W. and Hedges, R. B. 'Male and Female Differences in Elite Political Participation: an Examination of the Effects of Socio-economic and Familial Variables', *Western Political Quarterly* 34, 1 (1981): 31–45.

Weber, M., Odorisio, C. C. and Zincone, G. 'An Analysis of the Political Behaviour of Women in Europe', preliminary report submitted to the Council of Europe, December, partly revised May 1984, Strasbourg, 1984.

Welch, S. 'Women as Political Animals? A Test of Some Explanations for Male–Female Political Participation Differences', *American Journal of Political Science*, 21, 4 (1977): 711–29.

Welch, S. 'Recruitment of Women to Public Office: a Discriminant Analysis', *Western Political Quarterly*, 31 (1978): 372–80.

Welch, S. 'Are Women More Liberal Than Men in the US Congress', *Legislative Studies Quarterly*, 10, 1 (1985): 125–34.

Welch, S. and Secret, P. 'Sex, Race and Political Participation', *Western Political Quarterly*, 34, 1 (1981): 5–16.

Welch, S. and Studlar, D. T. 'British Public Opinion Toward Women in Politics: a Comparative Perspective', *Western Political Quarterly*, 39 (1986): 138–54.

Welch, S. and Studlar, D. T. 'The Effects of Candidate Gender on Voting for Local Office in England', *British Journal of Political Science*, 18 (1988): 273–86.

Welch, S. and Studlar, D. T. 'Multi-Member Districts and the Representation of Women: Evidence from Britain and the United States', *Journal of Politics*, 52, 2 (1990): 391–412.

Welch, S. and Studlar, D. T. 'The Opportunity Structure for Women's Candidacies and Electability in Britain and the United States', *Political Research Quarterly*, 49, 8 (1996): 861–74.

Welch, S. and Thomas, S. 'Explaining the Gender Gap in British Public Opinion', *Women and Politics*, 8, 3 & 4 (1988): 25–44.

Westkott, M. 'Feminist Criticism of the Social Sciences', in J. McCarl Nielson (ed.), *Feminist Research Methods* (Boulder, CO and San Francisco, CA: Westview Press, 1990), pp. 58–93.

Whelehan, I. *Modern Feminist Thought* (Edinburgh: Edinburgh University Press, 1995).

Whiteley, P. and Seyd, P. 'New Labour – New Grass Roots Party?', paper presented to the Political Studies Association Annual Conference, University of Keele, 1998.

Wilford, R. 'Women and Politics in Northern Ireland', in J. Lovenduski and P. Norris (eds), *Women in Politics* (Oxford: Oxford University Press, 1996), pp. 43–56.

Winterson, J. *Oranges are Not the Only Fruit* (London: Vintage, 1991).

Wood, D. M. and Norton, P. 'Do Candidates Matter? Constituency-specific Vote Changes for Incumbent MPs 1983–1987', *Political Studies*, 40 (1992): 227–38.

Wood, S. 'The British General Election of 1997', *Electoral Studies*, 1, 1 (1999): 142–7.

Woods, P. *Successful Writing for Qualitative Researchers* (London: Routledge, 1999).

Young, I. M. *Justice and the Politics of Difference* (Princeton, NJ: Princeton University Press, 1990).

Young, I. M. *Throwing Like a Girl and Other Essays in Feminist Philosophy and Social Theory* (Bloomington and Indianapolis: Indiana University Press, 1990).

Young, I. M. 'Social Groups in Associative Democracy', in J. Cohen and J. Rogers (eds), *Associations and Democracy* (London: Verso, 1995).

Young, I. M. *Intersecting Voices* (Princeton, NJ: Princeton University Press, 1997).

Young, I. M. 'Unruly Categories: a Critique of Nancy Fraser's Dual Systems Theory', *New Left Review*, 222, March–April (1997): 147–60.

Index